"Intriguing, absorbing . . . fascinating. . . remarkable. . . . I am sure [this] book will be a source of considerable comfort to anyone whose life has been touched by depression."

—Irvin I. Blose, M.D.
American Journal of Psychiatry

"Sensible, practical, balanced and encouraging are some of the adjectives that characterize this genuinely helpful book."

—*Science Digest*

". . . a fascinating and illuminating book concerning the ways in which depression can become a source of strength and creativity rather than deteriorate into weakness and despair."

—*Wichita Falls Times*

"This is a very interesting and enlightening study of the effect of stress on a person, and what a person might accomplish under stress that they would otherwise be unable to master."

—*News-Chief*
Winter Haven, Florida

". . . a good competent overview of the current trends in treatment . . . readable and lucid."

—Irving M. Rosen, M.D.
Journal of Religion and Health

"This is a popular book, written in straightforward language by a well-informed, sensible, non-doctrinaire psychiatrist. . . . He has much sensible advice to offer, both to depressed people and to relatives who have to live with them."

—Anthony Storr
Washington Post Book World

"I can think of no better book to recommend on the subject than this one."

—John R. McCall, Ph.D.
National Catholic Reporter

Also by Frederic Flach, M.D., K.C.H.S.

Choices
Resilience
A New Marriage, A New Life
Rickie
The Secret Strength of Angels
Faith, Healing, and Miracles

Textbooks

Chemotherapy in Emotional Disorder
(with Peter F. Regan, M.D.)
The Nature and Treatment of Depression
(Ed. with Suzanne Draghi, M.D.)
The Creative Mind (Ed.)
Diagnostics and Psychopathology (Ed.)
Psychobiology and Psychopharmacology (Ed.)
Affective Disorder (Ed.)
The Schizophrenias (Ed.)
Psychotherapy (Ed.)
Stress and its Management (Ed.)

Audiocassette Programs

Take Command!™ Stress Management Program

The Secret Strength of DEPRESSION

Fourth Revised Edition

Frederic Flach, M.D., K.C.H.S.

Foreword by Peter C. Whybrow, M.D.

hatherleigh

PRINTING HISTORY
J. Lippincott edition published August 1974

Excerpts appeared in FAMILY CIRCLE MAGAZINE
And MACLEAN'S MAGAZINE

Bantam Edition / September 1975

2nd printing......September 1976
3rd printing ....October 1977
4th printing ....October 1979
5th printing.........August 1981
6th printing ....August 1982
7th printing .....December 1983

Bantam revised edition / September 1986
2nd printing March 1988

First Hatherleigh Press Edition: September 1995

Hatherleigh Press is committed to preserving and protecting the natural resources of the Earth. Environmentally responsible and sustainable practices are embraced within the company's mission statement.

Hatherleigh Press is a member of the Publishers Earth Alliance, committed to preserving and protecting the natural resources of the planet while developing a sustainable business model for the book publishing industry.

www.hatherleighpress.com

Library of Congress Cataloging-in-Publication Data is available.

ISBN 978-1-57826-275-5

All Hatherleigh Press titles are available for bulk purchase, special promotions, and premiums. For information about reselling and special purchase opportunities, please call 1-800-528-2550 and ask for the Special Sales Manager.

10 9 8 7 6 5 4 3 2 1

hatherleigh

TO MY CHILDREN

who have kept me in touch
with the way things are
in a changing world

Contents

Foreword

What is depression? Over thirty years ago, back in the early 1970s, judging from the national surveys of the day, the majority of Americans gave a confident answer to that question. Depression was a form of laziness; tangible evidence of a moral turpitude that was best hidden from the public eye. Whether in one's family or in oneself, depression was something to be suffered alone and in silence—as an unwholesome secret. So when Frederic Flach's *The Secret Strength of Depression* was first published by Lippincott in 1974 and started to appear in bookstores nationwide, there was some scratching of heads. Surely the title was a bad joke, an oxymoron: depression, we all knew, was weakness—and usually a secret—so where was the strength amidst such malaise?

Within the first few pages of reading *The Secret Strength of Depression* the answer was readily apparent. Dr. Flach's message was simple and compelling: for the majority of us, a single episode of depression is destructive only if we fail to manage it successfully. Indeed, working through the experience and coming to understand the roots of sadness offers an opportunity not just to learn about oneself, but to be enriched and to grow stronger as a person. For those who had suffered in depression's dungeon, confined in public silence, it was a message of hope—as evidenced by how the book flew rapidly off the bookstore shelves. Within a few months *The Secret Strength of Depression* was released in paperback and went through seven printings before a new, revised, edition appeared in 1986.

Frederic Flach's own reason for writing *The Secret Strength of Depression* was his fascination with the complexity of human behavior, and his hope of advancing public and professional appreciation of that complexity. Dr. Flach was entirely comfortable in tearing down the usual fences that give comfort in thinking about complicated things in abstract, linear ways, circumscribing precise categories such as sociology, psychology and biology. Thus in the early 1970s, when mainstream psychiatry was casting aside the cloak of Freud's dynamic parapsychology in preparation for a leap into the vortex of psychopharmacology and neurotransmitters, Frederic Flach took pains to avoid such fractionation. As a consummate psychotherapist and physician, who earlier in his career had been involved in basic research, and was above all a teacher, Dr. Flach's goal with *The Secret Strength of Depression* was one of dynamic integration of the best thinking in the field, presented in engaging, simple prose. With similar concerns for accessibility it is a book filled with personal stories, for stories are the way we make sense of the world. Moods—including sadness, Dr. Flach insisted—are part of the human condition and can only be successfully managed through an understanding of the central role that emotional experience plays in the narratives we construct for ourselves.

Frederic Flach was right in his insistence and in his focus, which is what has made *The Secret Strength of Depression* a timeless, classic text for the general reader. The shifting pendulum of emotion is vital to staying alive and to negotiating everyday stresses and strains. Emotions are part of a pre-verbal system of social communication that we share with our mammalian forebears. Even though, as human beings, we have the extraordinary facility of language, we use emotion everyday to communicate our desires to each other, and to monitor our social environment. Emotion is part of the brain's early warning system, intimately linked to the body's ancient mechanisms of survival. When the swing of the emotional pendulum signals that events are not moving favorably, feelings of anxiety and irritability are commonly mixed with a mood of sadness, especially if adverse circumstances persist. At the opposite end of the spectrum, as exemplified by the wonderful energy and optimism that accompanies falling in love, we experience happiness. Thus our emotions are constantly changing as the brain monitors the ups and downs of a shifting social world.

For most of us, the challenges and opportunities of everyday life lie in our relationships with others—in the intimate bonds of family and the affection of lovers and friends—and in understanding the intricate social systems of the workplace while learning the skills that are essential to economic survival. These are extraordinarily complex tasks demanding vigilance and mental agility and generating continuous challenges. Remarkably, most of the time we succeed in navigating these social complexities. But then there are those weeks when nothing seems to go our way; when plans come apart and friendships are called into question. We remember those weeks; we feel them. There is a sense of anger and tension, a distracting preoccupation with the details of the problem and irritability towards those who don't seem to understand. But, then, slowly the feelings pass. We find some compromise and the struggle resolves, or seems less important. The memory recedes. We move on.

What Dr. Flach teaches us in *The Secret Strength of Depression*—and it is a lesson as important today as it was in 1974—is that blindly pushing ahead at such times, without thoughtful reflection, is a mistake. It is when under stress that we witness the emotional brain at work, and with self-reflection such moments offer opportunity. Each and every one of us can become depressed, given the right set of circumstances. Most common are those challenges that present chronic insoluble problems, usually of a social nature: divorce or a loveless marriage; a demanding and difficult work situation with little personal reward; the death of a lifelong companion. It is then that we encounter such obstacles and depression threatens, as is virtually inevitable during the span of a lifetime. After the ensuing turmoil, appropriately harnessed, we are then able to move forward on a path of self-knowledge. This is the secret strength of depression.

For Frederic Flach the experience of hope came from an understanding of resilience. He was fascinated by this dynamic inner strength that we each possess and wrote about it extensively in his book, *Choices*, first published in 1976. The argument goes something like this: in its early stages the experience of depression is very similar to that of profound grief. But most of us, even under complex and difficult circumstances, do not stay despondent. This is because the emotional brain, like all brain systems, is self-correcting. In the same way that a thermostat returns to a set point when maintaining the temperature of a room, so does emotion balance itself around the habitual temperament of an individual.

Without mindful self-awareness, however, resilience is compromised. Conflicting situations awaken alarm mechanisms in the brain and body that are intended to defend against acute emergencies. But, when this state of affairs coincide with another illness, like the flu, or is magnified by life changes that compound the stress, such as menopause or retirement from work, then a depression commonly follows. Resilience is lost. It need not be so, Dr. Flach instructs us.

With self-knowledge informing sensible choice and good health practice, resilience can be strengthened and we can guard against such challenges that depression can pose.

Frederic Flach was a man ahead of his time in resisting the plunge into rote pharmacology as the sole solution to our mental ills. For Dr. Flach it was self-knowledge and life-long learning that held the key to emotional health. While extraordinarily important, technical advances in genetics, pharmacology and neurobiology, cannot alone resolve depression. Depression, or any other mental illness for that matter, is not simply an irregularity that has invaded a body organ, as an illness might invade the liver. With depression, the organ of disability is the brain and in disturbing the chemical regulation and integrity of the brain's emotional monitoring systems depression enters and disturbs the person—and in turn perturbs the relationships the afflicted individual has with others. In other words, as Dr. Flach taught in his writings and in his clinical practice, depression is a disorder that afflicts the integrity of the self—that collection of vital feelings, behaviors, and beliefs that together shape each of us as unique human beings.

There is an important lesson to be learned. In seeking to understand mood disorder we cannot easily isolate the illness from the experience of being human, for in truth all of us have seen the shadows of these afflictions in our own lives. Such experience can either be considered a comfort and an opportunity to understand the origin and true meaning of emotion and its disorder or, through fear and studied ignorance, it can lead to a stigmatization of those who visibly suffer. It was Frederic Flach's passionate opinion that to take the latter route is to deny one's own humanity. I agree with him.

—Peter C Whybrow, M.D.
Los Angeles, January 2008

Dr. Whybrow is the Director of the Semel Institute for Neuroscience and Human Behavior and the Judson Braun Distinguished Professor of Psychiatry and Biobehavioral Sciences at the David Geffen School of Medicine, University of California, Los Angeles. His book A Mood Apart: The Thinker's Guide to Emotion and Its Disorders, *is published by HarperPerennial.*

Preface to the Third Revised Edition

It is hard to believe that more than twenty-five years have gone by since the very first edition of *The Secret Strength of Depression*. For me, it is extremely gratifying to know that it's still out there, giving many thousands of people a different and encouraging way to look at the experience of depression and motivating them to reach out for professional help when they need it. Not only has the book contributed significantly to reducing stigma associated with being depressed, but it has also influenced the way in which many of my colleagues approach their depressed patients, affirming that a depression may be a normal, expected response to a wide range of life stresses and becomes an illness requiring treatment when patients' physical and/or psychological and environmental resilience is not adequate to enable them to deal with it on their own.

Several developments have occurred to make this updating particularly timely. More people than ever appear to be suffering with clinical depression—diagnosed by psychiatrists as major depressive disorder. It is now estimated that between 10-25% of women and 5-12% of men will meet the medical criteria for clinical depression within their lifetimes. Visits to physicians for depression have also increased, from about 11 million in the mid-1980s to more than 20 million by the late 1990s. Depression seems to have become a much more acceptable condition to acknowledge and for which to seek treatment. The availability of safer and better-tolerated antidepressants has undoubtedly contributed to this. However, more patients are receiving psychotherapy from non-medical therapists, while being referred for medications to psychopharmacology specialists. This has placed a unique responsibility on the psychologist or social worker caring for the patient to be able to recognize when patients need antidepressants—or mood-stabilizers if they suffer with a manic-depressive (bipolar) type of disorder—make the referral, confer with the treating psychiatrists, and encourage those patients to comply with the medication regimen. A similar obligation rests with the doctor whose job it is not only to find the most effective drug for the patient and monitor him/her for possible side-effects, but also to be sufficiently familiar with the patient—through direct contact and via communication with the non-medical therapist—to be on top of interactions between situational and interpersonal stressors and the patient's emotional state and his/her response to medications. Only in this way can the doctor make truly informed judgments about altering the dosage of drugs, changing from one drug to another, or staying the course.

Treatment for depression has been made even more available—and more challenging—since the vast majority of clinically depressed people are being taken care of by primary care physicians. But a non-psychiatric physician may not be as familiar as most psychiatrists with the subtleties of psychopharmacological drug management, so more complex cases must be referred. Moreover, the financing of medical care can seriously limit the amount of time any doctor can spend with patients, so that the diagnosis of clinical depression is often missed and treatment scantily supervised.

Over the last decade evidence has accumulated to support a close relationship between clinical depression and cardiovascular disease. The failure to recognize and successfully handle depression may increase a person's risk for heart disease. Moreover, people who have suffered heart attacks or strokes or undergone coronary bypass surgery often have significantly more difficulty regaining their health if they also have untreated clinical depression.

Finally, recent years have seen an awakening of the medical profession—and of psychiatry in particular—to the importance of religious faith and spirituality in promoting health. Religious men and women still get depressed when it's appropriate. But they seem much less likely to become ill with depression, and, if they do, they usually recover more quickly and fully.

In today's chaotic and frightening world, the need to understand and know how to deal with depression has never been more urgent. One encouraging note is the readiness of the "under 50" generation to be more open about emotional and interpersonal issues than generations past. They are far more willing than most of us were to reach out for help when it's needed. I hope that today's new readers will find The Secret Strength of Depression as much or more of a source of insight and inspiration as did so many others over the years. Even now, quite unexpectedly, strangers will approach me at a medical meeting or in the lobby of the hospital, holding a copy of the book, its pages frayed from many readings, its paragraphs highlighted in yellow. They reach out to shake my hand as they say "Thank you." No author, or doctor, could ask for more.

Frederic Flach, M.D., K.C.H.S.

Preface to the Second Revised Edition

More than 20 years have passed since the first edition of *The Secret Strength of Depression* was published in September 1974, and 9 years since its second edition in 1986. My purpose in writing *The Secret Strength of Depression* was to encourage people to recognize and accept depression in themselves without shame, with hope, and with the realization that being depressed, in itself, was not necessarily a form of illness. Rather, the real illness lay in refusing to acknowledge being depressed; in becoming so depressed that one's ability to cope with life was seriously threatened; in being unable to recover from depression on one's own in a reasonable period of time; or in being unable to learn from the experience and be more of a person for having successfully transited such an episode.

I've frequently been asked about the book's title. "What is the 'secret strength'?" It's this: If you know how to manage depression successfully, you can be more of a person for having done so. In part, it generates a feeling of competency and power that comes from having successfully weathered a period of great pain and distress. But more than that, it's a catalyst for important changes, not just once, but again and again throughout life. Depression forces us to take a good look at ourselves and at our lives. When it involves grief, it's an outlet for the intense feelings of loss that accompany the end of a relationship. When it's a signal that something's wrong—in a marriage, in a work situation—it fuels us to do something about what's wrong, an effort we might be tempted to ignore or ride along with until even more devastating consequences ensue. Depression is surely a preferable way to react to certain stresses than pretending they don't get to us, or translating our distress into a physical language and succumbing to serious illnesses, such as cancer, or suddenly dropping dead of a heart attack.

Depression is an inevitable part of any healthy life. The secret of dealing effectively with these episodes is something I have come to call "resilience." I first began to formulate my concept of resilience in *Choices*, published in 1976 (republished under the title *Putting the Pieces Together Again*). By 1988, when my book *Resilience* was published, I was able to present the resilience hypothesis as a fundamentally different model by which to define health and illness. According to this model, various stresses that we experience throughout the life cycle—accidents, illnesses, the death of loved ones, unexpected success and the profound changes it can bring, simply moving from one normal stage in the life cycle to another—such stresses must, by their very nature, provoke a disruption in how we are put together, with psychological, environmental, and physiological dimensions. This state of disruption is often accompanied by, and perceived as, depression. It serves a critical purpose in reorienting us to whatever changes may have occurred and preparing us for what is yet to come. In the healthy individual, reintegration follows, with the creation of a new, different, more complex level of adaptation to oneself and one's life.

This model permits us to view depression in a completely different way. Being depressed, *per se*, is not the illness. Failing to manage it and recover from it is. Such an illness can result from:

1. *A lack of psychological resilience.* You may be too rigid and inflexible, you may have little or no insight into yourself, you may be so frightened and humiliated by being depressed that you fall even more deeply into your negative mood, and not infrequently into a state of severe panic and immobilization. This is where psychotherapy can be of tremendous help.

2. *A lack of physiological resilience.* Significant stress can have the effect of depleting the levels of brain chemicals such as serotonin and norepinephrine, which help transmit messages from one nerve network to another. This leaves the person less able to deal with smaller day-to-day stresses, which are managed much more easily under normal circumstances. Antidepressant medications bring these chemicals back up to normal baseline levels and restore a more normal biological resilience; the person is

consequently more able to deal with the roots of what is causing his or her depression.

3. *A lack of an adequate support system*. Friends and confidants are necessary for resilience. If you are isolated, without friends, or if you are surrounded by people and conditions at work or at home that block your recovery and reinforce feelings of hopelessness and low self-esteem, your illness is, in fact, the world around you. Changing the conditions of your life is therefore critical to recovery.

Many of my colleagues in psychiatry still persist in thinking of depression as an illness. Much of their effort has gone into clarifying the definitions of mood disorders to permit more accurate diagnoses. Diagnostic formulations—such as Major Depression, Unipolar Depression, Dysthymia, and Bipolar Disorder—have been helpful in selecting specific antidepressants and mood regulating medication. For example, in patients with Unipolar Depression, antidepressants may be used effectively, whereas they are not sufficient in patients with Bipolar Disorder (often referred to as manic-depressive disorder) in which mood stabilization often requires the use of the salt lithium or anticonvulsants such as carbamazepine. Diagnostic terms are useful for communicating from one doctor to another, and when used in conjunction with code numbers, they are essential for submitting forms for insurance coverage. In research, they have been useful in directing attention to genetic influences in certain kinds of depression, although it is quite unclear what such genetic influences have to do with depression or, as I believe to be more likely, with a biological capacity for resilience.

However, my profession's current preoccupation with diagnosis has some serious drawbacks. The traditional diagnostic model often engenders feelings of confusion and embarrassment, an inability to understand what one is experiencing, and a serious reluctance to admit to being depressed or to reach out for any kind of help. When combined with financial trends and the emergence of managed care delivery systems, it contributes to significant prejudice in the choice of treatment for depressed patients. In 1974, a survey of psychiatrists revealed that nearly half of those in practice had *never* given an antidepressant medication to anyone, even though the first such drug, imipramine (Tofranil), had been on the market for about 15 years! Today, most patients diagnosed as suffering from depression are urged to use antidepressants—which may well be an appropriate choice in many instances. However, less attention is being paid to the other two aspects of resilience: the psychological and the environmental. This trend has grown in spite of the fact that careful studies of psychotherapy have shown it to often be as effective as antidepressants, with a combination of drug treatment and psychotherapy appearing to provide the best outcome.

I hope that this revised edition of *The Secret Strength of Depression* will continue to help many of the millions of people who are or will become depressed, not just in their efforts to overcome depression but also in their ability to recognize the positive role that depression plays in our lives. Why we human beings have to experience episodes of emotional pain as part of our journey through life is anybody's guess. This question is a little like asking why we have to love, to care about anything or anybody. Not having invented human nature, I certainly don't have the answers. It seems best to me to accept that it's just the way things are, at least until we discover some new information to go on.

Frederic Flach, M.D., K.C.H.S.

Author's Note to the First Edition

A book is usually not written once but many times. In the preparation of this manuscript, I owe sincere thanks to the editors whose advice and direction helped shape its character: Grace Bechtold of Bantam Books for her enthusiastic and continued support; Beatrice Rosenfeld of J. B. Lippincott Company for her precise and careful clarifications; and Wilhemina Marvel for her creative and incisive editorial contributions throughout the writing of the book. I also wish to thank Dr. Oskar Diethelm, Emeritus Professor of Psychiatry at Cornell University Medical College, for reviewing the material for historical and scientific accuracy and for uncovering the seventeenth century treatise on melancholia by my namesake, Fridericus Flacht, in the archives of the University of Basel in Switzerland.

The men and women described throughout the pages of the book are people I have encountered over the 25-year period in which I have been practicing psychiatry and training residents in psychiatry. The patients'names and certain details regarding their life situations have been changed to preserve their anonymity.

Chapter 1

♦ ♦ ❖ ♦ ♦ ❖ ♦ ♦ ❖ ♦ ♦ ❖ ♦ ♦ ❖ ♦ ♦ ❖ ♦ ♦

The Nature of Depression

There is a strong wind called the *mistral* that blows across the south of France—a dry and chilling current of air that brings with it a sharp rise in the incidence of depression. In Bavaria, a warm wind called *der Föhn* blows north from the Alps when the snows melt; as it descends on Munich, the suicide rate increases for a period of several days. For many people, Christmas is traditionally associated with a mood of heightened sadness and loneliness. Spring is a time when people frequently become depressed; common, also, are what are known as "anniversary reactions"—depressed moods that recur at the same time of year as events that in prior years had been upsetting: "Two years ago this month my father died," or "Last year at this time I was going through the worst part of the divorce."

Depression is not limited to specific times and places, however, because it is essentially a reaction to stress. Hence, depression is a mood that can occur *at any time to anyone.* More than 17 percent of the adults in the United States have been significantly depressed at one time or another in their lives. Unfortunately, however, far too many of these people are not aware of their depression.

Many people have a hard time recognizing that they're depressed. Depression is often confused with ordinary unhappiness. To be unhappy is to be sad or discontented when things go wrong; it does not involve a loss of perspective. Circumstances occur in everyone's lives that cause some unhappiness. Depression, on the other hand, is a mood that affects people's basic emotional dispositions, determining how they experience and perceive themselves and their surroundings. "There's a real difference between being unhappy and being depressed," commented one man in therapy. "When my wife and I have an argument, I'm unhappy about it. I don't like it. But it's part of living. We make up in a fairly short time. I may be concerned over it, but I can sleep all right, and I still feel in good spirits.

"But when I'm depressed, that's a different matter. It hurts all over. It's almost something physical. I can't get to sleep at night, and I can't sleep through the night. Even though there are still times when I'm in pretty good spirits, the mood comes over me nearly every day. It colors the way I look at everything. If my wife and I have a fight, our marriage seems hopeless. If I have a business problem, which I would normally react to with some tension and frustration—but which I would deal with promptly and appropriately—I feel as though I'm really a lousy businessman and I battle with the problem of self-confidence instead of just dealing with the issues in front of me."

The difficulty in recognizing depression is strongly reinforced by popular misconceptions about the nature of the mood. Although many people will say that they are depressed, they are not really speaking of depression, since they believe that true depression is a serious mental illness. Fearful of the implications of mental illness, they consider depression to be exclusively a severe condition that may be part of the manic-depressive cycle or that seriously incapacitates people, forcing them to be hospitalized. But only a small segment of the vast pool of depressed individuals is represented by such dramatic instances of depression. The great majority of depressed individuals experience comparatively mild forms of the condition—dangerous but readily ignored. As a result, it is often difficult for most of them to identify with the more serious illustrations of melancholia. Therefore, to them, depression is something that happens to someone else.

Furthermore, a large number of people consider being depressed in the face of stress to be a mark of weakness and hence a source of embarrassment. In short, many of us would prefer to ignore signs of depression, rather than to acknowledge that *the only healthy reaction to many life situations is depression.*

Becoming depressed is a common psychobiological response to stress. In the course of a lifetime, every individual must cope with a multitude of stresses. Because humans are psychobiological units, with every thought and feeling producing a correlative change in the chemistry of the nervous system, they will react to, and cope with, stress on both a physical and psychological plane. Hence, a severe viral infection may trigger a period of mental depression, and the death of a loved one may produce feelings of depression that have physical components. Because humans are also social beings, their reactions will affect their environment, and will, in turn, be affected by the response from the environment.

One may view ordinary, day-to-day fluctuations in mood as mild episodes of depression. Nearly everyone has moments of experiencing a sense of futility, of being more sensitive than usual, of crying easily. The characteristic signs of depression include a lowering in spirits, difficulty in sleeping, a loss of self-esteem, and a loss of perspective. Other changes associated with depression include fatigue, a loss of energy, a desire to avoid being with people, decreased libido, poor appetite and weight loss, hypersensitivity, fearfulness and irritability, and physical complaints without any diagnosable basis. Rarely do they all occur together. More often, one or another sign is prominent—sexual difficulties, for example. Many psychiatrists notice in their practice that men and women who complain of decreased libido and problems with sexual performance are actually suffering from depression, which contributes to and aggravates their sexual difficulties.

Many people do not realize that they are depressed because they fail to make a connection between the one or two signs of depression that they have noticed and the overall change in their mood. Since they don't consider jumping out of windows or overdosing with sleeping pills, they are unable to see that they may be as affected by depression as others who, in a severe and acute reaction to stress, experience weeks of fear and despondency, and fall apart in a paradoxical effort to cope and not cope at the same time.

Acute Depression

Depressive reactions can arbitrarily be divided into two forms: an *acute*, immediate type and a more enduring or *chronic* type. Acute depression is a short-lived, intense, painful, directly experienced change of mood from which the individual can usually recover in a reasonable period of time. It may run on for weeks and even months, but as a rule the intensity and duration of the reaction are appropriate to the nature of the events causing it. While it would be clearly inappropriate to become deeply depressed after two or three job rejections, a period of depression lasting 6 months or more following a divorce would be quite natural.

An acute depressive reaction may be extremely mild: a few hours of sadness, a transient feeling of being rejected, a day or two of disappointment. It may become intense when the stress giving rise to it is serious and the person experiencing it is especially sensitive to that stress. A 42-year-old woman became acutely depressed after her mother and her 18-year-old son were killed in an automobile accident. She was beside herself. She could not sleep, refused to eat, and would not talk with anyone. She often thought of wanting to die. With medical help, she pulled out of the more intense phase of her reaction in a few months and gradually learned to come to terms with the disastrous happenings. Her acute reaction, painful and disruptive as it had been, protected her from becoming chronically and bitterly depressed.

Acute depressive episodes serve as an outlet for strong feelings and, as such, are a necessary and desirable way of reacting to certain major life changes, such as loss. Some events—loss of employment, death of a husband or wife, serious childhood illnesses—are clearly threatening to most people. The termination of a love relationship or marriage is equally likely to set off a depression, particularly when the element of personal rejection is added. The increased divorce rate over the past several decades has made family disruption a common trigger for depression in children as well as parents. The extent of an individual's reaction to a particular loss is determined by his or her personality. Certain people will be more affected by loss as a result of childhood experiences, like losing one or both parents through death or divorce.

In addition to the connection between depression and loss, a sufficient number of stresses occurring within a limited time frame can evoke a depressive reaction in almost anyone, as has been pointed out by psychiatrist Eugene Paykel and others. Nor do these events have to be exclusively misfortunes. If, for example, a man receives an important promotion and is transferred to a new part of the country, loses a large sum of money in the stock market, and attends the college graduation of his only child, all in a few months' time, he is likely to become somewhat depressed—a natural response to cumulative stress. His reaction may well be puzzling to himself and others because most of these changes could generally be thought of as good.

In other words, a series of major changes, for better or worse, compacted into a small enough span of time, is apt to produce depression in most people. The relevance of such a finding to this society, replete as it is with disruption in life patterns and values, is at once apparent.

The human being must react psychobiologically to stress. Too great a response, and too little, are equally problematic. If no reaction at all is apparent in the face of a critical stress, the individual should be suspected of blocking out depression. He or she runs a high risk of having a delayed reaction months later, or of entering the chronic and more insidious form of depression. Chronic depression may also be the aftermath of an acute depression that the person has not had the resilience or insight to cope with successfully.

Chronic Depression

In contrast to acute depression, which affords an opportunity for insight, chronic depression is nearly always disabling and will complicate one's life in ways that may be hard to correct. The immobilizing quality of the mood change persists, as if the nervous system continues to short-circuit, constantly reinforcing its crippling effect.

The signs of chronic depression are similar to those of acute depression: low self-esteem, a high degree of personal sensitivity, insomnia, withdrawal, a low tolerance for criticism, difficulty in making decisions, and a tendency to put things off. There is a strong urge to rationalize the depression. "I work too hard," commented a 34-year-old store manager. "With three kids at home, I don't have any time to myself; that's why I'm tired all the time." The tendency is to project onto the immediate environment the causes for the loss of drive or energy. People 60 years of age or older may correctly regard the slow, insidious personality change as a part of the process of "getting older," as if feelings of futility and immobilization were necessarily part of aging.

Chronic depression can be difficult to identify, because it is long-standing and more subtle than acute depression, and because it seems to be a part of the person's temperament or personality rather than a mood. "He's a pessimist, a born worrier," said one woman in describing her depressed father. In some people, the only evidence of chronic depression may be a persistent or recurring nervousness and tension, which cannot be relieved by mild tranquilizers or recreation. During a vacation, away from ordinary pressures, people who are in an acute depression often feel a sustained lifting in mood. By contrast, chronically depressed individuals may, in fact, feel worse while they are away; even if they do experience some relief, they will rapidly re-enter their depression when they return to their usual life situations. The key to chronic depression is its persistence; it will not go away by itself.

The exact point at which a chronic depression may have begun is hard to spot. Unlike acute depression, the chronic form is usually detached from its causes in the person's mind. Feelings which should have been experienced at the time of the stressful events may have been denied and blocked out. Sometimes the depressed person may even be misled into being "proud" of how calmly he or she seemed to have handled a particular misfortune. The importance of the causal events may escape notice because the person failed to become sufficiently upset by them at the time.

A case in point is a 24-year-old man who was quite upset because he felt that he had made a serious error in his choice of careers. He had studied to be a marine biologist but had quit 6 months before fulfilling the requirements for his doctorate to take a job teaching at a private high school. Within a few months, he left his work again, this time returning to his parents' home. There he was frequently silent and morose. He and his family spent hours going over ideas about his career dilemma without arriving at any solutions.

At no time did anyone recognize that he had really been depressed prior to ending his studies and that the original trigger for his depression was rejection. His girlfriend, with whom he had been deeply involved for several years, had abruptly ended the relationship some time earlier. He seemed to have taken the rejection in stride and there was nearly a year's delay between this event and his quitting his graduate program.

This kind of delay between the change responsible for the depression and the first evidence of a change in mood is common in chronic depression. Because the mood change is not recognized for what it is, other problems *caused by* the depression can become paramount. Marital problems, financial difficulties, sexual frustrations, and many other conflicts often result from the effect the chronic mood has over the person experiencing it. Psychiatrists can attest to the fact that far more time must be spent dealing with the difficulties accumulated by chronically depressed people because of the depression than with the origins of the depression itself.

People frequently mistake complications of chronic depression as miscellaneous problems that seem to have sprouted out of nowhere. Millions of men and women worry about their sex lives but are unaware of the subtle interplay between mood and sex. Marital conflicts often stem from communication difficulties caused by unrecognized depression and can become painful enough to bring husband and wife to the verge of divorce. Depression commonly disrupts communication. Because depressed people are hypersensitive, they may misconstrue silence, for instance, as rejection and a lack of love. Because they are withdrawn, they themselves may be misunderstood as rejecting others. They feel alone.

One situation in which chronic depression can be advantageous—and then only if it is correctly recognized and managed—is when the persistent mood serves as a *warning* to the depressed individual, telling him or her that there is something of a recurrent or ongoing nature in his or her home or work environment that is continually undermining his or her self-esteem. A woman married to a man who is ready to criticize her at the least provocation and is unappreciative of her contributions to family life; the vice-president of a company whose president is shortsighted, exploitative, and untrustworthy; the adolescent son or daughter of parents who are blindly arbitrary—any one of these people may be chronically depressed as long as he or she remains in the present environment and accepts such deprecation, however passively or unconsciously, without trying to correct the imbalance.

Why do certain individuals become chronically depressed rather than dealing with stress in an open and direct way through acute depression? The acutely depressed person is usually one who is in better touch with his or her emotions and feelings on a day-to-day basis, and who has learned ways of expressing them more effectively. The chronically depressed person does not have this ability. The acutely depressed person is more flexible, hence less likely to get trapped in a depressed mood. There may also be important biochemical factors that determine whether or not a depressive reaction will be resolved within a reasonable period or go on to become chronic. The work of Bunney and Schildkraut in the 1960s set the stage for a long series of studies of the neurophysiological operations of the brain, which point to the tendency of depressed patients to show alterations in the metabolism of the substances called biogenic amines, which affect the transmission of impulses within the nervous system. My own studies have demonstrated that depressed patients show changes in the metabolism of hormones and of minerals such as calcium that are reversed only after the depression lifts.

Regardless of whether people become acutely or chronically depressed, however, depression is still preferable to other ways of reacting to stress, such as psychosomatic disorders. As people work their way out of depression, whether on their own or by means of newer approaches to psychotherapy combined, when appropriate, with new antidepressant medications, they gain the insight essential to strengthen their ability to cope with their futures.

By contrast, psychosomatic illnesses—another form of stress reaction—carry with them a poorer outlook for recovery. Stress is known to be a major contributant to the development of cardiovascular disease, such as hypertension, as well as asthma, colitis, peptic ulcers, and other conditions. To have a heart attack or an ulcer is socially acceptable; it shows, somehow, that one has been a hard-working, success-oriented kind of person. Even though his or her health forces such a person to slow down, this is considered reasonable inasmuch as it is required for his or her physical well-being. It is not socially acceptable to be depressed.

Yet, whereas depression is nearly always completely reversible, the patient who has taken the heart attack or ulcer route for coping with stress must face the fact that these illnesses often leave in their wake physical damage that is irreversible. Still, the majority of men and women would, if asked, unwittingly prefer a physical illness to depression. This widespread attitude encourages millions to avoid facing depression in themselves and doing something about it.

It is time that we recognize the ubiquity and contagiousness of depression—as much a public health problem as yellow fever or smallpox in their time—and realize that depression is not only a highly common way of reacting to stress, a reaction that sometimes requires medical attention, but that, when acknowledged, it is also for millions a unique opportunity to redefine themselves and resolve long-standing destructive conflicts within themselves and their environments.

Chapter 2

♦ ♦ ❖ ♦ ♦ ❖ ♦ ♦ ❖ ♦ ♦ ❖ ♦ ♦ ❖ ♦ ♦ ❖ ♦ ♦

An Opportunity for Change

Any event or change in our lives that forces us to break down some of our defenses, for whatever reason, is going to be painful. To experience acute depression is an opportunity for us not just to learn more about ourselves, but to become more whole.

"Falling apart" not only affords us a chance for insight, but it can accelerate the process of reordering one's life after a serious stress—a loss, for example. Becoming depressed is an inevitable concomitant of letting go—of a person, a position, a piece of oneself. The greater the attachment, the more involved it is with one's self-esteem and dependency needs, the greater the reaction will be.

The most common situation in which depression accompanies such a letting go is the reaction to the death of a loved one, or the breaking up of a relationship in which intense love has been involved. In his monograph "Mourning and Melancholia," Freud attempted to distinguish between such grief reactions and depression. According to Freud, when a loved one is lost, the normal response is grief; the abnormal response is depression. He conceived of the difference as rooted in the kind of relationship that had previously existed between the two people, in particular whether there was any unconscious hostility and guilt toward the one who had died.

This distinction has proved misleading. It is much more useful to think of grief as being a form of acute depression, which becomes a more complicated problem when the person is extremely sensitive to the loss, or the loss is of such a nature that he or she cannot manage the intense feelings without professional help. Far more serious is an inability to experience the depression at the time of the loss. The failure to become depressed drives the reaction underground, where it can silently exert its influence over the person's life for some time to come.

In our culture, we are discouraged from experiencing and expressing our feelings. We are expected to conceal our emotions, often even from ourselves. No matter what the nature of the stress, we are expected to continue functioning efficiently unless we are physically unwell. Hence, people prefer such somatic manifestations of stress as cardiovascular disease or intestinal disorders, which permit them to become dependent and more or less incapacitated without embarrassment or censure.

Yet it is precisely the person who cannot respond with emotional pain when confronted with a significant loss who later becomes subtly and seriously compromised by chronic depression, frequently masked by physical ailments. When the situation warrants it, when letting go is a necessity, it is much better simply to break down. Acute depression affords such an opportunity.

Allen Stark was 40 when his father died suddenly of a heart attack. As the shock waned, he found himself wanting to be alone, waking in the night, remembering, crying. His wife, who had always considered Allen the epitome of stability, was frightened by the intensity of his feelings. As weeks passed, she became increasingly critical of him. "Haven't you cried enough?" she insisted, to which Allen replied: "How much is enough?"

How much *is* enough?

It took Allen nearly 6 months to fully recover from the impact of his father's death. During that time, he experienced repeated episodes of acute depression. Tension and sadness would recur and last from a few hours to several days. At these times he found it difficult to concentrate and to communicate with his friends and family. Wondering whether his wife might be right, feeling embarrassed by the persistence of his grief, he spoke with his minister. After a few talks, he was reassured that his depressive feelings were quite normal. Through these discussions, he was able to free himself from feelings of guilt and inadequacy, realizing that his wife's inability to understand his mood stemmed from her own fear of emotionalism. Once aware of this interaction, he could accept his own feelings in a sensible way and work through with his wife her tendency to see any show of emotion as "weak."

In addition, he reconsidered the nature of his relationship to his father, what his father had really been like, what his strong points were, and in what ways his father had been a disappointment to him. He thought carefully about what it meant to be a father himself. He felt a gradual lifting of his sadness and ultimately described himself as being "better put together than I was before."

In a changing society such as ours, in which changes occur rapidly and often without warning, the opportunities for loss are especially commonplace. Psychiatrists who have studied the effect of culture on various emotional states have observed that overt depression occurs more frequently in tightly knit and highly organized societies, where the value systems are readily identifiable and the ways and means of avoiding coming to terms with depression are few and far between. These psychiatrists argue that a society in flux is characterized by an extremely high incidence of hidden depression because of the great confusion in value systems—to the extent that one hardly knows where to draw measures for self-esteem—and the innumerable environmental changes that people encounter in relatively short periods of time. The depression is often hidden because in such a loosely structured society, the individual has many options for reacting to life stresses other than by becoming depressed: options that range from indulging in antisocial behavior to becoming dependent on drugs or alcohol to resolving problems in communication simply by terminating the relationship, as in divorce.

Change of any type, if it involves something or someone of importance to the individual, is usually a catalyst for depression. The process of growing up and growing older involves a series of changes; every transitional phase of life, from childhood to marriage to old age, requires some degree of giving up, of letting go. In order to move successfully from one phase to the next, a person must be able to experience depression in a direct and meaningful way.

Children can be depressed; when they are, the mood change is likely to show up primarily in their behavior; they may become obstreperous, do poorly in school, become shy and withdrawn, or have trouble relating to other children. The beginning of adolescence is when the individual first becomes truly conscious of the nature of his or her inner emotional life and can recognize and feel depression as such. It is common for adolescents to be depressed. They are experiencing themselves as individuals for the first time and determining their impact on, and relationship with, other people. It is the second major period of separation, the first real separation between them and their parents. Fourteen-year-olds begin to feel a need to break away, to be alone, to be with others their age. Nonetheless, they have a continuing attachment to their families and feel varying degrees of guilt about rejecting them.

Today's world is a particularly difficult one for adolescents. The adolescent has been described as the pulse of society. If teenagers are in a state of confusion and turmoil, they reflect a society that, analogously, is disturbed and out of touch with itself. The contemporary climate in America makes it especially difficult for adolescents to acknowledge and deal with being depressed. Faced with a multiplicity of standards and a plethora of readily available distractions, from TV to text messaging, many have become bewildered, disenchanted, and seduced into quieting their distress with sex, drugs, alcohol, and apathy. Adolescents who sometimes experience overt depression do not present as great a problem to themselves or to society as the adolescents who cannot tolerate sadness or disappointment, are out of touch with their emotions, and have little understanding of what is happening to them. They are the adolescents who are likely to submerge their depression and replace it with such self-defeating behavior as dropping out of school, joining a gang, or getting caught in unwanted pregnancies.

Getting married is another example of a major transition likely to bring on depression. Marriage, regardless of how long the couple may have known each other before, and even if they have lived together for a time, requires major alterations in attitude and a reassessment in expectations. It no longer consists of just a man and a woman in love with each other or sharing each other's companionship. In addition to the details of living together in new roles, there is also the necessity of coping with friends and relatives in a new context. Economic considerations change. It is not surprising, therefore, that some degree of acute depression accompanies the giving up of the old freedom—even if such freedom only involved keeping one foot out of the door—and the initiation of a new and more permanent kind of commitment. When an acute depressive mood is unexpected and misinterpreted, or, as the family physician can readily support, disguised by the appearance of various psychosomatic problems such as headaches, urinary tract disorders, or fatigue, it can start to undermine the very core of the new relationship.

Becoming aware of, and making an effort to change, a pattern of behavior that has been self-defeating will often bring on an acute form of depression. Frequently, the behavior pattern itself reflects an underlying and unrecognized chronic depression. How the acute reaction may alert people to their predicament and force them to deal with it is illustrated in the case of Robert Duncan, a 50-year-old engineer, married for 20 years, who became acutely depressed. Three years before this mood change, several disturbing events had occurred. His mother had died. The company for which he worked had lost several government contracts, and, as a result, he had been laid off.

With several former associates, Robert had set up his own consulting firm, which struggled for existence in a poor economic climate. Not wanting to upset his wife, he concealed from her the extent of their financial crisis. When it came time to meet certain personal expenses, such as school tuition for their two children, he borrowed money, telling her that his new venture was growing.

Robert was under a great deal of pressure to make his new firm solvent. At the same time he did not sleep well, awakening at three in the morning anxious and worried. He put off making calls on prospective clients. His paperwork fell behind. Meanwhile, he was rapidly constructing a web of deception with his wife in order to maintain his self-esteem in her eyes.

Suddenly Robert's system collapsed. The banks from which he had borrowed money demanded immediate payment of his loans. He could no longer hide the situation from his wife. She was, of course, shaken by his confession. For several days afterward, he thought of suicide. "I can't face her again. She'll never trust me," he thought. His self-defeating behavior which had dated back to his mother's death and his dismissal, was interrupted by events that set off an acute and painful depression.

Robert confided his desperation to a close friend, who suggested psychiatric counseling. He reluctantly decided to visit a psychiatrist, who started him on antidepressants and proceeded to explore with him the important issues relevant to his depression. He had been hurt and angered by his dismissal, but could not deal with these feelings because they had been largely blocked out. He also felt guilty about losing the job, as if it had been a personal failure. His insecurity had caused him to fear that his wife would lose respect for him, so he fell back on a series of lies to hide his problems from her. While part of him was trying to make his new firm work, another part was working against him to undermine his efforts.

After 6 weeks of therapy, Robert felt much better. He and his wife then had several joint sessions with the psychiatrist, in which they were able to renew communication and set a basis for the restoration of trust. He was not only relieved to have the facts out in the open, but he was also sleeping well, more energetic, free from his tendency to worry and put things off. He was surprised by the increase in his productivity. As he began to cope more aggressively with business matters, he and his associates obtained several important contracts that assured their survival as a firm.

Robert Duncan had approached professional treatment gingerly, partly because he still assumed that psychotherapy was indistinguishable from psychoanalysis—that it would take 3 years and thirty thousand dollars to help him—and partly because he was skeptical of its value. "What can therapy do for me when my problems are real?" he thought. "Therapy can't get us contracts or restore my wife's respect for me." With the aid of therapy and the disappearance of his depression, he was able to accomplish both these aims.

Depression is an opportunity for change. Acute depression, then, is a genuine opportunity to settle long-standing, unrecognized depression that has been operating in a subversive way for years. One 55-year-old woman came to terms with her chronic depression only when she became acutely depressed after her daughter developed severe rheumatoid arthritis. Until then, she would never have considered herself depressed. Her hypersensitivity, her poor sexual adjustment, and her tendency toward social isolation had been viewed by her and her family as "personality traits" rather than signs of an underlying depression. She was just another human being subject to the usual stresses and strains of life, whose frustrations could best be handled by avoiding conflict and taking a drink or two when things became too rough. Her daughter's illness, which triggered an acute depression and forced her to seek counseling, gave her the very first realization of the way her chronic mood had been depriving her of a fuller life.

Finally, depressive episodes serve another, more complex function. They can provide the individual with an opportunity to become more of a person, more sensitive, more creative, more effective after the depression has lifted.

Depression reduces vitality. The mood makes it difficult, if not impossible, to envision solutions to problems. Yet the majority of creative people, whether the term creativity is used in the narrow, artistic sense or in the broader sense of being able to see things in a fresh way and to combine concepts in an original manner, will attest to the fact that they have experienced significant episodes of acute depression from which they have rebounded to reach new levels of creativity.

Why is this so? Why would a period of being depressed and feeling hopeless be a prelude to a heightening in creativity? The answer lies in the nature of creativity itself. To be creative in any sense, a person must be able to relinquish old and fixed assumptions that block a fresh appraisal of a situation. Forty years ago, for example, people assumed that a woman's femininity was contingent on an early marriage and having several children. In recent decades, people have assumed that women will pursue graduate studies and/or a career even if this means that marriage and family life must take second place. In either case, there is immense pressure on young women to conform to the particular bias that is in vogue.

The inability to be free from such influences cripples many young women in making decisions about their future, preventing them from using their imaginations and their knowledge of themselves to create the particular kind of life for which they would be best suited.

Pavlov and B. F. Skinner pointed out that society and the family inevitably condition people along a variety of lines. Such conditioning helps form an integrated personality structure. At the same time, however, many irrelevant, archaic, and even destructive patterns can become ingrained. The more rigid and intense the conditioning, especially when the individual is also insecure, the more unbending the personality. The more inflexible the personality, the less resilience and imagination he or she has to adapt to new or unexpected situations. Acute depression is a necessary vehicle for releasing a person from the bondage of such conditioning and freeing the vital elements of creativity. This phenomenon is regularly seen in the course of psychotherapy, where episodes of depression are followed by insight and greater flexibility.

Arthur Koestler, in his *Act of Creation*, refers to psychotherapy as an artificially induced regeneration, relying on the basic process of *reculer pour mieux sauter*—to take a step backward in order to make a better leap forward. Koestler writes:

> We found this pattern repeated on the level of human creativity: the scientist, faced by a perplexing situation—Kepler's discrepant eight minutes' arc, Einstein's light-traveller paradox—must plunge into a "dark night of the soul" before he can reemerge into the light. The history of the sciences and arts is a tale of recurrent crises, of traumatic challenges, which entail a temporary disintegration of the traditional forms of reasoning and perception . . . [and] a new innocence of the eye; followed by the liberation from restraint of creative potentials, and their reintegration in a new synthesis.

Chapter 3

♦ ♦ ❖ ♦ ♦ ❖ ♦ ♦ ❖ ♦ ♦ ❖ ♦ ♦ ❖ ♦ ♦ ❖ ♦ ♦

The Common Traps

"I'm 33 years old, and as far as I'm concerned it's over," remarked Walter Bergman. "Married to a woman who finds any excuse not to sleep with me. Doing a job I hate, way below my level of competence. The only thing I really enjoy is being with my kids. I'm caught in a trap."

Walter Bergman was depressed. He had been able to manage an ungratifying life situation for nearly 3 years until, one morning, after weeks of tiredness and irritability, he telephoned his superior at work and impulsively quit. The previous day he had been reprimanded for a minor error in his preparation of some sales information. In the ensuing weeks, he became increasingly withdrawn, silent, and sulky. His wife insisted that she would have to leave him if he didn't see a psychiatrist.

Insidiously and with relentless precision, Walter had constructed a complex trap, tailor-made for himself, which had finally emptied his life of meaning. Talented, one of the best students in his class at Yale, he had imprudently changed his career direction three times in 10 years. First he flunked out of his first year of law school by simply not studying. Then he worked for a bank for several years, but quit because he was "bored" and not getting ahead quickly enough. Finally, he quit his job with a fund-raising public relations group because he felt unappreciated. In each instance, he placed the blame for his dissatisfaction on people and things outside of himself. Now, unemployed, his work trap had snapped tightly shut.

Not content with an occupational trap, Walter built a personal one as well. In spite of his strong need for warmth and support, he had married a woman who was basically critical and undemonstrative. He had initially been attracted to her sharp, analytic mind and impressed by her high level of energy. He made what seemed to him a rational decision, but in the process he denied obvious emotional needs that were not likely to be met in the relationship.

Walter's career confusion and his poor choice of a wife were linked to a period of low self-esteem that had begun shortly after he had finished college. At that time he was very much in love with a girl who ultimately broke off the relationship, leaving him painfully hurt and rejected. Rather than becoming acutely depressed, he rapidly suppressed these feelings, pretending to himself that it really didn't matter. Whereas he had originally thought of studying journalism and political science after graduation, he suddenly felt that this direction would not afford him enough prestige or money. He decided on law and applied to the law school at the University of Michigan, where he was quickly accepted. In his social life, he adopted an attitude that becoming too emotionally involved was a poor idea since it would only lead to hurt feelings. He became aloof and inaccessible in his relationships with women. The denial of his intrinsic career interests for the sake of prestige and money, and the denial of his emotional needs in order to defend himself against the possible hurt of another rejection, were Walter's first steps in building his own trap.

Walter Bergman is the prototype of millions of men and women who are busily constructing traps for themselves. Such people are on the verge of experiencing acute fear and hopelessness, which sweep in on them once they realize that the trap has snapped shut.

Why and How People Build Their Own Traps

Trap-building often follows the same basic blueprint. The individual fails to cope adequately with a stress or a series of stresses. Instead of reacting to them appropriately and working the issues through, he or she denies the feelings, shuts them out of consciousness, and conceals them through the formation of mechanisms designed to protect him or her against future hurt. Rather than facing his own complicity in his career problems, Walter Bergman projected the blame for his difficulties onto his environment. By denying the importance of warmth and sex in his relationships with women, he ended up marrying a woman who could offer him neither.

For many people, there is a compulsive quality operating in the formation of the trap. One of the more common trap situations is seen in the efforts that people make to reproduce in their own marriages the kind of family life they knew when they were growing up. This occurs regardless of the attitudes that they may have had about their upbringing. For example: A young man is raised in a home in which his father is a strong and dominant figure, whereas his mother is quiet, uninvolved, and somewhat withdrawn. He sees his mother as ineffectual and his father as unkind. He resolves never to find himself in a similar position and ends up marrying a woman who is strong and independent, only to discover himself engaged again and again in a power struggle for control. If he makes a different error in judgment, he may marry a woman who appears quite self-reliant, only to find out, within a few years, that she too, like his mother, lacks initiative and a healthy respect for herself.

In either instance, by attempting to go to the opposite pole or by inadvertently overlooking personality characteristics in his wife-to-be, the young man has succeeded in constructing a trap for himself that has its origins in the kind of relationship his parents had.

Another route that people can take in building their traps is through *using their environment to reinforce and confirm their inner conflicts and constrictions.* As a result of an unusually repressive childhood and adolescence, for example, in which initiative and creativity were seldom encouraged and conformity was demanded, a young man may develop serious obstacles to his ability to mobilize his energy and direct his inherent aggression outward toward self-selected goals. At the same time, afraid of his own urges toward independence and unable to release his emotions, he cannot respond promptly and appropriately to stressful situations. His adaptation to life is generally passive, and he is readily controlled by others.

Failing to select a lifestyle in which his inherent need for freedom and initiative could be fostered, he chooses instead an environment that reinforces his low self-esteem. He then projects onto that environment the obstructions that had previously been internalized. For example, he obtains a middle-management position with a large manufacturing concern, where his decision-making authority is very narrow and he is discouraged from introducing innovative concepts lest he be ridiculed and criticized.

The real trap now confirms the inner trap. The circle is closed. The options available to the person become progressively more limited.

If and when some part of himself, through a shift in equilibrium provoked by a particular stress situation, becomes aware of the trap, he may begin, finally, to hurt. Human beings have a strong tendency to reaffirm inner constrictions and deprivations by building external traps, and then to live within them in unhappy equilibrium until something sufficiently dramatic occurs to wake them up to their dilemma. In the process of creating such traps, they choose the wrong people as romantic partners. They place their trust in friends and business associates who prove untrustworthy. They handle money with special irresponsibility and choose occupations replete with frustrations and designed to block personal fulfillment.

Winifred Regan, at 29, was unmarried and worked as a rewrite editor for a large weekly magazine. Although she had graduated *magna cum laude* from Mount Holyoke, she had always been haunted by a sense of inadequacy. "I don't really see any point in girls having careers," her father had maintained. "No man is good enough for you, Winifred," her mother pointed out repeatedly, but then added, "Don't be too aggressive or you'll never get a man."

Winifred herself felt that she was a good student, but had no special talents. "I don't have the energy to go on to graduate school. I really don't know what to do." In this mood, she took the first job offered her after graduation with the production department of a magazine, for which she was still working 7 years later. The nature of her work prevented her from introducing her own ideas into articles. Most of the time she was engaged in a glorified form of proofreading. She was paid a relatively meager salary that barely allowed her to meet her expenses.

Great demands were placed on her time, leaving her with little freedom or motivation to do any writing of her own. She was too demoralized to actively search for another position. She was caught in a trap that repeatedly reinforced her low self-esteem, feeding again and again the inner conflict that had created it in the first place.

Traps can be built just as easily—and effectively—by men and women who have collected all the external evidence of social and material success. Adam Barclay was born poor. His family lived in Detroit. His father was an unemployed alcoholic and his mother worked as a clerk-typist. Adam was an unusually bright student and won acclaim again and again for his academic achievements. He was awarded a scholarship to the Wharton School of Business, from which he was graduated at the top of his class. "Damn it," he said to himself, "I'm going to make a million dollars before I'm 30." And he did.

He started a chain of computer software stores with two other men, which quickly flourished. He worked 11 hours a day and on weekends. He was asked to be on numerous boards and to involve himself in community activities, all of which he accepted. In fact, he could not say no, since each new offer brought with it a new occasion to associate with wealthy and prominent men and women in his community.

By the time he was 37, he began to lose interest in the various enterprises he had built. "I want out," he told his wife, Ruth, repeatedly, "but I don't know how to get out. There's no one else who can run things if I leave." Ruth, in turn, had begun to drink more and more, out of loneliness and a sense of social inadequacy. She had grown up with Adam in Detroit and had never felt comfortable with their new friends. She avoided the country club and important social occasions as often as she could. They had two children. The eldest, a boy of 11, was an underachiever in school. He was very bright, but because of a painfully low level of self-confidence and a generally apathetic attitude, he could barely pass his classes.

Adam Barclay's house in suburban Westchester had become a trap, a solidly constructed one built by his own hands as he drove himself relentlessly on to accept every new opportunity that came along. What had begun as his determination "never to be poor like my parents" became a compulsive need to accumulate more wealth, more power, more recognition than ten people would need in a lifetime. Adam realized this—painfully—but had no idea what to do about it.

Traps are constructed, on the whole, by human beings who are chronically depressed or who lack inner freedom, who are not what the late psychologist Abraham Maslow called "self-actualizing." According to Maslow's concept, healthy and mature adults should be capable of identifying and moving spontaneously toward goals which are in keeping with their value systems, reflective of their personality needs, and at the same time attainable within the environment, even though such achievement usually involves overcoming obstacles. The late psychoanalyst Lawrence Kubie stated that mature people in touch with their feelings and abilities can consider and choose among legitimate options and can move toward worthwhile objectives with a freedom unknown to the compulsive or phobic people. The latter must repeatedly exhaust themselves using "will power" to overcome inner resistances and fears. Only a small segment of the adult population can be said to be self-actualizing. The rest of us are more vulnerable to the game of building traps.

Western society, while in many ways facilitating the conditions for self-actualization, has in other ways become a civilization of traps. Millions of people feel that the roads to sexual fulfillment, self-esteem, work satisfaction, financial security, equal opportunity, personal dignity, and spiritual meaning are closed at every turn. They are, however, sharply aware of a social and economic mobility that seems to promise, somewhere, somehow, the fulfillment of these needs. A society undergoing rapid change is a society of people painfully aware of unfulfilled ambitions. The white upper-middle-class couple in Lake Forest, Illinois may hurt as much because of a lack of sexual and emotional fulfillment in their marriage as does the black family in metropolitan Los Angeles because of neighborhood violence and limited economic and educational opportunities. Obviously, the nature of the deprivation is different in these two instances. The role of the environment in preserving the deprivation is different. Nonetheless, the upper-middle-class couple and the family in the ghetto are caught in similar traps—expanding expectations with few visible signs of fulfillment.

One of the most dangerous traps of all is the failure to recognize the presence of depression and respond accordingly to its message. Denial on the part of the individual is reinforced by social values that encourage resistance to insight. What are these values?

In certain sections of our society, it is considered better to engage in empty sexual affairs, to exploit others financially within the limits of the law, and to pursue self-defeating forms of behavior—as long as these do not directly involve suicide or physical injury to someone else—than to spend a few sleepless nights contemplating with some measure of anguish who one is and what one's life is all about.

In our society, people frequently use drugs such as alcohol, benzodiazepines, and marijuana to dull emotional pain. Regardless of the overt efforts to control such drug abuse, the continued spread of the problem strongly indicates the presence of factors in society that covertly encourage the use of such methods to block awareness and avoid facing depression.

One of the more popular mechanisms used to avoid facing depression and gaining insight is to place the blame on others—especially on someone close to you or on large, readily identifiable groups such as blacks or whites, employers or employees, youths or adults, men or women, that can serve as targets. Denying one's own problems and placing the blame on someone else is not only a temporarily effective way of postponing depression; it can also be a brilliant device for obscuring the real issues and elaborating on the original trap.

Jean Carter was a 43-year-old divorcée who worked as an interior decorator for a department store in Kansas City, Kansas. For 7 years she had lived alone with her two children, a boy who was now 17 and a daughter who was 14. During the previous 11 years of her marriage to Roger, they had rarely engaged in disagreements. Their sexual adjustment had been quite unsatisfactory for her and for him as well, but they never discussed it. Silently, each blamed the other for lacking in affection. They made no efforts to explore or improve the relationship.

Together they had created an adequate social life and achieved a place in their community. They were financially secure. They were a successful American middle-class family. Suddenly Roger demanded a divorce. Jane was shocked. She started to feel acutely depressed. After a few sleepless nights she discovered that a drink or two before bedtime would help ease her tension.

Three months after the divorce, Roger married his secretary. "We have a lot in common," he told a friend, "and what a sex life!" The marriage lasted 18 months. Meanwhile, Jane drank steadily as loneliness pressed in on her. She dated occasionally, and went to bed with a few men who would take her to dinner. When she became aware of some feelings of depression and disdain in regard to these experiences, she could suppress them rapidly with a few martinis before her date arrived. "I liked my freedom. It's quite a surprise. Roger was a horror. I know that now."

When her son dropped out of his senior year in high school, she called Roger. "He's *your* son. Do something about it." But by now Roger was into his third marriage and busily working in Boston. "The kid hasn't been in touch with me in nearly a year," he thought. "Besides, it's his problem. Let him work it out."

Jane Carter and her family can be considered victims of the trap of denial. They avoided communicating with each other about sensitive issues during their marriage. When the trap finally closed, she handled her depression through drinking and her husband handled his by rapidly building new traps for himself. They would not permit themselves to acknowledge and understand the depression warranted by the situation. Had they done so, they might have recognized the nature of their dilemma earlier. With this insight they might have resolved their emotional and sexual impasses. Or they might have terminated their marriage more sensibly and sustained their parental relationship.

Breaking Out

Becoming aware of living in a trap—whether it is imposed by the environment or created by one's own machinations—will induce an episode of acute depression. *Awareness of self-made traps is the first in a series of steps leading to insight and to the ability to free oneself from the traps.* One usually experiences this awareness as a realization of its external fabric—the job, the marriage, the social situation—which is seen as the main cause of the hopelessness and tension. "I've married the wrong woman." "My husband has changed; I can't live with him any longer." "I've been passed over for a promotion twice, and there isn't going to be a third time."

The next step in the process of insight also involves acute depression as the individual realizes how effectively he or she has collaborated with his or her environment in constructing the trap. "I had just gotten my accounting degree," said a 39-year-old man in therapy. "I was only 24. I felt I wasn't ready to get married. But Susan pushed it. When she said she'd break it off if we didn't get married right then, I should have stopped to wonder about what her real feelings toward me were. I was afraid to, so I gave in.

"When the children came, I was making out well in practice. We had a nice house, a good social life, lots of friends. Sex was just O.K. What made me tense a lot of the time was the way she could go after me when she was angry. She made me feel that it was always my fault whenever something went wrong.

"I remember once we were supposed to meet some friends at a restaurant. I showed up early and Carol and Jim were there on time. Forty-five minutes later Susan showed up, angry. 'Why have you kept me waiting?' she insisted. 'You told me it was the Steak House, not the Lobster Pit. Luckily, I called home to find out what you told the baby sitter. The least you could do is apologize.' I know I told her the right place, but to this day I feel guilty.

"Somehow or other I felt I really needed Susan. She knew that

I felt I'd fall apart or something without her. I never had a real mother. My parents were divorced when I was 4, and my father brought me up with a housekeeper. Mother married someone else and I didn't see much of her.

"Susan and I have been married 15 years now. Last summer I really got depressed—couldn't concentrate, had to take three weeks off from work, felt nearly suicidal. Somehow I pulled myself together and went on, but from then on I realized that I was caught in a trap with Susan. I can't get angry at her. I can't stand my ground when she goes after me. She goes after me like a truck. I guess if I divorced her that might solve something, but I don't even think I can do that. I need her too much.

"I've been pretty depressed again this year, but now I know it isn't just Susan beating on me. It's how I can't handle it . . . how I actually encourage it . . . why I married someone like Susan in the first place, someone I thought I could depend on for strength. It's me I've got to change."

A third step in the process of escaping from the trap involves changing the environment: finding another job, getting a divorce, or encouraging one's partner to cooperate in a process of improving the relationship. At the same time, there must also be an inner reaching for freedom from the conflicts and constrictions that induced the creation of the trap in the first place and nurtured it over a period of years. Each aspect—physically getting out of the trap, changing the environment, or modifying behavioral and emotional patterns conducive to trap-building—inevitably involves experiencing acute depression. One of the most important reasons so few people free themselves from inner or external traps is their natural—though unfortunate—reluctance to experience the pain of acute depression. Again and again psychiatrists see in their patients the acute depression that results from having attempted to interrupt an ingrained pattern of behavior that was detrimental to their lives.

Acute depression, in other words, alerts people to the fact that they have become entrapped. It will be activated by any efforts they make to escape their traps. The successful management of acute depression is an inherent part of the process of changing their personalities, which makes it possible for them to free themselves from the need to construct new traps.

To acknowledge that one is depressed is the first step toward escaping an entrapment or freeing oneself from chronic depression. It is essential, therefore, to recognize the many forms in which depression can appear.

Chapter 4

♦ ♦ ❖ ♦ ♦ ❖ ♦ ♦ ❖ ♦ ♦ ❖ ♦ ♦ ❖ ♦ ♦ ❖ ♦ ♦

How to Recognize Depression

Most people find it difficult to acknowledge that they are depressed. In fact, it has been reported that there is an average time lag of 3 years between the event responsible for an individual's depression and the point at which he or she recognizes that he or she is experiencing depression.

We can easily misinterpret a clinical depression for which we may need help as a normal episode of depression that is part of the human condition. Most men, commented Thoreau, "lead lives of quiet desperation." "Man's life oscillates like a pendulum between boredom and sorrow," wrote Schopenhauer. Sartre and other existentialists have emphasized that people must go through an awareness of hopelessness and experience the emptiness and anguish of life as part of becoming capable of determining their own future.

Then again, depressive moods are often suppressed or blocked out because most people would like to sustain a feeling of euphoria as much of the time as possible. Thus, depression, being painful, is frequently denied.

A lowering of mood may cause a general slowing up in the thinking and actions of anyone who is depressed. This change is misleading; depression is, in fact, an intensely active process, and hence painful. Even though the depressed person may withdraw from social contacts and experience a greater or lesser degree of immobilization, this response is the *effect* of the depression rather than the cause. Beneath the surface, at times beyond the person's real awareness, is a highly turbulent mixture of fear and anguish. The right questions, the right remarks, can readily tap it. It is not surprising, then, that fatigue is a common symptom of depression. Hypervigilance of the nervous system can be exhausting, and the tension produced by making an intense effort to work against the inertia caused by depression can be exhausting.

Because this inner anguish can be intolerable at times, there is a natural tendency to seek temporary relief through the use of commonly available drugs, whether they are "ups," "downs," or alcohol, which itself is a depressant. There is also a tendency to ward off depression by such "antidepressant" forms of behavior as overspending, sexual promiscuity, compulsive overworking—patterns that ultimately reinforce the underlying depressive conflicts. Since depression is itself a new stress to which a person will react, one's response to it can take many forms, ranging from boredom and ennui to overwhelming panic.

Among the more common ways of coping with depression are: to be dimly aware of it, to procrastinate about coming to terms with it, to engage in formidable rationalizations, and to deny the significance of its signs: "I can't get to sleep at night, and I wake up at four or five in the morning. That's why I'm tired and haven't any interest in what I'm doing. If I could sleep I'd feel a lot better. Depressed? Of course not."

Basic Signs of Depression

Many of us fail to recognize depression because we do not know what signs to look for. There are certain basic changes associated with depression, not all of which are present in every case. No two people manifest each and every emotional and behavioral change at the same time or even in the same way.

First, depression is commonly associated with a sleep disturbance.

Most depressed individuals will notice a disruption in sleep habits. It may take them longer to fall asleep. They tend to waken more often during the night and sleep more lightly. They are likely to wake up very early, well before their normal time for rising. Waking hours—before falling asleep and after awakening in the morning—are spent stewing over problems and pressures. Though unaware of it, they are often afraid of going to bed at night and find any excuse to stay up. They are equally afraid of facing the day that lies in front of them. Anyone with a significant or a long-standing sleep disturbance should consider the possibility that he or she is depressed.

The second important sign of depression is a decrease in sex drive. This can be especially troublesome in our culture, which places much value on sexual athletics. Such a change may indicate that the conflicts giving rise to the depression are of a sexual nature; more often, it reflects a general decrease in energy or a rechanneling of energy into an effort to cope with the lowered mood. A waning of sexual interest should always raise the question of depression.

Closely related to the decrease in sexual drive are a loss of appetite and the disappearance of normal enjoyment in eating. These in turn lead to a significant loss in weight. People may not even be aware of the fact that they are eating less than usual until they find that their clothes are a bit too large and that the scales show a weight loss of five or ten pounds.

Finally, there is the subjective experience of the depression—how people perceive what they are feeling. "I hurt all over inside." "I feel like crying most of the time, but I can't." "I cry too easily; I can't control it." "I'm just plain unhappy." "I've lost interest in everything I used to care about." "I'm scared as hell." "I'm bored." "I can't make a decision." "I can't concentrate effectively." "I feel just hopeless."

For many, the mood of depression is experienced as a lack of self-confidence. There is a close link between mood and self-esteem. People who feel that they are "failures," "worthless," "ineffective," "undeserving" are often, in fact, depressed.

If people are aware of the issues that seem to have triggered the depression, they may tend to dwell on them ruminatively. "Mother died 5 months ago. I can't get her out of my mind." "I really feel boxed in at work, by the people under me and by my supervisors." "This marriage isn't going anywhere." "I'm so terribly lonely since the divorce." "Why the hell can't we communicate?" Depressed people often have a feeling of urgency and of being trapped. They can see no solutions to their impasses. There is no way out. Their mood ranges from apathy to despair.

The basic signs of depression are: insomnia, a waning of sexual interest, a marked decrease in appetite, a loss of self-esteem, fatigue, and an inner mood change ranging from boredom to frank hopelessness. It is as if the biological energy flow that normally reaches out from a person to his or her environment has been blocked, while inner agitation and anguish churn around within the nervous system. Preoccupied with their own distress, depressed people appear on the surface to be self-centered, unresponsive to outside stimulation, and apparently indifferent to the needs of others. It is easy to see why they may initially provoke sympathy, then impatience, anger, and finally outright rejection—the very thing they most fear—from those with whom they live and work but who do not understand what they are experiencing.

A special group of people fail to recognize that they are depressed because of a tendency to cope with the stress of being depressed through counterreactions. Instead of losing weight, they overeat. Instead of waning sexual interest, they seek out sexual experiences almost compulsively. Instead of insomnia, they oversleep, partly as a result of tiredness but largely as a way of withdrawing from an environment they find unbearable. These behavioral changes are called "atypical" and probably indicate somewhat different psychological and biological mechanisms at work.

There are other changes that result from being depressed that can serve as important clues. Difficulty in making decisions that otherwise could be made with little effort, problems with concentration, and a marked tendency to put things off are common. Depressed people may find it more difficult to write and read, but this is often rationalized as a loss of interest. They procrastinate in making plans or commitments, delaying everything from arranging a weekend social schedule to rewiring a lamp to looking for a new

job. This, too, is often rationalized: "I'd do it if I had r
"I'm basically lazy."

Depressed people usually need to withdraw fron
others, even those who are normally gregarious and outgoing.
aversion toward social contacts is not really a desire to be alone; they are often painfully lonely and fear rejection. Instead, it reflects a fear of interpersonal contact, caused partly by the inner pain and the exquisite sensitivity to careless or unkind remarks. It is also a result of the overall reduction in the outward flow of energy and in their ability to give of themselves to others.

Because of a change in the perception of time, events seem to occur more slowly. For depressed people, the Bergsonian concept of mutable time is a reality. The person may feel slowed up, regardless of inner agitation. Consequently, the resolution of issues which in fact may be only days or weeks away seems to him to be an interminable distance in the future. "There is no turning back no going forward. I feel helpless. The hours and days drag by. I can't stand it," is the way one woman described her hopelessness.

A person's ability to piece together these various subjective changes and to admit that he or she is depressed is certainly sharper when the depression is acute, and particularly when the triggering events are easily identifiable. It is much more difficult to detect depression when it has settled into a long-standing pattern, even to the point of being confused with personality characteristics ("This is the way I am, negative, a pessimist"), and when the mood cannot be related to its causes. Therefore, in determining whether someone is depressed, it is important to go beyond the questions "How do I feel?" and "How has my behavior changed?" and consider, in addition, "Am I the kind of person who might become depressed?" and "What kind of environment am I living and working in?"

One should ask oneself: "Have I experienced anything in the last few years likely to set off a depression? Have I been rejected by someone I loved? Has anyone died? Has anything happened at work to threaten my self-esteem?"

There are certain events that *should* cause some degree of depression; for example, a major change in one's life situation, for better or worse: a promotion, a divorce, the death of a parent or child, leaving home in adolescence, retirement, loss of physical health, financial reverses, marrying, having a child. When the reaction to such events is prompt and appropriately intense, the depression, being acute, is not hard to detect. However, when it begins slowly and builds up over a number of months or years, the insidious immobilization, insomnia, fatigue, withdrawal, and unresponsiveness may be hard to link to the source of these symptoms, and hence harder to account for.

Martha Wrightson was 61 years old when her husband died. She had been very close to him during the 33 years of their marriage. They had no children. She worked as a secretary to the president of a large bottling plant and continued, after her husband's death, to live in the same apartment they had occupied during his lifetime.

He died in June. Martha found it hard to cry. She shared her grief with no one. Instead, she tried to lose herself in her work. During the late summer she took a 2-week vacation, but, finding herself bored and restless at the seaside resort, she cut it short and returned to work. The following Christmas holidays were especially difficult. She was lonely, often waking at night and missing having her husband in bed next to her. During the fall and early winter, she noticed a tiredness that grew progressively more intense. She attributed it to her age and the weather.

In the early part of February, a few days before the anniversary of her husband's birthday, Martha found it hard to get out of bed in the mornings. She was late to work several times, which was most unusual for this very punctual woman. On the job, she began putting things off more and more. On several occasions her normally pleasant, but by now impatient, employer responded with annoyance to her slowness and seeming lack of responsibility. Although she felt that she was "in the wrong," her feelings were deeply hurt by his criticism. One day she impulsively handed in her resignation.

Fortunately, her employer did not accept it. Instead, he insisted that she speak with her family doctor about her health. She was initially tempted to reject his suggestion as an intrusion into her personal life, but, sensing his real concern, she eventually decided to follow his advice.

Martha's physician recognized that she was depressed. He started her on an antidepressant drug and arranged to see her twice a week for half an hour, during which time he encouraged her to review and release the feelings she had stored up about losing her husband. A piece of guilt emerged. She had not pressed her husband strongly enough, she thought, to get an annual physical examination. "Had I done so, his cancer might have been picked up sooner. He might still be alive."

Within 2 months, Martha was more cheerful and energetic, though still experiencing mild bouts of fatigue, as if she had recovered from a long illness. She was again doing her usual fine job and enjoying it.

For Martha Wrightson, the slow emergence of her depression—in this case an inadequately handled grief reaction—prevented her from dealing directly on an emotional level with her loss. She did not relate the disintegration in her performance to her husband's death and her reaction to it because of the long delay between the causal event and the surfacing of her depression. She had not even considered herself depressed until her doctor pointed it out to her. She was amazed to discover that the release of her feelings and the relief afforded her by antidepressant medication could so quickly restore her normal spirits.

Special Vulnerability

In assessing her vulnerability to depression, Martha Wrightson could have considered another important clue: the kind of person she was. The personality of the individual is highly relevant to whether he may become depressed under certain circumstances.

Susceptible people are especially vulnerable to loss. Studies indicate that if a person has experienced a significant loss during his or her formative years, such as the death of a parent or other important family member, the vulnerability to depression is heightened. Susceptible people are also conscientious, responsible, and have a high personal ethic. They are quick to feel guilty, whether warranted or not, whether consciously or not. They may be ambitious and energetic when in normal spirits, and competitive as well.

In spite of a tendency to be self-absorbed, susceptible people do care about the feelings of others, sometimes too much so, and may be overly cautious lest they inadvertently hurt others' feelings. They have a strong need to be liked and respected. They tend to find themselves in deep and sometimes overwhelming involvements and quite dependent on those they love. They are inflexible and have difficulty in setting limits. They are highly sensitive to anything that would reduce their self-esteem in their own eyes or in the eyes of others. They find rejection especially painful. Their need for self-control is strong; yet, paradoxically, they are often vulnerable to being controlled by others without always appreciating what is happening. They also have a need to maintain control over their environments, as a way of handling insecurities and avoiding hurt, and may become quite frightened when such control is jeopardized.

Susceptible people have difficulty managing their hostility. At times they are not even aware of their own anger. It is difficult for them to mobilize their emotions in their own defense, even when it is justifiable and necessary to do so. Patience, usually a virtue, is often their liability. When their hostility is repeatedly provoked, whether openly or covertly, in a job, a marriage, or in an environment in which the normal expression of anger is severely suppressed, they may find it hard to maintain their emotional equilibrium.

A further clue to the presence of depression is the quality of the interaction between oneself and one's environment. An important question to ask is: *"What kind of psychological climate do I live in?"* In certain homes, a free expression of ideas and feelings is simply not tolerated; in others, angry, deprecatory, and vicious feelings are repeatedly voiced. In working with depressed patients, the therapist can often identify a lack of communication within the patient's family and a lack of respect for ordinary sensitivities.

Similarly, the environment of an organization can reinforce the self-esteem of those within it. On the other hand, it can also sabotage them by encouraging destructive competitiveness, stifling open communication, setting impossible expectations, or, by indifference or undue permissiveness, not fostering any expectations at all. People who work in such a setting may have a hard time holding onto their identities. They may become insecure and afraid of assuming responsibility. "If it works and is profitable, the organization gets the credit. If it fails, the blame is all yours!" They may become immobilized in their efforts: withhold their comments, refuse to introduce new ideas, do only what has to be done to maintain their positions, and reinforce the demoralizing atmosphere within the entire organization. Such homes and offices can be considered depressogenic; that is, likely to induce depression in most of their inhabitants.

Certain occupations are also especially depressogenic: medicine, for instance. Physicians have extremely high rates of suicide, divorce, and psychosomatic disorders. Corporate executives represent another group with a high incidence of stress-related conditions, such as alcoholism, cardiovascular disease, and other types of psychosomatic disorders. These conditions often result from the presence of underlying depression, unrecognized and unmanaged.

Here are *five major questions* to ask yourself to help determine whether you may be depressed:

1. Are you experiencing one or more of the cardinal signs of depression (sleeplessness or oversleeping, poor appetite or the tendency to overeat, a marked decease or increase in libido, a drop in self-esteem, fatigue, a loss of energy, persistent nervousness and tension, down moods)?

2. Have any major changes, good or bad, taken place in your life over the last few years that might have set off a depression?

3. Are you the kind of person likely to be susceptible to depression?

4. Could depression be lurking behind self-defeating behavior patterns, like abusing alcohol or drugs, compulsive gambling, underachievement, or provocative, irritating interpersonal behavior?

5. Are you living or working in a demoralizing environment?

Even after such a self-assessment, depression may sometimes be hard to detect since it is often concealed behind the particular way in which each person reacts to any stress including the stress of depression itself.

Chapter 5

♦ ♦ ❖ ♦ ♦ ❖ ♦ ♦ ❖ ♦ ♦ ❖ ♦ ♦ ❖ ♦ ♦ ❖ ♦ ♦

Camouflage

Although it is important to envision depression as a way of reacting to stress, it is equally important to realize that *depression is itself a stress* to which the individual inevitably reacts. In some people, a mild depression that transiently impairs concentration and encourages indecisiveness may be barely noticeable. By contrast, a person with another type of personality may experience the same degree of depression as highly painful and irritating. In other words, it is often difficult to tell *how much* depression is present from the overt reaction of the individual, since different people will react differently to the same degree of depression.

One case in point is William Agess, a specialist on the New York Stock Exchange. He worked on the floor of the trading center, where he was constantly involved in rapid-fire bidding and had to closely follow the swings in prices of various securities. He was conscientious, ambitious, and perfectionistic.

As a result of domestic problems, he became slightly depressed. Unable to sleep for several nights, preoccupied with his wife's complaints about their life together, he found it more and more difficult to attend to his work. He became frightened that he might make an important error involving thousands of dollars. This fear reinforced his depression until finally, seriously immobilized, he had to ask for several weeks off. During his absence from work, he began to fear that his firm would find someone else to take his place. He had hoped to be named a partner within a year or so. Now feeling that this was less likely, he experienced a growing rage at himself for his "incompetence." His anxiety mounted to such a degree that he often paced aimlessly about his apartment, further frightening himself and his family.

What had begun, in this instance, as a minor depressive reaction rapidly evolved into a nightmare—not because of the intensity of the depression, but because of William Agess's rigidity and perfectionism. Having a compulsive need to perform at a high level of efficiency at all times, he reacted to depression with panic.

Panic, like depression, is itself a psychobiological reaction to stress. Some severely depressed patients have an elevated level of corticosteroids—hormones formed in the adrenal glands in response to stress—circulating in the blood. This elevation in steroids may not, however, be related to the depression itself, but to the stress of being depressed, since the abnormally high level usually returns to normal during the first week or 10 days of hospitalization, long before the depression itself has begun to lift. Such a biological change would indicate a lessening in the panic the patient had felt during whatever circumstances led to hospitalization.

How you react to being depressed depends very much on your personality and environment. Some people are conditioned to giving up; others tend to drive themselves on more and more relentlessly. Compare these two instances:

Alice Larvin was a junior in college when she first became depressed over her relationship with a boyfriend who seemed considerably less interested in her than she was in him. She became increasingly apathetic about her schoolwork—putting off term papers, finding it difficult to concentrate in class discussions. Though normally an active participant, she was now silent and slightly morose. She began to cut classes and spent her time in her room, ruminating about her situation. She occasionally thought of dying, but dismissed such thoughts quickly. After a month or so of lethargic, apathetic behavior, she decided to drop out of college and go home. Her parents did not seriously object. With their help, she obtained a part-time job at the local library. She felt "unhappy" but was also convinced that there was little or nothing for her to do about her state. When former boyfriends called her up, she avoided speaking with them and refused to make any dates.

Except for some boredom and discontent, and occasional bouts of diarrhea and intestinal cramps, she settled into her new routine for over a year. Alice, in the face of being mildly depressed, had given up.

By contrast, Simon Rank, the executive director of a research institute in biologic sciences, became depressed when he was faced with sudden stresses both in his professional career and in his marriage. He felt torn between concentrating on improving his home life and maintaining his heavy responsibilities at the institute, where he was threatened by conflicts with his board of directors.

Simon began to work 10 hours a day, preparing reports, going over plans and budgets. Being somewhat slowed down and having trouble paying attention to details, he attempted to compensate through time and effort for what he had lost in concentration and decisiveness. At home, his wife increasingly complained about the long hours he was spending at the office and expressed concern about his health. Their time together deteriorated into arguments; Simon pleaded with his wife for more patience with the pressures he was under.

He slept about 4 hours a night, skipped meals, lost eight pounds, and felt utterly exhausted. Nevertheless, the worse he felt, the harder he pushed himself—until he could push no longer. Unable to resolve his depression, and at the same time unable to withdraw from the field even temporarily, he suddenly developed chest pains that forced his family physician to hospitalize him for a careful checkup, in the course of which his depression was recognized and treatment for it began.

An individual's personality—how he or she usually responds to stress—will have a strong influence on the particular way he reacts to a change of mood. One of the most common ways of reacting to depression is the activation of anxiety and tension. The prominence of such feelings can often totally camouflage the underlying depression. Anxiety is, essentially, a state of apprehension, nervousness, mild fear, and uneasiness. If it has an irrational focus, it is called a phobia; common phobias include fear of heights, of enclosed places, and of crowds. Anxiety is often "free floating," unattached to any object but readily zooming in on ordinary preoccupations that concern everyone, such as financial difficulties or health problems. "If only I had a little more money, I wouldn't have any more problems." "Could this little lump in my breast be malignant? Maybe the doctor is wrong."

Anxiety is often associated with physical symptoms as well: heart palpitations, profuse sweating, dizziness, and weakness. It is physically distinct from tension, which involves a generalized tautness in the skeletal musculature of the entire body. People with severe tension often say that they feel as if they are in a "vise," a suit of armor that is too tight and that presses in on them. Tension, of course, may also be localized and involve only parts of the body, causing neck stiffness, chest pains, difficulty in breathing, headaches, or a tightness and heaviness in the muscles of the legs.

Anxiety is caused by the awareness that something is wrong without one quite knowing where the danger is coming from. Tension, however, is usually caused by recurrent stresses that require one to maintain control over one's emotions and the situation simultaneously. A salesperson, for instance, confronted with a series of potential customers who are both rude and demanding, may have to resist the urge to flail out at them in a temper, thereby building up tension during that particular day. A highly conscientious computer technician may build up tension when his or her machine keeps delivering erroneous information and he or she cannot rapidly locate the error in the program.

Anxiety and tension are common ways of reacting to stress. When the stress is depression itself, they may become pronounced. Unfortunately, if a depressed person consults a physician, he or she is often treated only for anxiety and tension, and the underlying depression may remain camouflaged for a long time. *A depression should always be suspected if episodes of anxiety and tension persist month after month, and are not relieved by such ordinary measures as recreation or a vacation and do not respond to tranquilizers taken for a short time only and on the advice of a physician.*

If an individual has any psychoneurotic anxiety symptoms—and most people have some, such as mild phobias—he or she may respond to becoming depressed by a sudden upsurge in fear.

At the age of 23, Edna Markey consulted a psychiatrist because of severe phobias that clustered around traveling. She was afraid to ride in cars, trains, planes, buses. These constrictions had begun to develop in the course of her first sexual experience with a young man about whom she felt quite uncertain.

When Edna terminated this relationship and gained insight through therapy into the guilt and ambivalence she felt toward sex and men, her fears subsided. She subsequently got married, had three children, and lived a quiet, uncomplicated life. Although she never fully lost her fear of traveling, she was able, with the help of her husband, who did the driving, and by taking a drink or a tranquilizer before boarding planes, to get about quite well.

When she was 43, her mother died of cancer. At the same time, her 18-year-old daughter became pregnant and had an abortion. Edna herself was then about twenty pounds overweight and was feeling somewhat old and unattractive.

Her husband, wanting to cheer her up after the funeral and her daughter's abortion, arranged for a trip to the Caribbean. She was pleased. But, as the day of departure approached, her fear of flying reached near-panic proportions. She insisted that the trip be canceled. Angrily, her husband complied.

Gradually, over the next few weeks, her fears expanded. At first she would not go anywhere in the car. Then she would not even leave her house. Any attempt to do so caused her to feel faint, frightened, tense. As long as she remained at home she was comfortable, although she did not sleep well at night. These fears forced her, of course, to avoid social engagements, and she was even unable to bring herself to attend her son's graduation from high school. Her family, having no understanding of what was happening, grew increasingly impatient with her behavior. This impatience, in turn, only reinforced her sense of hopelessness.

Edna Markey's traditional way of handling conflict and stress was to employ a mechanism known as dissociation; that is, to shut out of consciousness the conflicts she encountered and the feelings associated with those conflicts, and to develop in their place a network of phobic fears. This is a common maneuver employed by men and women with what is termed a "hysterical psychoneurotic pattern of reaction." Naturally, when she became depressed, she reverted to her usual way of managing stress.

However, the clues to what she was experiencing could be found by looking at her behavior and, for the moment, ignoring her phobias that camouflaged the depression. She was immobilized and felt a growing sense of futility that she blamed on her immobilization. She slept poorly. She withdrew. All the elements of a depression were visible, but neither Edna nor her family recognized them. Even the precipitating event, her mother's death, followed the classic pattern: the loss of a person important to her.

Depression, then, is a reaction to stress that itself becomes a stress and is handled through the particular mode of behavior characteristic of each person. For certain people, it is vitally important to function at a high level of effectiveness, and the slowing up and constriction ordinarily associated with being depressed represent a special threat to them. Others tend to overeat under pressure and, when depressed, will show a marked increase in weight, rather than a loss, as they fill up with food to relieve their sense of emptiness. For some, direct physical tension is the primary way of acknowledging the change in mood.

Whenever Harold Vetter was under pressure, in business or in his personal life, he could "feel it." The muscles on the back of his neck were tight. He felt a tautness in his calves, and would often play squash or walk a couple of miles to loosen up. Because of chest pains every now and then, he was afraid that he might be having a heart attack, and he was reassured only when an electrocardiogram showed that his heart was normal. From time to time he developed headaches, but aspirin would usually relieve them. "I'm a tense guy. When you're involved in the textile business—a hell of a lot of risk and one uncertainty after another, tough, competitive—you're going to get tense. A lot. But I've figured out ways to beat it. They always work."

When Harold became depressed after his only son's failure to obtain admission to law school and Harold's discovery, a few months later, that his wife had been having an affair, he did not recognize his depression as such. He felt no despair; though he was resentful, he felt no more pessimistic about life than usual. Moving out of his home to a small apartment, he continued to play golf on weekends, occasionally took out models and buyers, and began to show up for work at 6:30 in the morning.

Now, however, his ordinary methods for releasing tension began to fail. Tension kept him awake at night. His headaches increased in frequency and duration, and aspirin barely touched them. After a game of squash, he felt tighter and more fatigued than he had in the past. At work, the ordinary pressures in his everyday life now affected him profoundly. Being tense, he was frequently sharp and angry with his partners and employees. He felt as if his body were constantly in a strait jacket, which sometimes closed tighter and tighter around him until he could hardly breathe.

Harold saw his doctor several times. The physician's reassurance about his physical health was no longer enough to quiet his fears, and during his last visit he stormed angrily out of the office, shouting that he would find himself another and more competent doctor. When his wife's lawyers attempted to initiate a reconciliation, he made it clear that he was not about to go home again, nor would he give her a divorce.

At no time did it occur to him that he was depressed. Tension, irritability, and concern about his physical health combined with his conviction that the "world was against him" to deprive him of the insight that he was reacting, true to his form, to the stress of being depressed.

Attempts to reduce tension or anxiety that conceal depression usually fail, whether such attempts take the form of a vacation, a divorce, or a change of jobs, since the real mood change remains unrecognized and unresolved. Because depression can manifest itself in so many different ways, the average person may be confused over what he or she is experiencing.

Often, with the mention of the word "depression," a patient will acknowledge, "Oh, yes! I am depressed." A sense of relief may occur when the patient is told that his or her fatigue are not due to physical problems such as loss of appetite, weight loss, or illness. At last it all makes sense. The patient can now understand that what he or she has been experiencing is depression.

Different Ways of Experiencing Depression

Existential psychoanalysts, such as Ludwig Binswanger, departing from the traditional psychoanalytic mold of seeking answers primarily in the patient's history, have encouraged therapists to ask not only what the patient is experiencing, but *how* he or she is experiencing it. This is a crucial question in the matter of depression. Many people will use the term "depression" loosely, saying that they are depressed when in fact they are not. And many, because of the way in which they react to being depressed or because they are out of contact with their inner feelings, will deny being depressed when, in fact, they are.

> "I'm not really depressed," stated a young woman of 28. "I'm lonely. I'm so lonely that it hurts. As long as I have a boyfriend, I'm fine. I can be alone then, and read or putter, and it doesn't bother me. But when I don't have anyone, I get so agitated that I could jump out of my skin. I can't do a thing. I can't bear being by myself."
>
> "Frightened, I'd say," said a 40-year-old woman.
>
> "I'm always afraid, of losing my husband to another woman, of losing my job, of something terrible happening to one of my children. These fears haunt me. I haven't always been this way, only for the past year, since we moved to our new house."
>
> "Afraid of being a homosexual," answered a third-year medical student, "Ever since last term when we had our lecture on sexual abnormalities. It really troubles me. Sometimes the thoughts crowd in so much I can't concentrate on my work. I feel like quitting school for awhile. I must really be in bad shape. I haven't had any homosexual experiences, of course.

But I have had a hell of a lot of difficulty making it with girls I like."

"Angry," said the middle-aged social worker.

"Angry at the whole goddamn world, day in and day out. Not bitter, you understand. Just angry."

"Empty. An emptiness that makes me want to die."

The existential analysts emphasize that the way in which people describe what they are experiencing is an invaluable clue to the nature of the underlying problem. For instance, when Edna Markey, whose depression was manifested as a rash of phobias, was asked in therapy how she experienced her phobic condition, she replied: "It's crippling. I feel like a prisoner, as if I have been guilty of some crime. My husband and children are angry at me, and that makes me feel really worthless. I don't want to see my friends. I feel like a failure as a mother. Somehow I feel it's my fault that my daughter had to have an abortion. If my mother were alive now, she'd feel it was my fault."

At once the depressive quality of Edna's experience and the enormous guilt contributing to her state are apparent when the "how" of what she is experiencing is explored, when one goes beyond the more visible manifestations of her reaction.

The case of Simon Rank is similar. "There's no other way," he said, describing his compulsion to overwork. "I am convinced that if I stop moving, everything will fall apart. I won't be able to get started again. I have no choice. I can't be spontaneous any more. Life drives me, I don't drive it. I am really scared of being helpless. There isn't anyone to depend on. If I stop, I'm dead."

The complex ways in which people experience themselves make it difficult to measure "how much" depression may be present. Simon Rank, with his strong determination to keep his life in one piece, his energetic attack on the world in the face of falling apart, may indeed have been quantitatively "more depressed" than Alice Larvin who quit school, went home for a year, and gave up rather than push against obstacles built by depression. To the casual observer, Simon Rank's ability to cope might well conceal the depth of his despair, whereas Alice Larvin's compliance with her unhappiness might conceal the mildness of her depression.

Recognizing depression, therefore, is complicated by the fact that depression, being a shock to the human system, will be handled by each person in his or her own way. Sometimes people handle depression by acting out.

Acting Out, and Alcohol and Drug Misuse

The psychiatrist uses the term *acting out* to describe the translation of an inner conflict into a behavioral change. Releasing anger in a direct way, for example, is not a form of acting out. By definition, acting out implies that a person is not aware of how his or her action pattern is determined by inner conflict. Hence, until the person who is acting out gains insight, it is beyond his or her control. Depressed teenagers who repeatedly provoke their parents and teachers by not studying and by defying rules are not likely to establish for themselves the connection between their inner sense of hopelessness and the behavior that evokes, again and again, the disappointment of, or punishment from, their elders. A 50-year-old man who is involved in an affair with a younger woman at work may not realize that his sexual and emotional arousal is protecting him from coming to grips with a fear of aging, and may indirectly reflect anger against his wife and family.

Alcohol and other drugs supply one of the most common methods of translating an inner conflict into a behavioral one, as a way of reacting to an unrecognized depression. Alcohol is a temporarily effective way of blocking out the painful feelings of being depressed; it enhances sociability (the depressed individual often has to work against his or her tendency to withdraw from social contacts), dulls the emotions, decreases inhibitions and permits the liberation of anger (which the depressed person finds difficult to cope with), and promotes the further suppression of the idea that there is anything wrong.

But it is a double-edged maneuver. Alcohol is, in fact, a central nervous system depressant that will ultimately intensify the underlying depression. "I feel so rotten," one habituated drinker often complained, "I'd like to die." Then, taking a drink to feel better, he inevitably felt worse.

To be habituated means to be dependent on a particular drug, in this case alcohol, or on a behavior pattern, such as promiscuity, as a way of coping with stress. Addiction is another matter. People who are addicted to alcohol experience a biochemical change—the nature of which is not fully understood—so that their bodies require the continued use of alcohol in order to feel comfortable and meet certain physical demands. Addiction is the result of the interaction between the alcohol and the cells of the central nervous system. Once it has taken place, it is irreversible. All heavy drinkers are not addicted, but for those who are, a single drink is enough to activate the underlying chemical process of craving.

Alcoholism is only one of a number of drugs that people use to escape a confrontation with depression. Insomnia, a common sign of depression, is often combated with benzodiazepines and other sleeping tablets used regularly over a period of years, causing the person to lose confidence in his ability to fall asleep spontaneously and inducing habituation and addiction. Other drugs that affect behavior—cocaine, amphetamines, marijuana, lysergic acid diethylamide (LSD), and even heroin—are often taken in an attempt to cope with unrecognized depression.

A 17-year-old girl was brought to a psychiatrist by her parents because she had been using alcohol, barbiturates, and amphetamines for over 2 years. She attributed her drug usage to experimentation, but a careful review of her history revealed that she had been depressed, without knowing it, ever since her parents' divorce three years earlier. Shortly thereafter she had become pregnant and had had an abortion. Afterward she had started to feel some degree of depression, which she could temporarily obliterate by using various drugs.

Acting out is a common phenomenon among teenagers. It was not surprising, therefore, that this teenager attempted to cope with her reaction to the disruption of her home through drugs and by becoming pregnant. Studies that psychiatrist Lawrence Downs conducted suggest that many women whose pregnancies end in abortion have become pregnant to resolve—subconsciously—a problem in self-esteem caused by a period of depression.

The many different ways that people react to depression may camouflage the depression itself, causing them to delay coming to terms with it. Behavioral disguises are the most blinding and the most likely to promote trap-building. In a culture characterized by a multiplicity of value systems and by a high degree of personal and geographical mobility, there is more than ever a trend toward translating depression into patterns of behavior rather than patterns of feeling—behavior that may occasionally be frankly antisocial, but that always and ultimately does harm to the individual who seeks, in motion alone, an escape from depression.

Chapter 6

♦ ♦ ❖ ♦ ♦ ❖ ♦ ♦ ❖ ♦ ♦ ❖ ♦ ♦ ❖ ♦ ♦ ❖ ♦ ♦

What to Expect of Psychotherapy

Too often, people who are aware of being depressed postpone seeking professional help because they don't know what therapy has to offer them. For many, psychotherapy is synonymous with a kind of cartoon conception of traditional psychoanalysis. The bearded therapist sits behind the patient, nodding, about to fall asleep, as the patient, supine on the leather couch, stares up at the ceiling and rambles on. Or he is caricatured in film as someone who listens impassively as a patient struggles for words; then, as soon as the patient begins to articulate feelings that matter, he abruptly looks at his watch, ends the session, and informs the patient they will have to continue next week, same time, same place. In cartoons and films, these images may be amusing. For millions, however, they confirm the lurking suspicion that psychotherapy is a rather ineffectual, costly, and perhaps exploitative procedure, and that they have little choice but to go on living and battling their unhappiness by themselves.

Since depressed people already feel hopeless, it is not difficult to convince them that there is no resolution to their problems. And since they often see their difficulties only in terms of their life situation, and not in terms of how they view and cope with it, they logically ask themselves: "What can a doctor or counselor do for me, anyway—find me a new job? Change my wife's attitude toward me? Balance my budget?"

The psychiatric profession has itself contributed to this resistance by cultivating a philosophy of therapeutic exclusiveness. Therapeutic exclusiveness basically means that therapists are familiar with one or two approaches to the resolution of emotional conflicts and tend to use their skills in a narrow way, without due reference to the patient's condition or particular set of problems. Traditional psychoanalysts psychoanalyze their patients on a couch four or five times a week. Group therapists meet their clients weekly, or for an encounter session on a long weekend, with seven or eight participants, and focus on interpersonal relationships or transactional analysis. Biologically-oriented psychiatrists give antidepressant drugs or electric convulsive treatments, often without much attention to the psychological components of the patient's state. Primal-scream therapists wait for their patients' primal scream, and gestalt therapists encourage them to punch a pillow as a substitute for their mothers, whom they hate. Breathing exercises are used to reduce anxiety. Transcendental meditation is designed to reduce intellectualization and bring the individual into greater contact with sensory experiences, reducing tension in the process.

The diversity of therapeutic approaches makes it difficult for any single professional to be trained in depth in all the methods available. Psychiatrists could, if they abandoned therapeutic exclusiveness, be better able to understand the usefulness and limitations of the methods they have mastered and to know how to adapt them to the particular needs of various patients. They would also know when to call upon outside consultation or when to direct a patient elsewhere for therapy.

Fortunately, many psychiatrists and other mental health professionals have become increasingly oriented to a more eclectic, integrated, flexible approach to treating depression. However, the professional, like everyone else, is profoundly influenced by the popularity of particular points of view. Until the 1950s, psychiatrists considered traditional Freudian psychoanalysis to be the cornerstone of treatment, whereas they regarded other approaches, such as the cultural focus of Karen Horney or the psychobiological concepts of Adolph Meyer, as watered-down versions of the "real thing." With the advent in the mid-1950s of the tranquilizer chlorpromazine (Thorazine) and in the early 1960s of the tricyclic antidepressants, the emphasis slowly shifted to a more biological approach to the treatment of emotional disorders.

Approaches to psychotherapy changed as well. By the early 1970s, a major break from long-term analysis had occurred, with an upsurge in interest in group therapy, encounter groups, transactional analysis, and Abraham Maslow's self-actualization model. At the same time, psychiatrists were no longer the primary therapists for people in need of emotional help. Psychologists, social workers, clergymen, nurses, and teachers were increasingly recognized as vital members in the network of mental health services. Family therapy became more commonplace, with the regular inclusion of family members of depressed patients.

During the 1980s, antidepressant medications were used widely, not only by psychiatrists but by family physicians as well. Many professionals were beginning to distinguish between depression as a normal experience and the elements that made depression an illness. As the decade came to a close, patient advocacy groups, such as the National Alliance for the Mentally Ill (NAMI) were demanding an environment in which people with mental illness would not be discriminated against or made to feel ashamed; these groups were also increasingly urging the government to fund research and treatment. NAMI and others primarily emphasized the biological aspects of depression, and helped pave the road for the growing dominance of medication as the primary way to manage depression.

The trend toward a predominantly biological viewpoint was intensified in the early 1990s by the move toward managed care and by the rapid growth of health maintenance organizations designed to control the costs of medical care. To many, the use of medication seemed the most economical route to follow, and what limited support had been provided for psychotherapy was limited even further. Simultaneously, studies of special approaches to psychotherapy—the cognitive, the interpersonal, and the behavioral—seemed to establish that these approaches could often be as effective as antidepressants in alleviating depression. Other studies indicated that combining psychotherapy with antidepressant medications offered superior results. By the early 2000s, it had become apparent that an increasing number of people were being prescribed medication, then left to assume the responsibility for dealing with the important personal aspects of depression on their own.

For many depressed individuals, it is bewildering to consider when, how, and to whom to reach out for help. A marked tendency for professionals to compete with one another, often quite critically, is confusing. Many people are misinformed about the effects of various medications and are therefore afraid of taking them. Nor are their fears entirely misplaced; many therapists, including physicians, are not adequately trained or qualified to administer medications efficiently, or even to know when they are indicated. As for psychotherapy, many people still believe it largely smacks of charlatanism. Everyone seems to know someone who has been in therapy for years with no apparent results, and many patients recount their past experiences with therapists who have proved inadequate at best. Besides, whether you're referring to medication or psychotherapy, both involve dependency. Isn't the mark of a real person to handle everything on his or her own? And if you are thinking about reaching out for help for depression, how can you find a professional who is truly competent? It's not quite like finding a surgeon whose success in the operating room is largely a matter of record.

So it is not surprising that millions of people who are clinically depressed hesitate—or refuse—to seek professional help. Moreover, shame and embarrassment are still powerful influences. It can be very difficult to seek out treatment when one lives in a culture that insists on handling life's problems entirely on one's own and regards the willingness to engage in psychiatric care as a sign of personal failure.

The decision to reach out for help is often half the battle.

Consider the variety of ways in which people express their reasons for consulting a professional:

"I came to see you, doctor, because my wife said that she would leave me if I didn't."

"I've hit a plateau. I had some therapy years ago and it helped me a great deal. Recently I've noticed a loss of interest in my work and a kind of boredom with things. I'd like to see if I can get going again."

"I can't finish my term paper. A friend of mine said you might be able to give me some pills to help me get more energy."

"I really came to see you about my mother. But I've always had the idea of straightening out a few things in the back of my mind. I'd like to go on with some therapy for myself for awhile."

"My parents told me to come. I don't want to. I don't see why I have to see a psychiatrist just because I smoked some pot and didn't pass my math and French."

"I want to leave my husband. I want you to see him so he doesn't fall apart."

"I asked my doctor for the name of a therapist. I know I'm depressed because I can't sleep at night and I can't concentrate on my writing. He was reluctant, wanted to give me pills, but I insisted."

"I didn't intend to commit suicide, doctor. I cut my wrists because the physical pain took away the hurting inside."

Some people seek psychiatric care because they have some insight into their depression and want professional help. Some go to a psychiatrist because they are not getting what they want out of life. Others go because someone in their lives such as an angry husband or wife or an irate employer forces them to come. Yet others put themselves in a position of having little choice by taking an overdose of barbiturates.

Because of the feeling of hopelessness inherent in depression, many do not expect to be helped. This negative attitude is often reinforced if they have already built a set of traps from which it seems difficult to extricate themselves. It is further aggravated if they see the problems primarily in terms of unchangeable external circumstances.

Therapists' Responsibilities

The first few contacts people have with their therapists are critical in establishing a basis for recovery. The quality of these contacts depends largely on the experience and approach of the therapists. There are certain things they must do.

Establish Rapport

Therapists must contribute to the establishment of rapport. So much has been written and said of transference—in which the patient projects onto the therapist fears and expectations that belong to earlier relationships with a parent, a sister, a friend, a lover—that not much has been said about the importance of rapport. Rapport is essentially a harmonious relationship that exists between two people, an interaction that permits the evolution of trust, communication, and sharing. The factors that give rise to good rapport, or poor rapport, are complex, but we have a few clues. The studies of psychiatrist Frederick Redlich and sociologist August Hollingshead strongly indicate that therapists are most effective when working with patients from similar cultural backgrounds and least effective when these backgrounds are grossly dissimilar. Paradoxically, therapists with very different backgrounds from those of their patients will probably be much better able to write up the cases and present them in medical journals or at hospital rounds precisely because they cannot identify with the patients and can maintain the doctor-patient separateness that contributes to a scientific understanding while, at the same time, interfering with empathy.

It is remarkable how seldom patients, in their early consultations, try to find out such relevant information as the experience, training, and approach of the therapists. Patients have a curious tendency to accept therapists on faith, and occasionally make no attempt to evaluate, in direct contact with them, the kind of people they are. Many patients have actually continued for years in counseling and treatment situations with people they have intensely disliked, on the assumption that this was somehow irrelevant or might in fact be part of the treatment process.

For therapy to work, there must be a mutual trust and respect, a confidence and a liking, between the parties involved. Both therapist and patient must determine early on whether this is present or not. Rapport is the matrix of therapy, and only within this framework can what happens eventually happen at all.

Empathize

As part of this rapport, the therapist should be able to empathize with the patient's feelings and predicament. Empathy is the ability to put oneself in someone else's shoes. Empathetic people understand what others are experiencing. In some way, they have experienced similar events or feelings themselves. It is quite a different phenomenon from sympathy, which is to "feel sorry for." At some moments, it is appropriate to feel sorry for another person, such as when a therapist listens to a patient relate how, in a single month, she lost her father, her husband, and her job. But it is not the therapist's sympathy that promotes her confidence. It is his or her empathy that encourages the patient to feel she is confiding in someone who will really understand. This quality in the therapist will lessen the patient's fear of further losing self-esteem by having entered therapy.

Combine Authoritativeness with Understanding

"I need you" is a difficult admission for many depressed patients to make, and the response of the therapists is a delicate one. Somehow they must be able to respond to this need without putting their patients down in the process. The position they cannot afford to take is "I'm the doctor, you're the patient, and that puts me one up." At the same time, they must retain the authority that their patients have invested in them because of their professional role. The situation is not unlike that of parents or teachers in dealing with adolescents; it is necessary to relate to them as individuals, on an equal and respecting basis, but without completely relinquishing the authoritative role intrinsic to being a parent or a teacher.

From this authority base, therapists communicate, verbally and nonverbally: "I know what you are experiencing, and no matter how you regard yourself now, I can be of help in restoring your self-esteem and your ability to cope. I know you hurt, but hurting this way and coming here to do something about it are the beginning of a cure. I don't like to use the word 'sick.' It's misleading. It's much better to consider that something difficult has happened in your life or that there is something wrong in your way of coping with life, and that now, finally, you have decided to do something to correct it. Most patients are a great deal better off after therapy than they were before they became depressed."

Acknowledge the Patient's Right to Be Depressed

When the onset of depression can be traced to a period of stress, change, or adverse events in a patient's life, it is helpful if the therapist acknowledges his or her right to be depressed. "Considering what's happened, it seems to me that depression is a normal, expected reaction. If there's a medical problem here at all, it must have to do with something that's keeping you from pulling out of this without professional input—something physical maybe, or something in your life situation, or maybe the way that you look at what you're going through."

Carefully Collect Information

In the first few contacts, therapists concentrate on acquiring data. Is their patient actually depressed? If so, when did the depression start and what seems to have triggered it? To what degree has the depressive immobilization interfered with the patient's ability to function? What kind of person is the patient? What about the patient's life history: Where did he or she go to school and what kind of marriage has he or she had? How many jobs has the patient held and how well were the jobs done? Why and when were jobs changed? What losses has the patient experienced, what blows to his or her sense of self-worth? What does the patient think is the cause of his or her mood? Is there a family history of depression?

Patients will often be confused about the actual cause of the depression, particularly if it has been of long-standing duration. The very process of reviewing the facts provides a sense of coherence, and the establishment of rational links in the chain of emotional reactions helps reduce their fear of losing control.

In the traditional psychoanalytic process, and to a lesser degree in the nondirective approach to counseling advocated by Carl Rogers, therapists allow patients' stories to evolve over a series of sessions without asking pertinent questions or helping them to understand or to piece together the stories. "You haven't said anything to me," many patients complain. "Why don't you offer me some direction?" To which they receive the reply, "That's not the way therapy works." An extremely nondirective approach may be the method of choice in counseling certain individuals, but it is generally not well suited for the therapy of depressed patients. It quadruples the amount of time required to get results. It denies access to important information simply because patients do not realize its relevance. Most important, it encourages already discouraged and often guilt-laden individuals to project onto their therapists the anger and rejection that they expect to receive and that they feel, being "worthless," they deserve.

Communicate

Silence, inappropriately used by therapists in communicating with depressed people, allows the depression to intensify and permits the patients to make many false assumptions. One patient described his experience with his therapist's prolonged silences as follows: "He just sat there, staring at me. I felt uncomfortable. That's too mild a word—I was scared. I didn't know what to talk about. Besides, I felt slowed up, I couldn't concentrate very well, I found it hard to be spontaneous. So we both sat there for minutes that seemed endless.

"After awhile I began to feel that he didn't really like me, that he disapproved of me. I asked him whether he did or didn't and he simply wouldn't comment at all. When I asked him whether he thought I should break off the affair I was having with this girl, he just replied, after a long pause, that it wasn't his place to make decisions for me. If I felt rejected before I started therapy, I really felt rejected after a few visits like that."

Depressed people should expect some participation on the part of their therapists, a participation that does not preclude listening and does not represent a rude thrust of the therapists' biases and opinions into the far reaches of their personal lives. Therapists are not there to tell patients what to do. Nor can they be expected to comment or point out issues and reactions before they have a sufficiently comprehensive understanding of the patients and their difficulties. What therapists can be expected to do is initiate a certain amount of the exchange and to respond in an appropriate manner to the needs of the patients as they emerge.

One of the earliest needs patients express is the desire to have some idea of the actual structure of the therapy itself. They usually have some preconceived notions as to what is going to be involved. They often assume that they cannot afford either the time or the financial expense of therapy. "I couldn't possibly come three times a week for a year, as a friend of mine has been doing," said one patient, who was then surprised when he was told that one visit a week for a few months might well be all he would need. "How can you really help me without knowing my wife?" asked another patient, who was subsequently relieved when the therapist suggested having joint sessions.

When psychoanalysis was in vogue and the average analyst devoted 40 hours a week to the therapy of eight analysands, it was not uncommon for the person making the referral to ask the analyst: "Can you take on a new patient or are you 'filled'?" Under such circumstances, the individual, if accepted for the first visit, usually arrived expecting to be taken on as a patient. Still viewing the psychiatrist in the same way, many physicians and other colleagues, when calling him to ask whether he can "take on" a new case, expect a yes or no answer. A more appropriate reply would be: "It depends." It does depend on the nature of the problem. A consultation visit or two will give the psychiatrist a chance to evaluate the situation and decide, with the patient, what should be done.

Together, the therapist and the patient establish a structure and pattern to the therapy, based on the needs of the situation. Within this framework, of course, the patient should expect shifts and changes and modifications as therapy evolves. Such changes apply not only to the frequency and duration of visits, but also to the character of the patient-doctor relationship and the approaches or techniques the therapist uses in treatment.

Early in therapy, psychiatrists may withhold their own emotional reactions from their patients so that they can remain somewhat neutral figures upon whom the patients can project and form transference experiences. As therapy progresses, however, psychiatrists may reveal more of themselves as people, sharing their own feelings and reactions with the patients in the interest of a patients' insight. For instance, if a patient's pattern of being late for interviews begins to make his or her therapist impatient since their sessions are never long enough to pursue important areas for discussion, the therapist may confront the patient about his or her behavior, as well as with the frustration he or she feels as a result of the pattern. The chances are that the patient's tendency to procrastinate provokes anger and rejection in other people as well, and the therapist's reaction may well afford the patient a direct opportunity to understand and change his or her self-defeating mode of behavior.

"Decentralization"

Depression affects how patients think and feel in ways that therapists can usually anticipate. As a rule, a patient's attention is focused largely on his or her depression and on preoccupying concerns. "All I can think about," said a 41-year-old advertising executive, "is my loneliness. I keep going over and over again in my mind how my wife left me. I keep wanting to call her up and scream at her to come back."

The term for the technique for dealing with such persistent feelings is *decentralization*. Its purpose is to move the patient's attention away from his or her obsessive concerns so that he or she can see what is happening with better perspective and, if necessary, more thoroughly let go of what has already been lost.

Equally common in depressed people is a destructive preoccupation with what they might lose. Loss of financial security is frequently a cause of concern, whether it is a real danger or not. During a sharp drop in the stock market, for example, when interest rates were soaring, a young businessman was terrified of having certain loans called that would result in the loss of the working capital necessary to support his new business, and perhaps even make it impossible for him to meet the mortgage payments on his home. It was a legitimate concern. Feeling overwhelmed, he became agitated and depressed. He could not sleep and was irritable and abrupt. His continual preoccupation with the possibility of loss had made it impossible for him to think of any solutions that would prevent the loss.

The psychiatrist pointed out to him that his worrying about the problem was blocking his ability to deal with it. His dread was rooted in a fear of losing control, while his efforts to retain control were progressively more self-defeating. His frantic anger had already alienated several business colleagues who might have been of help to him. The therapist actively reviewed the facts of the matter with him, including the details of the patient's financial situation; the therapist agreed with him that there was a serious risk, but helped him gain perspective by pointing to certain compensating factors the patient had lost sight of. He emphasized that the patient's desperation to regain control was serving him poorly. As the immediate issue became decentralized, the patient's fear and hopelessness subsided, allowing him not only to feel better but also to consider realistic options.

In the process of decentralizing the depressive focus, therapists often have to take what is called a paradigmatic position—agreeing with their patients that their special concerns are legitimate, so that they can become allies in their solution. Then the therapists proceed beyond the problem at hand to an exploration of how the emotional state of their patients contributes to and aggravates their inability to cope.

A 36-year-old woman consulted a psychiatrist when she learned that her husband was involved with another woman and intended to seek a divorce. "I can't live without him. Our marriage is all that has meant anything to me. I keep writing him notes, but he doesn't answer. I called him at his hotel yesterday and he just hung up on me. I want him back so desperately!" The paradigmatic response of her therapist began: "I know how much this loss must mean to you. I can understand why you want him back. Life must seem meaningless to you right now." She concurred. But then he shifted ground: "It's remarkable how out of touch you are with your anger toward him. It must infuriate you that he has rejected you. My hunch is that you have been controlled by him for a much longer time than you realize." He now alerted her to her underlying anger, and, at the same time, she began to see that the husband in whom she had invested so much love and dependency was a little less lovable.

The therapist was also moving to accomplish three other goals at the same time. First, he was creating an opportunity for her to release both the grief she felt and the anger that had accumulated within her. Second, he was offering her some relief from her guilt, since he knew that at some level she felt primarily responsible for what had happened. At that moment, she was not likely to see the dissolution of her marriage as the result of a progressively demoralizing interaction between herself and her husband. Being depressed, she was more apt to assume that she had failed, had done something seriously wrong to warrant such rejection. Finally, the therapist was helping her to begin restoring some of her self-esteem.

Recurrent Themes in the Treatment of Depression

The release of emotions and guilt, and the restoration of self-esteem are recurrent themes throughout both short- and long-term therapy of the depressed person.

When Marian Johnson was referred by her family doctor to a psychiatrist for therapy, she was completely unaware of the connection between her emotions and her physical distress. Shortly after the birth of her first child she had begun to suffer from headaches and dizzy spells. She was afraid that she might have a brain tumor. In spite of a completely negative medical checkup, she still had serious doubts about the state of her health. Reluctantly she began therapy, stating, "Of course I'm unhappy. I don't think there's any hope for me unless the doctors can find something physically wrong to explain the way I feel. I can't work; I can't take care of my house or my baby. I can't do anything the way I am."

In taking her history, the therapist soon learned that Marian had been through a series of traumatic events in a short space of time. Her father had been operated on for a benign tumor 4 weeks before she delivered her baby. Shortly after the child's birth, her husband became preoccupied with business problems and showed little or no sexual interest in her. Her mother frequently accused her of not taking adequate care of the baby. At times her mother was frankly brutal, making such remarks as "You're a lousy mother. And you're pigheaded too," and "You just don't want to take any advice from anyone. You have always been selfish and ungrateful."

As Marian spoke, hesitantly and only with encouragement, about these experiences, her eyes filled up with tears. "I couldn't stand it if anything happened to my father," she admitted. Again, tearfully, she confessed to feeling rejected by her husband. "I don't know why he doesn't take any interest in me sexually. I know that there isn't anyone else; he's not the type. But at night he hardly speaks to me. He just reads and watches television and goes to bed."

Her mother proved to have been a chronic problem for her, frequently berating both her and her father, making her feel useless and unattractive. When she was in high school, her mother repeatedly compared her unfavorably with other girls. "Why can't you get any interesting boyfriends?" "Why did Sarah win the French competition instead of you?" To compensate for her feelings of inadequacy, Marian had worked compulsively to win the highest academic record she could. She became perfectionistic, but in spite of her efforts, she never received any praise from her mother. Nor was she allowed to express unhappiness. If she tried, her mother took her comments as a personal accusation and retaliated cruelly.

As her emotions surfaced, her physical distress gradually decreased. Again and again the therapist would have to ask "What do you feel about this?" and "What do you feel about that?" since

Marian was simply not used to being able to understand and express emotions. This was particularly true of anger. "Has anything happened since your last visit that might have made you angry?" the therapist would ask, gently, patiently, knowing that her initial denial would be followed later by a slow recollection of an incident or two that "might have angered me," and finally, "Yes, that did anger me."

From time to time she became angry with the therapist but found it painfully difficult to admit it. Once, for instance, she was 15 minutes late for Marian's session. This annoyed Marian because she had made a dental appointment following her visit, and she would now either lose some of her therapy time or be late for the dentist. She felt too guilty to express her predicament frankly. "How can I get angry at you after all you've done for me?" she asked. The therapist pointed out: "Why not? No matter how close a relationship may be, or how good it is, it has to allow for the privilege of getting annoyed at times when the situation warrants it." This was a fundamentally different response from that to which she was accustomed from her family, and it served as a vital opportunity for her to learn a new way of experiencing and expressing feelings.

"You must learn to be more direct in stating your ideas and emotions," her therapist encouraged her. With her support Marian began to test herself with her husband. She gingerly confronted him one evening with her feelings of sexual rejection. At first he was surprised. He had not been aware of neglecting her, although he had. He admitted to just as much affection and desire for her as always, but attributed his fatigue and low spirits to pressures at work. For the first time he began to share with her what those pressures were. "I didn't want to tell you. I didn't want to upset you, with a new baby and all. As a matter of fact, since you were feeling so unwell, I thought you might have lost interest in sex."

Over a period of 8 months, Marian's physical symptoms disappeared. She realized that these had been caused by her depression. She also realized that, true to form, she had been reacting to her depression with guilt, as if she had been entirely responsible for it. When she was able to understand that her feelings of inferiority were in large measure caused by the undermining criticisms of her mother and were compounded by her inability to cope directly and immediately with feelings and events as they occurred, she began to feel more self-confident and worthwhile.

Therapy is a series of reconsiderations, a reappraisal of feelings and experiences in a different light. As the emotional turmoil surrounding the acute phase of depression lessens, the patient and the therapist have a chance to explore the core premises on which the patient's perception of experience rests. An Adlerian technique for discovering such premises rapidly and releasing some of the emotions attached to them is to ask the patient what his or her earliest memory of life is, the earliest memory he or she can recall at that particular moment.

"I was sleeping on a mattress in my parents' bedroom. They had moved me out of my crib, and the junior bed hadn't arrived yet. I was torn between wanting to have the crib back, wanting to stay on the mattress in their room and wanting to grow up and move into a bigger bed of my own." This patient repeatedly reacted to major changes in his life with a paralyzing ambivalence, never sure of which direction to take and painfully weighing the alternatives again and again.

"I was in nursery school. The teacher asked how many of the children still slept in cribs. I put up my hand. Only one other little girl did the same. I was humiliated. It hurt. I was angry at myself and my parents for keeping me a child." In her adult years, this woman remained extremely sensitive to humiliation, often experiencing it when it wasn't warranted, and reacting to it with outbursts of rage.

"I was on a tricycle, pedaling quickly down the street away from the house. I was running away. Something had happened between my mother and me. I was being punished for something, I don't recall what. I was angry, hurt." In adult life, this patient reacted to any show of hostility toward him, however mild, by withdrawing. Sometimes he would become silent for hours. Sometimes he would stay out late at night or disappear for a few days after a disagreement with his wife.

"I recall Mommy coming home. I must have been 3. I remember she had just arrived from the hospital. She had been away for so long, and she had been so sick. I ran and hugged her. It was so good to have her back again." This patient revealed a high degree of sensitivity to loss, but an ability to give freely and warmly of love and concern.

A number of such themes run throughout an individual's psychological make-up; in the course of therapy, numerous opportunities exist to explore them. "I just don't like to talk to my brother," said one man. "I don't approve of his behavior. His sister-in-law had a drinking problem. She still does. He won't let her in the house and doesn't like the idea of his wife's having too much contact with her own sister. I consider his behavior selfish. I think he ought to help. It's downright immoral." The therapist suggested another way to observe and interpret the brother's attitude: Had he considered the possibility that his brother had his own equilibrium to maintain? The patient had already mentioned that his brother had had several episodes of depression over the years, one of which required hospitalization. "I often have to advise people to set limits on how much they can be expected to do for others without compromising their own health or well-being," the psychiatrist informed him. After some thought, the patient concurred that he had been unreasonably harsh in looking at his brother's behavior. This reconsideration also opened the way for an analysis of his own value system and the extent to which his own depression and feelings of guilt were rooted in a rigid and punitive evaluation of his own behavior.

Getting in Touch with Anger

It is difficult to convey with words an accurate picture of what happens over a period of time in psychotherapy. As a result, it has been easy for the public to misconstrue the nature of the therapeutic experience. Certain aspects of psychotherapy have been extracted and seized upon, in a somewhat simplistic way, as the cornerstone of treatment. Free patients from their sexual guilt. Help patients to be able to express their anger outwardly and immediately. Each of these goals is basically relevant in the therapy of depressed people, but the popular assumption that "cured" patients should be capable of hopping into bed with anyone, anywhere, as a result of their newly acquired freedom from inhibitions, or that they should be able to yell and scream at members of their family at will, could not be farther from the truth.

It is generally true that depressed people do have difficulty in expressing their anger when provoked. Sometimes, because of tension, they are irritable and react with too quick a temper. In the course of therapy, they will be encouraged to find new and better ways to handle hostility—ways that do not omit judicious self-control when it is indicated. If, as in the case of Marian Johnson, a patient has been seriously out of touch with his or her feelings, he or she will become more aware of his or her emotions during the actual experience. If justifiably angered, he or she will begin to see how anger can serve a useful purpose.

Frank Jensen found it very difficult to become angry at, or to set limits for, his 14-year-old son. He was patient and understanding to a fault. In contrast to many of his friends who had alienated their teenage children by refusing to listen to them and by pressing their own ideas and demands on them unreasonably, he had always tried to maintain a tolerant and open relationship with his son that afforded the two of them some degree of closeness. When the boy began coming home later than allowed, however, skipping school several times, and using his allowance money to buy beer against his parents' wishes, his father spent hours trying to coax him into complying with family rules. However, the problem of defiance only became worse. One evening, in a peak of anger, the father shouted: "If you come in one more night after the time limit without calling, that will be the end of your allowance!" It was the last incident of its kind. The boy had been asking for limits and for some demonstration of feelings to indicate that his parents intended to enforce those limits. Because of the basically sound relationship with his father, he had been able to respond to this demand without becoming alienated.

Anger, at the right time and when honestly provoked, can serve a vital purpose. But therapy is not designed to help formerly depressed people become bundles of rage. Much of the anger that the patients gradually become aware of and release in therapy is either stored up from previous failures to deal with it or has been the result of a misinterpretation of events around them.

Many depressed individuals have always been very dependent on positive feedback from the environment in order to bolster, again and again, a secure sense of their own worth. School is an ideal setting for such feedback. If intelligent enough, teenagers can work hard to obtain good grades. If athletically inclined, they can put his energies into becoming a star basketball or football player. Once school days have passed, it becomes much more difficult to obtain evidence of one's value from the environment. How can you measure it? By the amount of money earned? By the number of times each day one's husband or wife says "I love you"? By the number of invitations to social events one receives?

As the opportunities for positive feedback diminish, the opportunities for rejection increase. The world is so complex and so busy that it can hardly attend to normal sensitivities, much less to those of people who are in greater need of ego reassurance than others. The self-concern of depressed people sets them up to interpret as rejection what is only indifference, and as indifference what is sometimes actually a considerable amount of respect and affection. They are easily hurt. They can easily become angry as a result of feeling slighted.

Anger that is rooted in their sensitivity will be released in the therapeutic session, although they will certainly not be encouraged to release it wildly elsewhere. Rather, the emphasis will be on helping them to more correctly determine their own worth and set their self-esteem free from its compelling dependency on what others think or say about them. In this way, there will be fewer hurts and hence fewer opportunities for anger.

Depressed persons' tendency to procrastinate—not only in activities and decision making but also in responding to any stimuli—serves as a further source of frustration and anger. "I meant to place the order sooner," said a patient who worked as purchasing agent for a large company, "but I was slow in getting around to it. By the time I made the call, I was told there would be a 5-week delay in delivery. Damn it, I was furious. I told them that if they valued our business they'd better have it there in 2 weeks. It ended up taking 8 weeks, and cost us several thousand in lost orders. At first it was a matter of pride. Now, after our talks, I see that it was really a matter of my dragging my feet on the order for over a month. Why did I do that? I had plenty of time. Do you think it had anything to do with the idea I have of not being properly appreciated by top management for the job I do?"

Dependency Needs in Therapy

Throughout the entire course of therapy, psychiatrists must carefully assess and balance how they will fill the dependency needs of their patients without inviting an excessive dependency that would prolong and complicate the recovery process. Anyone who is afraid and feeling helpless is bound to become more dependent than usual. He or she is likely to invest this need in the doctor, the person to whom he or she turns for relief. The structure of therapy—regular visits with an understanding person who is helpful—as well as the opportunity to focus on troubling issues are both going to produce a certain amount of self-generative dependency.

A relationship exists between the number of weekly therapy appointments and the amount of dependency that builds up. A patient who has only one or two sessions a week is not likely to become as dependent as one who sees the therapist every day. Carefully defining the amount of time the therapist and patient will spend together—an hour, half an hour—provides a sense of security and sets a limit on the amount of dependency that may develop.

Dependency needs are aggravated when any relationship, including a therapeutic one, is riddled with inconsistencies and ambivalence. One patient, a young woman, kept changing appointments and canceling them at the last moment in an unconscious attempt to prevent herself from becoming too involved in therapy. Paradoxically, she was creating a state of uncertainty that reinforced her fears and consequently made her feel more helpless.

In the beginning, the average depressed person sees the therapist once or twice a week, as a rule, for sessions running about 45 minutes. Once a sufficient degree of well-being has been established, the subsequent frequency of visits will be determined by how much there is to talk about, how much turmoil there still is in the patient's life, and how much room there is for further insight. Throughout therapy, because of his or her susceptibility to developing strong needs for those with whom he or she is involved, the depressed individual will often struggle with the desire to see the doctor more often and, on the other hand, with the impulse to terminate therapy at the earliest possible moment.

Cognitive and Behavioral Therapy

One of therapists' most difficult tasks is encouraging their patients to break out of patterns of behavior that are self-defeating and damaging. This may require a considerable amount of persuasion and patience on the part of the therapists. A few patients stop the behavior as soon as they realize that it is injurious. Many, however, tend to procrastinate because they do not see the point of the advice, or because they are unwilling to forfeit the satisfaction they mistakenly believe their behavior affords them. It is usually not enough for their therapists to recommend a change. Their therapists must also point out to them that such a change will provoke some depression, but will at the same time release emotions that can be worked through in the sessions. The patient who has been compulsively engaged in a series of empty sexual relationships, for example, may be concealing a great deal of insecurity about himself or herself as a person.

Another important task is to encourage patients to break out of patterns of thinking and perception that are self-defeating and damaging in their own way. Psychiatrists such as Dr. John Rush at the University of Texas believe that such cognitive patterns are major contibutors to depressive moods, and this constitutes the basis of what has come to be known as cognitive therapy. Because the strategies used in the cognitive approach to psychotherapy have been carefully structured and defined, it has been possible to study the effect of cognitive therapy on alleviating depression and strengthening people's ability to deal more successfully with stress and change in the future. Numerous studies have shown that cognitive therapy—which usually consists of two hourly sessions with a therapist for a period of 10 weeks—is just as effective in reducing depression as antidepressant medications. Some existing evidence indicates that combining cognitive therapy with antidepressant medications further improves the chances of recovery.

What actually occurs? According to the cognitive theorists, three elements are essential to the development of clinical depression: cognitive triad, silent assumptions, and logical errors. The first consists of the negative views that people hold about themselves, their worlds and their futures; they *assume* that these lack something required for them to be happy. For example, they think of themselves as unworthy, or of their environments as too demanding and unsupportive, or of their futures as hopeless.

Silent assumptions are unarticulated rules that influence a person's emotional, behavioral, and thinking patterns. The kind that seem to set the stage for depression are obviously depressing, such as "*If* I make any mistakes, people won't respect me," or "*If* my friend doesn't call me up for a couple of weeks, it's because she really thinks I'm not a nice person." Logical errors are just that—logical errors. You receive a notice from the IRS and before you open it, you *feel as if* you're headed for jail. Nobody comes up to speak with you during the first 5 minutes after your arrival at a cocktail party, so you *feel as if* you are being rejected because of who and what you are.

In the process of cognitive therapy, the individual is helped to identify these negative views, silent assumptions, and logical errors, and encouraged to correct them intellectually every time they occur. At work here is the notion that one can change how one feels and behaves by altering how one thinks and perceives.

In fact, the principles used in cognitive therapy are employed by most sophisticated therapists. In some ways, the approach is reminiscent of the late Norman Vincent Peale's advice in his famous book *The Power of Positive Thinking.* As a research method, cognitive therapy is a valuable instrument; what has been learned from it can be processed and used in many forms of stress management education.

Interpersonal Psychotherapy

Twenty years ago, it was still more the rule than the exception that people who experienced depression consulted psychiatrists because of the distress that depression had been causing them, or they did so at the insistence of someone close to them. Nowadays, it is more common for depressed individuals to seek help because they are having serious problems with their personal relationships, primarily love and marital relationships. Thus, it is no surprise that another so-called short-term approach to psychotherapy for depression has emerged. It is called IPT, or interpersonal psychotherapy. Like cognitive therapy, it is a focused treatment, emphasizing the contemporary difficulties that a person has with a husband, wife, lover, and even with parents, children, friends, and co-workers.

The theoretical basis of interpersonal psychotherapy is that depression often stems from a disruption of attachment bonds—for example, depression that stems from the grief one experiences following the loss of a loved one. By the same token, people who have social deficits, such as the lack of an intimate, confiding relationship, are less protected against the development of serious or chronic depression in the face of life stresses.

Interpersonal therapists address four specific problem areas, emphasizing those that play an important part in a particular patient's depression: grief, role disputes such as those based on nonreciprocal expectations in a relationship, role transitions that require an individual to move from one phase of life to another (graduating from college, getting married, getting divorced), and interpersonal deficits, such as an inability to form close, trusting relationships or a lack of the repertoire of skills necessary for healthy interactions. Such problems may have set the stage for clinical depression; they may also have resulted from depression, which can itself put stress on relationships.

Interpersonal therapy is conducted in both individual and group settings. Ordinarily, one session is conducted weekly for about 4 months. Like cognitive therapy, IPT is structured; therefore, it lends itself to assessment. Studies suggest that over half of the patients who undergo IPT fully recover from depression. The overall effectiveness of treatment appears to be the same as that achieved through cognitive therapy and with the use of antidepressants, although antidepressant therapy seems to induce improvement more quickly.

As with cognitive therapy, experienced effective psychotherapists incorporate the concepts and strategies of interpersonal therapy in their regular work with depressed people. The fact that both of these approaches have produced results that are the equivalent to those achieved with antidepressant drugs—which are often the optimal way to manage intense or persistent states of depression—makes a strong case indeed for not abandoning the psychological management of depression in favor of a strictly biological one, as some third-party insurance payers and even some medical school teaching centers seem to be encouraging.

Humor in Psychotherapy

A certain amount of humor is a vital asset in psychotherapy. Psychiatrist Lawrence Kubie warned against the injudicious use of humor in therapy lest it be at the expense of the patient and reinforce his or her low self-esteem, but he also pointed out that it can "express true warmth and affection" as well. "The critical difference is between laughing with someone or laughing at them. . . . In the hands of an experienced therapist, humor can be a safe and effective tool." What Kubie was cautioning against is a particular kind of humor that puts down either the therapist or the patient, especially as it might be employed by a beginning therapist or a therapist who uses it as an outlet for his or her own hostilities.

Nonetheless, humor is a vital and necessary response to certain situations and an important counterbalance to depression. Humor restores and enlarges perspective. One middle-aged businessman, speaking with great earnestness, said to his therapist: "These have been the most difficult months I've ever had in business. Profit margins cut. Employee problems. Patent suits. But, damn it, in spite of everything, I've maintained my insanity throughout!" When he and the therapist realized his slip, they both laughed.

Involving Family Members and Spouses in Therapy

Many depressed patients can be successfully treated without involving their families in any significant way. It is always a help, if the patients and families agree, for therapists to meet key members of the family to determine for themselves something about the nature of their relationships with the patients. Families, after all, are groups of powerfully interrelated people who have contributed to, and are affected by, the patients' episodes of depression. No one is depressed in a self-contained vacuum. Patients often represent the pathology that runs through the entire family. Their recovery must necessarily cause waves—shifts in the values and the balance of power of the entire group.

One of the two most common situations in which therapists involve themselves more actively with families is in the treatment of depressed people whose marital difficulties have contributed to, or have been caused by, the depression. The second is the treatment of adolescents, in which some initial contact with their families is necessary to evaluate the environment and obtain a thorough history of the problem.

The therapist of the depressed adolescent rarely counsels the teenager's family, since such contact could jeopardize the trust and confidence the adolescent may have placed, slowly and painfully, in this unusual adult who listens. There is a great deal of risk of losing that trust through too much contact with the parents. When necessary, the family members are often referred to a colleague of the therapist for counseling.

It is common, however, for therapists to work with the husbands or wives of depressed patients, not only to help the partner understand how better to relate to the patient, but also to modify attitudes and behavior patterns that may have contributed to the depression in the first place. Occasionally, to improve the communication between patients and their spouses, both are seen together in a number of joint sessions after the patient's depression has lifted.

From time to time, relatives make themselves completely unavailable to the therapist. Such resistance is common when a marriage has deteriorated to the point where divorce is imminent. Sometimes partners feel that there is something they cannot or will not reveal. They may feel humiliated or guilty, often without cause, by the thought of being somehow responsible for the patient's depression. They may be afraid that the doctor will find "something wrong" with them, too. They may be unwilling to relinquish a position of power in the relationship. Frequently, they do not know what therapy is all about and hence why they should be involved in it at all.

When and How Regular Therapy Ends

Although the healing process begins from the moment one decides to do something to help oneself, the first few visits must be considered consultative in nature. The therapist cannot possibly decide what course to take and what to recommend until he or she has had a chance to know the person and the problem.

There is still a 60-minute hour and a 50-minute hour. There is also a 45-minute hour and a 30-minute hour and a 15-minute hour and a 3-minute telephone call. There are still patients who come for psychotherapy three times a week for 3 years, but there are as many patients who come for a dozen visits over a 3-month period. The emphasis should be on flexibility. Patients should make as many visits as they require to accomplish the particular goals of their therapy: relief from their depression, an understanding of what caused it, modification of their methods of coping and their perception of themselves so as to benefit as much as possible from their depression. An acute depressive reaction may be successfully managed in a few months. If the depression has been chronic, and particularly if in the context of chronic depression the patient has constructed a network of traps, therapy could easily extend over several years.

There are many factors that determine the duration of therapy and its outcome. How long had the patient been depressed before starting therapy? To what extent has the patient complicated his or her life by building traps? How stable and supportive is his or her present life situation? How flexible is he or she? How quickly does he or she learn? How skilled and experienced is the therapist in dealing with depression? The answers to questions such as these will influence the amount of therapy required for any particular person. For example, if one has serious marital difficulties or has positioned oneself in a job that is essentially demoralizing, therapy may go on much longer than if one's depression is a simple and uncomplicated reaction to a stressful situation, such as the death of an elderly parent.

The end of therapy is not the end of the relationship between therapist and patient. Each remains open to the other, and should the occasion arise in the future for the patient to come again—with a problem, an idea, an experience to tell about—the therapist remains available to renew communication. Freud, in his paper "Analysis Terminable and Interminable," wrote in a different age of a different process. In the course of analysis, a point should be reached, he emphasized, at which the analysis ends. Using the criterion of change in the patient's personality or the emergence of resistances that could not be worked through, the analyst, he felt, should call it quits. Enough is enough.

Unfortunately, the Freudian concept of ending therapy was a more or less final one. Unless the patient were to consider reentering analysis, the door to his or her analyst's consulting room was effectively closed. The result of this policy was that many a patient who had to struggle through life crises subsequent to a long period of analysis was denied the brief counseling that would have helped him meet the particular difficulties with greater resilience. Preventive psychiatry—which includes keeping the recovered patient in good shape—had not yet been born.

Currently, it is an increasingly common practice for therapists to encourage patients to keep in contact with them. In this way, they can keep track of what has been going on in the patients' lives, so that in the event of a future crisis, they will have the knowledge necessary to be of further help.

Psychotherapy offers depressed people the opportunity to free themselves from their depression and, at the same time, gain valuable and useful insights. This process has been accelerated by means of antidepressant medications.

Chapter 7

♦ ♦ ❖ ♦ ♦ ❖ ♦ ♦ ❖ ♦ ♦ ❖ ♦ ♦ ❖ ♦ ♦ ❖ ♦ ♦

Antidepressant Medications

The Discovery of Antidepressant Medications

A major breakthrough in the treatment of depression took place in 1957, when tricyclic antidepressants (TCAs)—called tricyclic because of their three-ring chemical structure—were discovered. Until then, there were no medications available that could so effectively relieve depression. Major tranquilizers (the phenothiazines e.g., Thorazine,Compazine) had been introduced a few years earlier; although they had proved useful in the treatment of severe mental disorders such as schizophrenia, they had no impact on mood.

As is the case with so many medical breakthroughs, TCAs were discovered by accident. The Swiss psychiatrist Ronald Kuhn was attempting to ascertain whether these compounds—in particular, imipramine (Tofranil), which chemically resembled the phenothiazines—might also be useful in relieving the acute emotional symptoms of schizophrenia. They were not. However, in the process of his study, he astutely noted a significant alleviation of depression in many patients. Because 3 weeks of regular use were required for these drugs to relieve depression, his observations were initially met with considerable skepticism. Some attributed his findings to what is called "the placebo effect."

The placebo effect is essentially a change in a person's physical condition or emotions that occurs simply because patients assume it will help them. "I will give you an injection of this new medication," the physician suggests, "and within a few minutes your headache will go away." Frequently it does, even though the injection consists of little more than salt and water.

The placebo effect always must be considered whenever claims are made that a substance produces a psychological change. People are suggestible—some more than others—and will respond to the combination of what is done to them and what the physician says is being done in a more or less compliant way, depending on the amount of trust they place in their physician and the extent to which they are receptive to his or her recommendations.

Evaluation of the tricyclic antidepressants required carefully controlled "double-blind" studies, or studies that are designed such that the evaluators of the results are unaware of which substance is being given to which patient and such that the patients have been selected on a random basis. Therefore, the researchers could definitively establish that the TCAs effectively relieved depression—not in all patients, but in most.

During the nearly 40 years since the discovery of imipramine, many other antidepressants have been developed and marketed, literally revolutionizing the treatment of depression. The best-known today are the "selective serotonin reuptake inhibitors" (SSRIs), including fluoxetine (Prozac), sertraline (Zoloft), paroxetine (Paxil), fluvoxamine (Luvox), citalopram (Celexa), and escitalopram (Lexapro). Their more recent siblings are the "serotonin-norepinephrine reuptake inhibitors" (SNRIs): duloxetine (Cymbalta), venlafaxine (Effexor), and desvenlafaxine (Pristiq). Then there are buspirone (Buspar), trazodone (Desyrel), mirtazapine (Remeron), nefazodone (Serzone), and bupropion (Wellbutrin), each of which affects levels of serotonin, norepinephrine, and/or dopamine in unique ways that do not fall into any clear category.

Antidepressants alter the brain's actual physical chemistry by affecting levels of these chemicals, which are called neurotransmitters because they enable messages to be carried across synaptic junctures of the central nervous system. It is believed that clinically depressed patients have insufficient amounts of one or several neurotransmitters at these critical locations, or that their brains cannot process the neurotransmitters that are available. One way antidepressants try to address this is by reducing the "reuptake" of serotonin, norepinephrine, and/or dopamine, so that more of the substances would be available for the transmission of neural messages in the brain.

Now, antidepressants are actually not specific for the treatment of depression; they also work well in a number of other distressing emotional disorders, such as generalized anxiety, phobias, obsessive-compulsive disorder, and bulimia nervosa. A better way to view these medications is as resilience-enhancing agents that are capable of restoring the physiologic pathways in the brain, enabling the nervous system to work the way it should. Thus it is not surprising that SSRIs, such as sertraline, have proven effective in treating patients with Post-traumatic Stress Disorder as well as those with Social Phobia, even if they do not manifest significant depression.

Pharmacotherapy of Depression

Antidepressant Medications

Antidepressants are distinguished either by their ability to block the reuptake of certain brain chemicals (norepinephrine, serotonin, and/or dopamine) or inhibit the production of the enzyme monoamine oxidase, which removes used neurotransmitters. Desipramine (Norpramin), protriptyline (Vivactil), and maprotiline (Ludiomil), primarily reduce the reuptake of norepinephrine. The SSRIs specifically work toward preventing serotonergic reuptake at the synapses. Imipramine, the gold standard of all antidepressants, prevents the reuptake of *both* norepinephrine and serotonin; so do amitriptyline (Elavil), doxepin (Sinequan), trimipramine (Surmontil), nefazodone (Serzone), venlafaxine (Effexor), and duloxetine (Cymbalta). Bupropion (Wellbutrin) primarily induces an increase in dopamine at synaptic junctions, while mirtazepine (Remeron) stimulates norepinephrine and serotonin release while blocking certain receptors.

Another group of antidepressants, called the monoamine oxidase inhibitors (MAOIs), block the enzymes that break down serotonin and norepinephrine. It takes many weeks for the systems to restore themselves after these drugs have been terminated. These medications, such as phenelzine (Nardil) and tranylcypromine (Parnate), appear to have a place in the treatment of a small group of depressed patients whose symptoms are "atypical"; that is, instead of presenting the classic signs and symptoms of melancholia—early morning awakening, appetite and weight loss, decreased libido—they tend to oversleep, overeat, and experience a generalized state of nervousness, tension, and fatigue.

A final category to consider here is composed of medications with mixed pharmacologic properties. Common examples include: trazodone (Desyrel), clomipramine (Anafranil), and amoxapine (Asendin). Clomipramine shares properties with the TCAs and SSRIs and, while used primarily for the relief of obsessive-compulsive symptoms, is also effective in alleviating symptoms of depression

There are important differences among these medications. Some, such as desipramine (Norpramin) and fluoxetine (Prozac), produce prominent stimulating effects. Others, such as amitriptyline (Elavil), cause sedation and, therefore, may be especially useful in patients with considerable anxiety, agitation, or insomnia. The newer SSRIs seem to have a more targeted effect on biogenic amines, with less of a "fall out" and a more benign side-effect profile; thus, they are easier to monitor, better tolerated by patients, and more useful in patients suffering from milder depressive states who cannot tolerate the discomfort (especially dry mouth and constipation) that the TCAs often produce. It is easier to use the SSRIs in treating patients with dysthymia—a low-grade chronic depression, characterized by years of low self-esteem, lack of drive, anxiety, pessimism, and negative thinking.

Some patients who fail to respond to a particular antidepressant in an adequate dosage administered for a sufficient length of time may respond to another antidepressant, for reasons that are not at all clear. In addition, many people report that SSRIs in particular gradually become less effective after a number of years of successful treatment (commonly referred to as "Prozac poop-out") and that they must switch to another antidepressant. However, this is by no means a universal experience. In practice, most physicians learn to master the use of several antidepressants in each category and prescribe them according to the perceived needs of their patients.

Central Nervous System Stimulants

Other medications have been used to treat depression, such as central nervous system stimulants—sometimes referred to as psychostimulants. For years, amphetamines were liberally prescribed to patients to relieve low spirits and fatigue. Not infrequently, they have been combined with barbiturates to quell anxiety. Not only is this approach unjustified and ineffective for relieving depression, but both of these types of drugs lend themselves to serious abuse. Amphetamines and barbiturates produce an immediate response in the person who uses them. The antidepressants, on the other hand, do not; their effectiveness occurs slowly, over weeks, and they do not induce behavioral changes that would set the stage for abuse.

Psychostimulants, which stimulate the central nervous system by releasing monoamines, include methylphenidate (Ritalin), dextroamphetamine (Dexedrine), methamphetamine (Desoxyn), and pemoline (Cylert). Although technically only approved by the FDA for the treatment of attention deficit disorder (with or without hyperactivity), these compounds are occasionally prescribed for patients suffering from milder states of depression. Methylphenidate is the most widely prescribed medication in this group, and is known for its remarkable ability to alleviate symptoms associated with attention-deficit/hyperactivity disorder (ADHD) in children. In fact, approximately 90 percent of children in the United States who take medication for ADHD are prescribed methylphenidate, which has proved effective in improving academic attainment and productivity, attention span, and peer interactions in such children. Its use, however, does remain controversial.

Hormones

Hormones, such as the thyroid hormone, the thyroid-stimulating hormone, and triiodothyronine (T_3) are sometimes added to a treatment regimen of antidepressant pharmacotherapy to enhance the therapeutic effects of the antidepressant medications. This strategy, known as thyroid augmentation, has met with mixed results and largely has been studied with regard to the TCAs imipramine, amitriptyline, and desipramine.

Estrogens have been tested, without success, on depressed women at the time of menopause. Many women who use contraceptive pills, which are essentially hormones that affect the menstrual cycle and ovulation, have reported a lowering of mood while taking the pill. That a link exists between variations in mood and alterations in endocrine functions seems apparent; however, what this link is and how it can be exploited in the interests of treatment remain to be clarified.

Antianxiety Medications

Anxiety frequently accompanies depression. In fact, it may sometimes be the most prominent sign of distress. Therefore, it is not unusual for physicians to prescribe antianxiety medications as a first-line intervention to help a patient feel better. Minor tranquilizers such as alprazolam (Xanax), oxazepam (Serax), diazepam (Valium), chlordiazepoxide (Librium), and lorazepam (Ativan) belong to a class of medications called the benzodiazepines; they are commonly prescribed to relieve nervousness, tension, and insomnia.

Ironically, these medications frequently intensify depression. Carefully tapering off the dosage of a medication can sometimes lead to a real improvement in the patient's mood, not to mention relief from the drowsiness and fatigue that often complicates the use of anxiolytic medication. It should be noted that whereas antidepressants are not addictive, benzodiazepines are potentially quite habit-forming and lend themselves to abuse. A benzodiazepine should be used only as a temporary addition to an established antidepressant medication, and it should be terminated as soon as the patient improves and it is no longer required.

Dosage of Antidepressants

In order for antidepressants to work, an adequate dose must be given over a sufficient period, typically a minimum of 4–6 weeks. In establishing an effective dosage for TCAs, the physician usually must increase the dosages gradually, to minimize untoward effects. Moreover, there may be considerable individual variation regarding the optimal dosage for any particular patient. When patients do not respond to treatment as expected, it is common practice to determine the level of antidepressant in the blood stream and compare it with the known levels established for efficacy. One of the advantages of the SSRIs is their ease in achieving an effective therapeutic dose. For example, for many patients, a single 20-mg tablet of fluoxetine or a 50–100-mg tablet of sertraline is enough to produce the desired effects.

Why it takes so long for these medications to work is unknown. A comparable situation can be seen in the use of hormones to correct endocrine disturbances. In the treatment of hypothyroidism, for example, several weeks administration of thyroid hormone is usually required to correct the dysfunction. It can take many weeks of estrogen therapy to produce the desired effects in estrogen-deficient women experiencing menopause.

Depressed patients taking antidepressants tend to show some lifting of mood and increased energy during the first week of pharmacotherapy. Within a few nights, they sleep better. They may or may not notice such changes themselves; in fact, the improvement may be more noticeable to others. During the second week of treatment, a plateau often is reached: no further improvement may be evident, and sometimes a sharp recurrence of emotional distress may occur, with an increase in suicide risk. By the end of the third week of treatment, patients usually begin to feel better and concentrate more effectively. They experience fewer episodes of depression, and the episodes they do have are usually short lived. As one patient put it, this effect is analogous to "a log-jam breaking up." When a disturbing event or a provocative remark upsets them, they exhibit greater resilience, rebounding from the impact far more quickly than before. Research indicates that higher doses of antidepressants may be required to effectively treat prolonged, chronic states of depression.

Side Effects of Antidepressants

As with all medications, antidepressants have side effects. For example, patients who are taking MAOIs must observe a strict dietary regimen, avoiding tyramine-rich foods such as fava beans, herring, certain cheeses, red wine, and chocolate. Otherwise, these patients will place themselves at risk of experiencing a rapid rise in blood pressure resulting from an adverse reaction between the MAOI and the amino acid tyramine.

The most common side effects associated with the tricyclic antidepressants include dry mouth and constipation, the result of anticholinergic activity causing a drying up of the mucous membranes. Some patients sweat profusely. Orthostatic hypotension, a potentially serious medical complication, may result as well. When a patient suddenly changes position—from lying or sitting to standing—a sharp, sudden drop in blood pressure can occur. This can cause lightheadedness, even transient blacking out. An episode of orthostatic hypotension can trigger a heart attack, primarily in patients who already have a significant degree of heart disease.

Patients who have any kind of cardiovascular disease or are at risk for heart disease must be carefully assessed before a TCA is administered, as well as throughout the entire course of treatment. These medications can cause changes in electrocardiogram tracings, reflecting changes in heart function; therefore, their use is contraindicated in patients with cardiac conduction disorders.

Other side effects of the TCAs include fatigue, blurred vision, sleepiness, skin rashes, and hypersensitivity to the sun's rays. A troublesome side effect is a decrease in sexual drive and performance, which may sometimes be difficult to distinguish from the decreased libido that commonly accompanies depression. When a medication's dosage is reduced or when the medication is discontinued altogether, the pretreatment level of sexual functioning will return.

The SSRIs seem to be less problematic. They are much more comfortably tolerated and can be used in a broader array of patients. However, they are not without side effects, not the least of which is a reduction in sexual drive and performance; this seems to be more pronounced with sertraline (Zoloft) than fluoxetine (Prozac). Should a reduction in sexual drive and performance trouble patients, there are several possible remedies. One is to taper and eventually stop the drug, see how the patient does, and, if necessary, replace it with another that is less likely to induce sexual difficulties, most notably bupropion (Wellbutrin), which by some accounts actually increases sex drive. Or see whether a lower dosage will do the trick. Another tactic is to suggest brief medication "vacations"—a day or two off the drug to allow for sexual activity. With a drug like sertraline, this method works fairly well; but with others, such as fluoxetine, which is more slowly excreted from the body, it may not.

Some patients on SSRIs, especially those taking fluoxetine, complain of anxiety, agitation, and insomnia. Interference with sleep is the reason why most of the SSRIs are taken in the morning. These drugs reduce a person's tendency to overreact to stressors or to worry excessively about them—a positive effect, to be sure—but sometimes a troublesome apathy can develop, diminishing a patient's motivation and drive. Fluoxetine has been said to lead to suicidal and violent ideation and behavior; if there are any signs of such a development, the drug should be appropriately stopped and replaced with another antidepressant.

Many patients who take TCAs gain weight. Carefully controlled studies substantiate that this weight gain is largely caused by an increased intake of food that most likely results from a heartier appetite. At one time, it was argued that weight loss accompanying depression reflected a breakdown and excretion of body tissue, which occurred regardless of food intake. But studies by the author and colleagues demonstrated that diet books have cautioned readers against using antidepressants while trying to lose weight, implying that the drugs themselves directly cause weight gain. All things considered, a sensible precaution is warranted with regard to this issue. Certain antidepressants, such as maprotiline (Ludiomil), appear to have an especially strong stimulating effect on appetite and might be useful in managing patients who are seriously underweight. In most instances, weight gain is uncommon among patients on SSRIs. But it can occur, and when it does, it can be quite counterproductive, leading to discouragement and non-compliance. Doctors and patients should take this seriously and see what dietary and exercise measures can be taken to better control it. Weight gain seems less of a risk with sertraline or fluoxetine than with paroxetine, and nefazodone is reported to carry an even smaller risk. The lowest risk for weight gain appears to be with bupropion. So, in some instances, it may be prudent to change medications, particularly since vulnerability to weight gain and other side effects of specific SSRIs are thought to be influenced by individual genetic patterns.

The experience and judgment of the physician are critical in the decision as to whether to prescribe an antidepressant. If he or she feels that the patient will pull out of depression rapidly, the doctor may refrain from implementing a course of drug therapy that takes approximately 4 weeks to work and normally runs 4–6 months. The physician also wants to ensure that patients who say they are depressed really are. Some patients who describe themselves as being depressed are not, whereas others who deny being depressed really are.

Responses to Treatment

Considerable variation exists in the time it takes for different people to rebound from depression once they have sought professional help and have undergone a few therapy sessions. A 30-year-old woman was seen in consultation because she complained of feeling depressed. She had recently broken up with her fiancé; prior to that she had never been significantly depressed. During the first two sessions, her therapist was able to elicit the hurt and anger she felt in response to the end of this relationship. "Even though I ended it, I felt rejected," she pointed out. By the third visit, she was in much better spirits and was sleeping well. The rapid disappearance of her depression made the psychiatrist defer prescribing an antidepressant. By contrast, another woman who presented to the same psychiatrist a 5-year history of insomnia, pessimism, irritability, social withdrawal, and a poor sex life, and who had never considered herself depressed until she read about depression in a popular magazine, was put on an antidepressant medication after her second visit. The psychiatrist's decision in this case was governed by the long-standing nature of her depression and the fact that psychotherapy alone was unlikely to break her disabling, chronic pattern.

Antidepressant pharmacotherapy will also be influenced by the complexity of the patient's depression. If the patient has a relatively uncomplicated depression—a lowering of mood, anxiety, insomnia, and weight loss—the physician can expect a good response to medication. However, the patient may also demonstrate a great deal of fear, agitation, and restlessness. The lowered mood may be associated with an almost-paranoid hypersensitivity: "Sometimes I think that everyone is out to get me. In fact, even this morning the phone rang three times and there was no one on the other end." Intense anger—which, at times, may even escalate to the point of physical violence—may also be a part of the clinical picture. Under such circumstances, the psychiatrist may add a major tranquilizer to the antidepressant medication regimen. Although the tranquilizer will not relieve the depressive symptomatology, it will control the rage, fear, sexual unrest, hypersensitivity, and agitation within a few days. In fact, at times, if the psychiatrist does not prescribe such combination pharmacotherapy, he or she will discover that the patient will not recover as anticipated by the end of 4 weeks of treatment because of the deleterious impact of these emotions.

Diagnostic considerations must be weighed as well. The decision to use an antidepressant to treat patients suffering from dysthymia or from unipolar depression—a condition in which the patient *only* experiences depression without mania—is one thing. It is something else to make a decision to use antidepressants in patients with bipolar disorder (also known as manic depression), in which episodes of depression alternate with episodes of mania, characterized by overexcitement, grandiose thinking, extreme egoism, anger, and irritability.

When a history of mania is present, a new set of treatment considerations enters the picture. In people with bipolar disorder, antidepressants can trigger a manic episode, so they are generally prescribed with a mood stabilizer. The most common mood stabilizer is lithium (Eskalith, Lithane), a salt compound that was originally introduced for the treatment of mania by the Australian psychiatrist J. F. Case in 1949, but did not come into common use for another 20 years. Lithium has proved to be an effective method to treat mania and prevent its recurrence in many bipolar patients. If, for any reason, lithium is ineffective or cannot be tolerated by a patient, anticonvulsant medications such as lamotrigine (Lamictal), carbamazepine (Tegretol), valproic acid (Depakene), and divalproex sodium (Depakote) can be used as mood stabilizers.

In 2005, after a series of studies, the US Food and Drug Administration required drug manufacturers to update the labeling of all antidepressants to caution that taking antidepressants may increase suicidal thoughts and actions among children and adolescents in the first few weeks of treatment. In 2007, the FDA extended that warning to young adults (age 18 to 24). However, the FDA noted that antidepressant treatment does not increase the risk of suicidality in adults over 24, and that it actually decreases it in adults over 65. Although the risk of suicidal thoughts and behavior is important to consider, it should not categorically rule out treating children, adolescents, or young adults with medication when justified. The physician's experience and judgement, as ever, should be the guide in balancing the risks of treatment against the risks of untreated depression.

Attitudes Toward Treatment

The attitudes of both physician and patient are important to the success of psychopharmalogic treatment. Many therapists have not been able to integrate the psychotherapeutic and pharmacologic approaches to treating depression. Some steadfastly believe in the psychogenic origin of depression; others, in its biological causes. The former group often withholds medication, even when it is clearly indicated; if and when they finally recommend it, their interest in continuing psychotherapeutic treatment often seems to wane. "When I was first seeing the doctor, he wanted two sessions a week. After 3 months, he started me on a drug. A week later, he cut me to half an hour once a week, without any explanation." Many biologically oriented psychiatrists tend to interview patients briefly and offer them medication, but have little interest in exploring with them the psychological or environmental factors associated with their depression.

The fact that a large number of patients are seen by professionals who do not have the right to prescribe—psychologists, social workers, mental health counselors—poses a special problem. Some may be reluctant to recommend a psychopharmalogic consultation for fear that a physician will intrude on their treatment relationship. Some will ignore the potential value of medication because of their adherence to a particular psychological model of therapy. And in this era of managed care, some simply do not have a relationship with a psychopharmacologist who has openings for new patients. Unless a collaborative, competition-free environment exists between these professionals and physicians, many depressed patients in need of antidepressant medication will not receive it unless a major crisis develops.

Does a physician's conviction that a medication works—or his or her skepticism—affect the outcome of antidepressant treatment? It has been clearly established that suggestion plays an important role in the effectiveness of medications designed to reduce anxiety and tension. A senior psychiatrist at a leading hospital in Great Britain had a reputation for obtaining remarkable results from a variety of medications. When he would inquire, in a most authoritative tone, "You are getting better aren't you?" a patient would usually find himself or herself replying, "Yes, sir, if you say so, sir!"

The time lag in the effects produced by the antidepressants, the tenacious nature of chronic depression, and the double-blind studies on these compounds argue strongly against any significant influence of the placebo effect in their usage. Physicians' attitudes, however, can and will influence how their patients perceive and use the medication. If they are skeptical and consider the drug relatively unimportant, patients may respond to this message by skipping doses, discontinuing the medication before it has had time to work, or denying that their improved outlook has anything to do with the medication. This, of course, will enhance many psychotherapists' egos, because they can remain convinced that their psychotherapeutic efforts have been the exclusive cause for improvement.

Physicians can also err by promising too much, thereby activating the curious negativism of many depressed persons. Even though they are reaching out for help, something within them wants to preserve their depressed state—the control it has afforded them over others, the sympathy it has elicited, the anger it expresses for which they know no other outlet. If therapists are too enthusiastic about offering relief through medication, they may stir up this unconscious resistance to recovery. "After I took the first pill at bedtime, I could feel the effect," said one patient who had been promised a rapid improvement through medication. "I couldn't sleep. The next day I was washed out, but I continued to use it as the doctor said I should. My legs felt weak, and I thought I was going to collapse.

"I called the doctor three times the next night. He told me to stop the drug and come by the next day for another prescription. I did. This was supposed to be a milder antidepressant. But I felt even worse. The day after I started on it, I could hardly get out of bed at all. My legs were shaky—so weak I had to hold onto the furniture to get to the bathroom. I called him again, and this time he told me to come in for a special appointment to discuss the problem.

"When I saw him, he told me that most of the changes I complained about could not possibly be part of the drug effect, and in the course of the discussion, I realized that I was reluctant to give up the subtle way in which I had been able to act out hostility toward my wife—without affording her fair grounds for retaliation—by being tired and depressed around the house in the evening and on weekends. If the drug really worked, I was going to lose that outlet and have to learn a new way of coping with the anger she aroused in me."

Many patients are reluctant to take a medication to improve

their mood because they are afraid of becoming dependent on it. Others feel that if they take a medication, the change in their mood will be artificial, that any improvement that occurs will not be "real." One patient, for instance, unconsciously feared becoming dependent on anyone or anything, so much so that he would frequently cancel appointments with his therapist at the last minute, on the pretense of having suddenly discovered that he had some other commitment. In another case, it took nearly three months of tearful and angry outbursts before one 24-year-old woman could finally accept the idea that her doctor's recommendation of an antidepressant was not a form of personal rejection. Still another patient reported that since he had been taking antidepressants, his wife had voiced her fear that his emotions might be somehow synthetic. "Would you still love me," she asked, "if you weren't on Zoloft?"

How Long Should People Take Antidepressants?

How long should a person continue to take antidepressant medication? Some patients, especially those who have never been clinically depressed in the past and whose depressions have lasted for relatively short durations, may be able to terminate medication altogether within 6 months. This is best accomplished by *gradually tapering* the dosage over several weeks' time. A useful guideline is to continue the antidepressant until significant improvements have been evidenced in the patient's life circumstances, such as reestablishing his or her life after a divorce or getting a new job after having been fired.

Patients who have been chronically depressed for years or who have a history of recurrent episodes of depression should probably continue using the antidepressant medication for a year or two. Recurrences of depression following termination are not uncommon, especially because people's conflicts and problems in their life circumstances may not have changed. It may be that the underlying physiologic deficit that accounts for a lack of biological resilience has endured. With new stressors, depression may return and assume an intensity and tenacity that require antidepressant treatment once more. Therefore, some patients would do well to continue using the medications indefinitely, or at least be prepared to restart them when stresses increase and depressive feelings reemerge.

Suggestions for Persons Receiving Treatment for Depression

There are several issues that anyone who receives treatment for clinical depression should consider.

1. If you're in therapy with a non-MD therapist, *be sure to assess his or her attitude about antidepressants.* It's important for you to be assured that your therapist is open-minded about this viable treatment option and willing to refer you to a specialist for medication if it is indicated.

2. A significant number of people can weather depressive episodes and recover from them without medication; some possess sufficient resilience to do it on their own, whereas others can require psychotherapy to accomplish this. But it's important to be *willing to consider the use of medications as an option.* Thinking of them as resilience-restoring agents will save you from falling into the trap of believing that they produce a "false high" or that somehow or other it's braver or smarter to get better without them.

3. If you're on an antidepressant, you must have medical supervision as long as you're taking the medication. *Don't stop the medicine on your own.* Terminating an antidepressant should be a joint decision between you and your physician. To prevent a sharp recurrence of depression, it's important to taper the dosage, thereby avoiding abrupt discontinuation.

4. If you're seeing a psychiatrist or physician who wants to treat you with an antidepressant, *find out what his or her*

> *attitude is about other approaches to therapy*. You want a specialist who will consider psychotherapy and other strategies such as marital or family therapy that you can use to modify inner and psychosocial conflicts that may be contributing to your condition. For most depressed people, drug treatment alone is not enough.

Antidepressants have revolutionized the treatment of depression. They have also underscored the importance of the role of biological factors in magnifying the intensity and tenacity of depressed moods. They have made it much easier for people to not only recover from depression and its otherwise potentially devastating consequences, but also to develop inner resilience, resolve interpersonal difficulties, and improve their lives within the framework of psychotherapy as well as on their own.

Chapter 8

♦ ♦ ❖ ♦ ♦ ❖ ♦ ♦ ❖ ♦ ♦ ❖ ♦ ♦ ❖ ♦ ♦ ❖ ♦ ♦

Sex as a Barometer

Sexuality and self-esteem are closely connected. In this culture, with its Playboy and Penthouse magazines and sex therapy clinics, physical attractiveness and the ability to perform in bed have become serious ego issues.

In the first half of the twentieth century, the focus of male-female relationships in the United States was marriage, and the emphasis in marriage was placed on the social and economic integrity of the family group. The raising of children was of primary concern. Interpersonal compatibility was vaguely relevant, and both husband and wife had their respective roles to play no matter how they regarded the quality of the marriage itself.

In the last 40 years, there has been a strong shift in emphasis toward the importance of the intimate, personal nature of the relationship between a man and a woman. Men and women alike are focusing more on their ability to communicate, to form a trusting and sharing commitment, and to sustain romantic and sexual interest over a period of years. "I wouldn't marry someone if he didn't turn me on" has often replaced the earlier expectation of "I wouldn't marry someone if he wasn't dependable."

The growing demand for intimacy and sexual fulfillment in human relationships, both heterosexual and homosexual, arises in part from the rejection of a culture in which the roles people played took precedence over the importance of being themselves. It also reflects the fragmentation of the family, with parents, grandparents, and adolescents all inhabiting their own separate worlds. In spite of crowdedness, loneliness is epidemic. The average individual feels isolated and alienated, and these feelings reinforce the need for, and challenge of, intimacy. Two young people standing naked in the bedroom must encounter each other in immediate and uncamouflaged terms—sexually and emotionally—without roles, without social props, without orientation to past and future.

This moment is made even more difficult because of the profound depersonalization that this culture fosters. "We try to make our employees feel like people," a spokesman for a large company once said. If his company has succeeded at this, his secret should be shared at once with the millions of people the computer has helped to feel like things. Transactional analysts use the term *thinging* to describe the process of regarding people as if they were objects. Social scientists aptly describe our society as a marketing society, and whether one is sitting in on a planning meeting at a large advertising firm or a conference of scientists, it is more than a little disquieting to hear people discussed statistically as if they were items for sale or rent. The individual begins to feel like an object, "a living object, but no longer a person," wrote T. S. Eliot in *The Cocktail Party*.

In the general process of depersonalization, sex too has succumbed to "thinging." Because of the intimate connection between sex and self-esteem, the phenomenon of impersonal sex has catalyzed the spread of depression. Loneliness and a feeling of being alienated have become common ways of experiencing depression. At the same time, many lonely and depressed people turn to sex as a way of relieving that inner emptiness.

Although the current culture places enormous value on sexual fulfillment, the underlying purpose of sexual encounters is often not sexual at all. During a period of low self-esteem, sexual conquests or the discovery of oneself as sexually desirable may temporarily ameliorate the feeling of being depressed; yet there is usually a sharp return of depression afterward, when the bogus reassurance wears off. Under such circumstances there can be no genuine ego reinforcement.

Erik Erikson, in *Childhood and Society*, stressed the importance of experiencing sexual excitement and fulfillment within the framework of a relationship that also includes love, mutual trust, and a sharing of the everyday concerns and activities of living. The existentialist Martin Buber outlined the relevance of the I-Thou relationship as the basis for real intimacy. Emotional closeness and a fulfilling sexual experience require the freedom to enter into a "we" relationship, in which the I and the Thou become one. The height of this experience, emotionally and physically, is represented by the moment of orgasm, which permits the individual to give up, for a few moments, the ordinary boundaries of self and "dissolve" into a common bond with the loved partner. Not every sexual experience has to have this unique quality, but it will appear from time to time in the sexual encounters of two people who love and care about each other.

In order to allow oneself to participate in such a union, two ingredients are essential: first, the individual personality must be sufficiently intact to let go of itself and promptly return after the experience is over. If such a transitory giving up of ego boundaries is too threatening to the person, the consequent fear will block his ability to fully participate in the sexual experience.

The second important element is trust, a belief that the person with whom the sexual moment is shared is also able and willing to give up the "I" for the sake of the "we." Trust is not created overnight. This kind of sexual experience is the product of hours and months of sharing many things other than sex, of setting the stage for a relationship in which intimacy and sex can be integrated.

Not all sexual encounters demand such a blending of personalities, but when a "quick roll in the hay" becomes the primary outlet for one's sexual drives, the inevitable enhancement of self-esteem that results from the complete experience does not occur and a slow, progressive waning in self-worth takes place, however it may be denied. Sexual harmony is not rooted in fine technique;

rather, its foundation lies in both partners generously sharing with each other their bodies and their souls.

Nowhere is this concept of integrating the personal elements of the relationship with the sexual so important as in a relationship that is expected to endure over a period of time. Erotic attraction and sexual interest, if not backed up by love, fade rapidly. It is the caring, the interdependency, the openness in communication that exist between lovers that keep the erotic component vital and alive over a period of years.

Low self-esteem makes it difficult to find the kind of relatedness Erikson and Buber are talking about. In fact, when sexual encounters are used to combat unrecognized depression, one's sense of self-esteem is compromised even further.

Jane Conway, age 29, is a striking example of a young woman who became more and more depressed as she sought to find in sexual relationships what could be found only in a serious reconsideration of her worth as a person. She had always felt unattractive, which she was not, and unpopular with boys in school, which she was since she clearly communicated her fear of and disdain for them.

Jane left home at 19 and went to Boston, where she finished college and subsequently obtained a job as a computer programmer. She was usually cheerful and outgoing—as long as she was able to maintain a relationship with a man. Whenever she was without a regular boyfriend, she was morose, lonely, unhappy, restless. She haunted singles' bars, where she picked up many men and went to bed with them. Neither her regular sexual experiences nor these transient involvements led to orgasm. As long as she could prove to herself—over and over again—that she was attractive to men, she did not have to face the painful fear that she could never establish a more enduring love relationship with a man, since she felt basically unworthy of it.

Then for several years she had an affair with an older man for whom she worked. She knew she did not love him, but felt secure in his constant affection for her. However, she gradually grew bored with the relationship and, at times, was actually contemptuous of him. When he insisted on marriage, she ended the affair.

A year later she became involved with an emotionally erratic man who was grossly ambivalent in his attitude toward women. The more he confused her—"I love you, but you're not the kind of girl I want to spend my life with"—the more she felt she needed him. Again, her sexual experiences did not lead to orgasm.

At no time did Jane consider herself chronically depressed. She saw her moods entirely as reactions to her life circumstances. It did not occur to her that she might benefit from professional guidance until she visited her physician because of recurrent intestinal difficulties and he suggested that she consult a psychiatrist.

In the course of several months of therapy, she rapidly assimilated the following insights: She had been battling against chronic depression and low self-esteem for years. She had a highly confused view of herself and her worth. Her father had always been a very withdrawn and unaffectionate man who gave little of himself to his family. As she grew up, she desperately sought to find in her relationships with men what she had not found in her relationship with her father. As she progressed from one affair to another in search of the "perfect man," feeling empty and afraid when there was no man in her life, she used sex and her relationships with men as a temporary relief from her low self-esteem.

Jane had become an addict, in a sense, and the ultimate resolution of her difficulty included the termination of her sexual promiscuity as a way of restoring self-esteem, and the rediscovery of herself as a more complete person, with her own individuality, gaining the "I" in the Buber "I-Thou" equation.

Sexual Desire and Depression

A loss of sexual desire is one of the most common signs of depression. When this connection between sex and mood is not recognized, most people fear that something fundamental has happened to their sexual capacities. Many men and women in their forties and fifties, for example, mistakenly assume that the loss of sexual interest is the result of some kind of biological change associated with getting older. Depressed people's sexual indifference can also be misinterpreted by their sexual partners as a loss of love and erotic attraction. Sometimes it is; more often it is not. There are many reasons why depressed people lose an interest in sexual activity. Making them feel agitated, pessimistic, anxious, discouraged, the mood itself forces their attention away from sexual desire. Their hypersensitivity to feeling rejected, their vulnerability to guilt, the difficulty they may have in releasing angry feelings, and sexual conflicts themselves combine to interfere with sexual drives.

Not all depressed people, however, lose their sexual desire. In fact, there are instances in which depression is associated with a heightening of sexual energy, a state referred to as sexual unrest. Sexual unrest is experienced as a direct stirring up of sexual urges. It is quite different from Jane Conway's essentially asexual attempt to gain self-esteem and ward off depression through sexual encounters. Sexual unrest may be due to hormonal changes but may also be the result of the anxiety and apprehension provoked in response to being depressed, since anxiety not uncommonly leads to a heightening in sexual urges.

A young woman who was somewhat depressed noticed a stirring up of sexual tension, caused by her fear and anxiety, whenever she felt overly pressured in preparing for college exams. Similarly, a 53-year-old man noted a sudden increase in the frequency of his erections and the occurrence of a series of sexually exciting dreams, many of which led to spontaneous ejaculations. Some of these dreams were homosexual in content even though he had never had any conscious homosexual impulses. He was deeply disturbed by all this until, with the help of his physician, he was able to relate it to a lowering of his mood that had evolved over a number of months. He was concerned about losing his energy and attractiveness. He was also shaken by his daughter's liberal attitudes about sex and the angry arguments they had had about their different value systems. As his depression lifted, the unusual upsurge in his sexual drives subsided.

Many women who have experienced depression after divorce and even after becoming widowed have noted a stirring up of sexual drives that seems, to them, somewhat out of keeping with their normal selves. Unless these sexual feelings are related to a hypomanic swing in mood—some people become mildly elated in the process of denying depression—they are often experienced as uncomfortable and distracting rather than pleasurable.

On the whole, however, depression is associated with a loss of sexual interest. In certain instances this loss reflects an unconscious hostility that is being expressed through the depression. Since people who are depression-prone or in states of chronic depression tend to withdraw into themselves when angry rather than cope with the disturbing situation directly, the withdrawal of sexual interest can be a highly effective channel for the expression of hostility. "What Bill doesn't realize," said his wife, "is that he provokes me with his sarcastic remarks, his criticisms. I feel that he's always putting me down. It hurts. I hate it. I suppose it would be better for me to blow up and get angry, but I refuse to give him that satisfaction. Besides, even if I did, I don't know whether he'd get the point. . . . The net result is I don't want to go to bed with him. It's a matter of pride, I guess. But it's more than that. How can I want to make love with him when I feel either tired and exhausted around him or hurt by his remarks?"

Rejection and Depression

Since people who are likely to experience depression have usually invested a great deal of feeling in, and dependency on, the object of their love, being rejected is one of the main triggers for activating or intensifying feelings of depression. This is as true of homosexual relationships as it is of heterosexual ones.

When the rejection is subtle, insidious, concealed, the individual may live in a state of chronic depression for years, unless and until an acute state of despair and upheaval terminates the malignant pattern. Jim Smith was 35 years old when he attacked and brutally beat his 29-year-old wife, Nancy. She called the police, and he was sent away by ambulance, humiliated and confused, to the psychiatric unit of his local hospital. The marriage was destroyed beyond hope. Jim's image of himself as a reasonable, well-balanced person was shattered in the process.

Four weeks of treatment quieted his agitation and to some measure relieved his hopelessness. After his discharge, he arranged with his attorneys the details of the divorce settlement and left town to reestablish himself as a lawyer in another community.

Jim had been brought up in a conservative, middle-class home in the Midwest. He was an honors graduate from his state university and attended Yale Law School. Although he was an attractive and sociable young man, he felt somewhat shy with girls. His sexual experiences were quite limited. When Nancy, his wife-to-be, sought him out and aggressively pursued him, he was first flattered, then very turned on sexually, then, finally, trapped by the involvement and his sense of commitment to her. The commitment arose from genuine love, but also from a sense of responsibility for the first person with whom he thought he had shared sexual and emotional closeness.

Unfortunately, at the age of 22, Nancy was incredibly naïve. She had many boyfriends, though none particularly interested her. She tended to regard men as a challenge. If they were attracted to her, she rapidly lost interest in them. If they seemed aloof and uninterested, she felt compelled to seek them out and make new conquests.

Before she married Jim, her sexual and personal interest in him had already begun to evaporate. Several days before their marriage, she had actually dated and slept with one of her old boyfriends, in what she regarded as a last gesture toward her exciting single life, a farewell to fun and youth. Asking herself why she intended to go through with the marriage, her answer was: "He's attractive, stable, a good catch, and besides, I do love him in my own way. I'll make him a decent wife."

During the 9 years of their marriage, prior to its tragic climax, they had two children. After the birth of the first child, less than a year following their marriage, Nancy's lack of interest in sex became apparent to Jim. She and Jim never discussed it. Whenever he tried to bring up the subject, she managed to evade it. She felt that she did not want to hurt him by telling him she didn't want any more sexual contact with him. For awhile he felt jealous, wondering if she was involved with someone else: a common reaction of one who is slightly depressed and feeling rejected. Gradually he became impotent, and then Nancy could point to the fact that the lack of sexual desire was mutual.

Jim's sense of self-esteem, though compromised, was nonetheless sufficiently reinforced by becoming a parent, having an attractive wife who was also a social asset, and progressing creditably in his law career. He could ignore the despair he felt whenever he thought of the lack of sexual and emotional intimacy in his marriage. Nancy could also ignore their lack of intimacy because she had never really experienced Jim in a close and loving way to begin with. She had never looked at him as a person, and so there was no way in which her initial infatuation with him could have developed into a relationship of love.

Then, after 9 years of marriage, she met someone else who turned her on and was a challenge, as in the old days. This affair enabled her to be free of the fears she had felt on approaching her fortieth birthday. She was "in love" again. She asked him for a divorce.

After 6 weeks of insomnia, of pleading with her to go with him for marriage counseling, of looking fruitlessly for an explanation for what had happened, Jim had too much to drink one evening. Dismissing the idea of suicide, which he had been seriously considering for several days, he cornered his wife and demanded that she stay with him. When she refused, he struck her several times with his fist, becoming more enraged and frightened as she fell to the floor, bleeding, screaming. For a moment he thought of rushing to the window of their twelfth floor apartment and jumping out. Instead, he reached for the telephone and called the police.

Throughout their marriage, Nancy had been curiously free of feeling any emotional dependency on Jim. Not wanting him sexually, and not loving him with any emotional depth, she was placed in a uniquely controlling position in the marriage. Jim, as a result, felt subliminally rejected and became increasingly more dependent on her. When she announced her intention to divorce him, it seemed to him as if his entire world were collapsing. He became acutely depressed, and might have succeeded in committing suicide had his hurt and rage toward her not been suddenly released.

Psychological theories stress that depressed people's sensitivity to a loss of love is rooted in the way such people love. Specifically, they tend to become too involved, to place too much dependency on the people they love, and to lose too much of their identities in relationships. If such individuals should become involved with people whose ability or willingness to give is considerably less than their own—as is often the case, unfortunately—a serious imbalance is set up. Unless both partners understand and accept the difference in the way of loving, the one who is more involved may frequently feel rejected, search frantically for evidence of affection, and intensify their anxiety over the possibility that the relationship may end. "He who loves the more," wrote Thomas Mann in *Tonio Kreuger*, "is inferior and must suffer. . . ."

Sexual Guilt

Another important link between sexuality and depression is the guilt that is activated when sexual experiences cause a loss of personal integrity. Throughout the centuries, cultural values, moral teachings, and the conflicts and personality characteristics of many parents have combined to inculcate a high level of guilt about many kinds of sexual behavior. But in the second half of the twentieth century, many people have extensively reconsidered their sexual values in regard to many forms of activity ranging from masturbation to marital infidelity to homosexuality. Some people are delighted by these changes, others are angered by them; most find them confusing and upsetting. One father described a typically contemporary dilemma as follows: "This guy's been coming to the house on weekends, and he sleeps in my daughter's room. She's only 17. I can't get him out. It makes me see red. My wife is afraid that if we take a firm stand, my daughter will leave and end up living with him somewhere. When I suggested he use the guest room, he thought I was being funny and just laughed."

While a more open and honest attitude toward sex has been long overdue, a more permissive environment has unfortunately obscured the healthy guilt that should attach itself to sexual activities liable to jeopardize a person's sense of worth. This kind of guilt is actually a protective device to help people avoid sexual liaisons that might diminish their self-esteem and lead to depression. Without such protection, many people are more susceptible, in the face of so many sexual opportunities, to engaging in behavior that may be inappropriate, premature, and at times degrading. In the process of getting rid of—with good cause—the undesirable inhibitions and restrictions that made sex "dirty," the capacity of many people to recognize and cope with healthy sexual guilt has been lost as well. The suppression of sexual guilt has become a widespread phenomenon: marital infidelity appears to be commonplace and has even been advocated by some as a palliative for an unsatisfactory marriage.

This situation poses a special problem for adolescents. Peer pressure forces more and more adolescents to engage in sexual activity long before they are emotionally prepared for sex. Teenagers have many tasks to accomplish, among them finding out who they are, to define the extent and limits of their own personalities. They are naturally somewhat shy. Sex has been a mystery to them and traditionally an experience to be explored gradually, experimentally, so that it can eventually become integrated into their whole personality.

Working against this evolutionary pattern is the push of instant sex, a pressure so intense that they begin to feel that if they do not follow this lead, there must be something wrong with them. For young girls to be faced at 14 with such issues as birth control pills and abortions, when their sexual needs are still intimately interwoven with romantic ideals, can disrupt healthy personality development. Many teenage boys are not ready for the complex emotional overtones that accompany full sexual activity. A certain amount of confusion, ennui, and even the extensive use of alcohol and drugs among teenagers must be attributed to the pressure placed on them to involve themselves in sexual and emotional situations for which they are not prepared.

The roots of depression are found in how one regards oneself. Nowhere is mood more likely to be affected than in matters of love and sex. A fulfilling sexual relationship gives enormous reinforcement to one's sense of being whole and desirable, providing it occurs in the framework of mutual respect, trust, and caring.

Chapter 9

◆ ◆ ❖ ◆ ◆ ❖ ◆ ◆ ❖ ◆ ◆ ❖ ◆ ◆ ❖ ◆ ◆ ❖ ◆ ◆

Anger and Aggression

The Healthy Side of Aggression

The word "aggression" means, essentially, to move toward. It is a simple word of Latin origin that connotes energy and direction. However, the word has acquired enormous moral and emotional overtones, especially in recent years. Many people think it is a virtue, interpreting it to mean the drive and force necessary to accomplish good. Others consider it to be a derogatory term that they associate with destruction, war, violence, and exploitation.

Moral precepts that have influenced Western civilization—such as "the meek shall inherit the earth," "turn the other cheek," and "it is easier for a camel to go through the eye of a needle than for a rich man to enter the kingdom of God"—have infused into the culture a certain amount of guilt over the process of taking decisive action to reach desired objectives.

In contemporary society, aggression has become synonymous with invading someone else's territory, whether militarily, as in Vietnam and Iraq; financially, as in the invasion of another company's sales region; or personally, as in the exploitation of one human being by another. To call someone "aggressive" nowadays is often to use the word as a pejorative label, implying that he or she is selfish, greedy, hostile, and at times dangerous. While it is true that the pursuit of one's goals may have a detrimental effect on someone else, it is more a matter of how and in what context aggression is mobilized.

Actually, aggressiveness can be considered a healthy and highly moral personality trait when directed toward legitimate goals and when the rights of the individual and the rights of others are properly balanced. The movement in education, for instance, toward a system that allows different pupils within the class to move ahead at different rates of learning speed, based on their inherent abilities, is a step toward a liberation of healthy aggression. Previously, brighter students had been penalized, held back for the sake of the group, while slower students were painfully aware of their slowness whenever they compared their grades with those of their classmates. The efforts of more progressive corporate groups to expand—not so much by merger, acquisition, and the setting up of new divisions, but rather by establishing new small, innovative companies whose managers own a "piece of the action" and have a greater degree of independence—is an example of releasing constructive aggression.

Any individual's ability to be constructively aggressive is closely tied to his or her mood, emotional state, and personality. The libido theory of Freud posited that every human being possesses a given quantum of energy—biological energy derived from organic and genetic sources. The extent to which that energy is free to be utilized may be limited by many factors. Even when environmental opportunities for being aggressive are present—when initiative and creative action are valued and not smothered—most people seem to have an inner block limiting their freedom to be aggressive.

"Creative people are hard enough to find," said one experienced business entrepreneur. "Dependable people are even harder to find, and people with energy and follow-through, those who keep moving and see that the job gets done, are rare indeed. Our society doesn't seem to breed self-starters, and when initiative shows itself, everyone seems quick to chop it down."

Because the majority of men and women have some degree of inhibition in the free outward flow of energy, they are often frightened by demonstrations of initiative in others. They may feel envious of, and competitive toward, those who have uninhibited aggression. For every person who really takes pleasure in the achievements of others, there are many more who envy, resent, and criticize these achievements to compensate for their own lack of aggressiveness.

Because of the normal need for acceptance, a great many bright and capable individuals are discouraged from being aggressive and thus running the risk of social rejection. Everyone recalls the pressures within school to minimize academic performance and to deny any pleasure in the learning process simply to avoid being ridiculed and ostracized by classmates. Peer pressure perversely demands mediocrity.

In addition to environmental influences, the ability of an individual to be constructively aggressive depends on elements within his or her own personality. One of the most important is the freedom with which he or she can manage anger. Aggression is not the same as anger, but the ability to be aggressive is closely related to the success with which a person handles angry emotions.

Anger and Depression

The depressed individual is usually unable to experience and express normal anger. Instead, according to psychological theory, the anger is turned "inward against the self." Often the anger rumbles around disguised as tension, agitation, intestinal distress, fear—anything but what it really is. Walter B. Cannon, the physiologist, described what he called the fight-flight reaction: the human being, when confronted with danger, will react either with anger—self-defense or attack—or fear and, if possible, flight. For the depressed person, fear and/or flight is the usual way of responding to stress, even when in a normal mood anger would be the more appropriate response.

There are a number of reasons why people who are chronically depressed or depression-prone have a difficult time managing their angry feelings. Perhaps the most important is the fact that the way in which people handle emotions is a learned pattern, passed on from generation to generation within families and cultures. If, for example, expressing legitimate anger was simply not tolerated within the home and if any show of independence or assertiveness was firmly thwarted, emotions would be driven underground. Feelings would be concealed and communication stifled.

A case in point is a 51-year-old woman who began to have insomnia and episodes of anxiety as she grew uncertain about her relationship to her husband, who throughout their marriage had offered little affection and support but ample criticism. He paid no heed to birthdays and anniversaries. He was abrupt with her whenever she disagreed with him even on minor points. He made all the major decisions in the marriage by himself.

For 19 years, she had collaborated with this pattern without complaint and supported him in many ways. Then, suddenly, her father died. During her period of grief, she began to question the quality of her married life. She had been hurt and angry on many occasions, but had ignored her feelings in the interest of harmony. The only way in which her feelings had expressed themselves was through a series of minor physical illnesses, which periodically disrupted their family and social life.

When she finally spoke up, as she emerged from her acute depressive reaction, her husband proved himself willing to work on his attitudes so as to demonstrate more warmth and a greater appreciation of her worth. "Over the years, it was almost as though she were inviting me to be indifferent," he complained. "Why didn't she speak up sooner?"

The answer was to be found in her own upbringing. Her parents, rigid and unemotional, had tolerated no disagreement within the home. Both were preoccupied with the role they played, that of husband or wife, mother or father, provider or housekeeper. Each role had certain expectations attached to it, and these were lived up to strictly and without complaint. Very little affection was shown; and never any anger. The children were discouraged from being spontaneous and assertive. They were rarely given any praise.

The inflexibility and emotional sterility of the woman's childhood proved to be a breeding ground for her problems in experiencing and handling emotions, especially anger. As an adult, she concealed her sensitivity and lack of self-confidence. Unwittingly, her husband played into the pattern by neglecting her feelings, thereby reinforcing both her lack of emotional spontaneity and her doubts about her worth. Nor could she bring herself to tell him about her feelings, since doing so might liberate some of the anger she had suppressed.

After her father died, she became acutely depressed and sought counseling. In the course of her therapy, she began, for the first time, to ventilate some of the hurt and anger she had felt, and to reveal the pain of her compromised self-esteem. As her emotions were released, not only did her spirits lift, but her level of energy also progressively increased. For the first time in years, she felt free to be more assertive, to speak up, and to take the initiative in communicating with her husband. The anger she had been accumulating was now directed outwardly in her own defense. As this anger subsided, it was replaced by a greater freedom of expression. She was able to confront and deal with issues as they came up, either calmly and directly, or with anger, if appropriate.

The discharge of hostility leading to a lifting in mood and the emergence of healthy aggression and assertiveness is a pattern commonly seen in the therapy of depressed people. It is as if they have stored up unexpressed rage that they subsequently let out in bits and pieces until it has all been released. Psychological theory stresses that depressed people tend to have a strong identification with the people they love, at times so strong that the lines separating the two individuals become blurred. Hence to be angry at a parent or a lover is to be angry at oneself. When this anger is redirected outwardly, self-esteem can be restored.

Psychoanalytic theory would place the major causal factors for depressed patients' fear of their own anger within the framework of childhood development, in particular at the oral and anal stages. In the former stage, traumatic events produce a great deal of difficulty in the way depressed individuals later experience dependency needs. When these needs are frustrated, in reality or in their imaginations, their response is an unreasonable rage.

During the anal phase of development, when children are approximately 3 years old, toilet training is completed. Too great a rigidity in child rearing at this time can serve to constrict children's normal spontaneity and enthusiasm; it can devitalize them, shut off their creative potential, introduce sadistic and masochistic components into their interpersonal relationships, and lead to a compulsiveness that denies them resilience in their later years. Such a combination of fixation points in childhood may produce adults with intense unmet dependency needs, which are a source of frustration and anger, and a rigid inability to express emotions, referred to by Wilhelm Reich as an "affect block." This sets the people up for chronic depression.

One of the most common reasons why people accumulate anger is because they are unable to be aggressive and assertive in a positive, constructive way. Whether as a result of a timidity that began in childhood, fear of rejection, low self-esteem, an intense need to please others, or an aversion to conflict, years of being unwilling or unable to speak up forthrightly—which can often be done in a polite, nonthreatening manner—sets the stage for deep internal rage and, of course, depression.

Freud himself postulated that biological factors would be identified and found to be closely linked to many of his psychological concepts, including those about the relationship between hostility and depression. It is now known, for example, that patients with hyperthyroidism (overactivity of the thyroid gland) tend to be exceedingly emotional, and to show irritability and anger at the slightest provocation, whereas those with an underactive thyroid gland tend to be apathetic and depressed. The treatment of hyperthyroid patients, either surgically or by means of drugs that suppress thyroid overactivity, leads to a reduction in irritability and hypersensitivity. The correction of hypothyroidism, through the administration of thyroid hormones, reduces apathy and restores patients' ability to experience and express anger when provoked.

Low Self-Esteem Blocks Healthy Assertiveness

Depressed people's sensitivity and low self-esteem are further intensified by a strong connection between lack of healthy assertiveness, anger, and depression and the concomitant block in spontaneity and aggressiveness. There are more opportunities for them to be hurt, offended, and threatened—precisely because their sense of worth is already compromised. They often read rejection into the slightest remark or indifference that ordinarily would not upset them. Paradoxically, depressed people's behavior frequently provokes anger and rejection from others, rather than the warmth they really seek. Depression can be especially irritating to those in contact with depressed people if and when the mood itself is an expression of their inner rage.

Harry Wright was associate dean of a small college in New England. He was 38 years old when the dean retired. Harry, having done an excellent job for the school, had expected to be chosen as his successor. For various reasons, however, the board of directors decided to look outside the school for a new dean. Harry did not receive the promotion.

He was deeply hurt. He felt, with good reason, unappreciated. This in turn set off a chain reaction in which he began to question his own ability and wonder whether or not he was good enough for the job. Perhaps he had overestimated his own abilities. He wondered whether he might have offended some key members of the college community. He was depressed.

Harry's anger, rather than being expressed in a direct and open manner, was repressed. Nonetheless, it surfaced in a "not caring" attitude. He no longer applied himself energetically to his work as he had. He was often late for faculty meetings or missed them completely. The new dean, only vaguely familiar with Harry's past contributions to the school, became irritated again and again by his indifference and reprimanded him for his irresponsibility. Harry felt even more unappreciated, since he failed to see the link between his behavior and the dean's impatience with him, and his hurt and anger doubled. When he was asked to resign, he was shocked; finally, when it was rather late, he was openly enraged by the situation.

Harry's disappointment at not receiving the deanship was quite understandable. However, his inability to initiate a discussion of his situation with the new dean, and the progressive accumulation of anger in the *form of depression*, prevented him from finding better solutions to the problem. He might have anticipated the possibility that the school would look elsewhere for a new dean. Inasmuch as he was well thought of, he might have communicated his interest in the position more definitively. Once the appointment had been made, if he felt the need to leave he might have handed in his resignation rather than forcing it by his behavior. He might also have continued to do his excellent work until the new dean was able to see and acknowledge his value to the school.

Because he could not handle his anger, Harry fell back on the use of depression to express his frustration and, in turn, received anger in response. This kind of pattern illustrates what is referred to as "passive-aggressive behavior," in which aggression, rather than being channeled actively and directly toward goals, is bottled up, and one sets out to make one's point by a circuitous route that permits one to disown—even to oneself—any responsibility for the outcome.

In such situations, one learns indirect methods for expressing hostility. All children recognize that if they hurt themselves, their parents will react. As children find better ways of eliciting a response, they gladly forfeit such dramatic and self-defeating ways of getting attention or expressing frustration. In the formative years of people likely to engage in passive-aggressive behavior, one usually finds a serious confusion in communication and a lack of responsiveness in the environment that impresses on children the idea that injuring themselves is the quickest and most effective way of "getting back at" those who may have hurt them.

This can easily become a habit of failure. For instance, adolescents who are somewhat depressed may express disappointment and anger with their parents by doing poorly in school. They cannot concentrate effectively. They consistently fail tests. They hand in their homework late, and even then it is sloppy. In a posture of failure, depressed teenagers bring home report cards that make their parents angry and frustrated. Any effort on their part to force a change meets with stubborn resistance.

Young underachievers are commonly depressed and angry. Their inadequate performance says to their parents: "I am hurt. I am angry, but you haven't offered me a decent way of expressing my emotions." The secretary who is repeatedly late for work and the customer who is always several months late in paying his bills in spite of having adequate cash on hand may not merely be demonstrating a kind of carelessness. Frequently, this kind of behavior pattern is unconsciously designed to disturb its target and is an oblique way of expressing hostility. The intense immobilization of seriously depressed individuals is often itself an expression of passive rage.

Cultural Influences on Anger

Cultural factors profoundly influence the manner in which people experience and handle anger. This is true in America even if the people are two or three generations removed from their origins. Not only are patterns for handling anger passed on, by contact, from generation to generation, but also through what Carl Jung described as archetypes within a cultural unconscious. It would be naïve to assume that a few thousand miles and a century or so would significantly change the inherent architecture of the emotional life.

In a society that is basically a "melting pot," there is no way to calculate the extent to which communication difficulties in a marriage are rooted in clashes of cultural characteristics. In one instance, a husband and wife found that though they were highly compatible in almost every way, the difference in the way each handled anger nearly destroyed their marriage. The husband, whose father was Spanish, felt quite free to explode in rage at a minor slight. It was all over in a few minutes and he was then ready to completely forget the incident. His wife, who was of Scotch-English origin, valued control over emotions and did not like to get angry. When her feelings were hurt, she tended to become silent and withdrawn, feeling a strong sense of rejection and futility stemming from her inability to discharge the emotions stirred up in her. When she retaliated, it was usually in the form of subtle, provocative remarks aimed at deflating her husband's ego.

Finally, in a counseling situation, they came to grips with this impasse. Until he appreciated the full impact of his outbursts and she learned to be more self-expressive, their relationship was seriously jeopardized.

In my work with patients over four decades, I have noticed that men and women brought up in strict religious settings, particularly if they are from families of North European origin, tend to withdraw in the face of anger. Becoming depressed is a common way for them to respond to provocation. By contrast, those from less rigid religious backgrounds, particularly if they are of southern European origin, show the opposite tendency toward less overt depression and more readiness to direct intense emotions outward when angered.

Expressing and Suppressing Hostility

Just getting out anger is not necessarily therapeutic for all people who are depressed. At first, this may seem to contradict the concept that depression itself is frequently an expression of hostility and that depressed people regain their energy and aggressiveness as they become more capable of emotional release. However, some of the anger depressed people experience comes from their hypersensitivity: their low self-esteem encourages them to feel rejected by others, whether they are or not. The hurt that they feel often derives as much from the way they perceive what is happening to them as from the actual facts of the matter.

If a certain amount of the anger depressed people struggle with is the result of having been wounded, in fact or fancy, being able to express this hurt angrily will discharge some of their tensions, but it will not automatically take away the underlying depression. In individuals who have had lifelong problems with hypersensitivity and have tightly controlled their hostile emotions, sudden outbursts of anger, which they might be encouraged to show in the course of a counseling or group therapy session, can hardly be expected to change their ingrained pattern. In fact, such an experience may backfire, causing them to panic in the face of the overwhelming and unfamiliar emotions that have been aroused.

The experience of being depressed is by no means always related to unrecognized or unexpressed hostility. Moreover, anger and violence are frequently as much the result of the depression as a cause. "I haven't been doing well in school," a 16-year-old boy said. "I can't concentrate on studies. I tried athletics, but couldn't make the team. At home, my mom is hell on wheels. She screams at me all the time. Uses lousy language. Calls me every four-letter name in the book. She's always after me, makes me feel like nothing. No wonder Dad left her. There's no future for someone like me. Get some money. Get out of this place."

The boy just quoted was not from a slum but from an upper-middle-class suburban home. He had been arrested by the police for breaking into a hardware store, striking the salesman, and stealing some merchandise that he hoped to sell in order to get enough money to leave town. Abused at home, lacking a father with whom he could identify, unsupported by any kind of achievement in school or among his peers, he was indeed desperate. His hopelessness had led him to resort to a violent act in order to escape and, at the same time, discharge some of the rage he felt at his situation.

When individuals are out of touch with their emotions, and especially when they blame others for their distress, it is common for hostility, rather than being suppressed or repressed, to be very much on the surface, hiding the underlying depression.

Anne Richardson was going through menopause. She was physically comfortable, except for some hot flashes and lightheadedness from time to time. She had had difficulty in sleeping and ate poorly, but seemed to be in good spirits. No one suspected that she was depressed.

However, she was extremely difficult to live with. She incessantly found fault with her husband and children. If the house was untidy, she screamed until the newspapers were picked up and the ash trays emptied. When her husband would come home late from work, she nagged him about his negligence. He found it hard to pin her down in making plans for weekends, but when the time came for them to go away on trips or entertain friends, she would belabor him for not having made adequate plans.

There is such a thing as an "angry" depression. Anne Richardson differs little from business executives whose depression shows itself as abruptness, irritability, impatience. At home, they are short with their families and do not want to hear about day-to-day difficulties. At work, they find fault with minor failures on the part of their employees. They come across as constantly angry. They may try alcohol or a brief affair as curative measures. They deny to themselves that they are—or ever were—depressed. Denial of this sort is commonly associated with open and, at times, intense anger and the tendency to blame others for one's misfortunes.

It is important to realize, however, that not everyone who is depressed is necessarily angry, either consciously or unconsciously. There is such a thing as a direct and uncomplicated depressive response that may be set off by a disappointment, a rejection, or a loss. While depressed, such a person may not be able to activate his or her anger when provoked, but anger itself plays no significant role in the origins of the depression.

Forgiveness Can Free Us from Resentment

No discussion of hostility is complete without considering the nature of resentment. Resentment is different from anger. It is also different from depression. In fact, an acute depression can often save a hurt and disappointed person from the ravages of resentment.

Resentment is a persistent and tenacious state of hostility. Resentful people feel hatred and cynicism that they justify by real or imagined hurts derived from their environment. Resentment is different from the repressed or suppressed hostility seen in certain psychoneurotic and depressed conditions, and is quite different from direct anger.

Resentful people lack insight. They are usually insensitive to the feelings of others. They are likely to be unhappy primarily when they cannot dominate or control others in their environment, and especially when their demands cannot be immediately fulfilled. They cannot forgive slights and rejections, many of which are unintentional or entirely apocryphal, and they appear to derive pleasure from finding fault with the people around them.

Resolving resentment demands the adoption of a fresh value structure that allows people to let go of slights and forgive others. It is not an easy change to make. Whenever resentment is a major emotional factor in any psychological picture, whether an anxiety state, a depression, or even alcoholism, the prospects for recovery are seriously diminished. Resentful people are too busy thinking up ways of getting even, of making others suffer, of denying their own complicity in their unhappiness to become overtly depressed. They are, in fact, depressogenic; that is, they are likely to make those in their environment who are continually in contact with their bitterness feel depressed.

By contrast, depressed people often reveal a willingness to *forgive*, and an eagerness to start anew as the depression lifts. Their value structure emphasizes the importance of love, and this endures even when their minds are full of angry and desperate thoughts.

It is only by learning how to forgive that resentment can be dispelled and interpersonal relationships (which are inevitably impacted by hurts and misunderstandings) can thrive. Forgiveness is a concept largely overlooked in psychological literature. This may be because it has religious or spiritual connotations. After all, "forgive us our trespasses as we forgive those who trespass against us" is a phrase found in the Lord's prayer. Only in recent years has forgiveness been given its rightful and essential emphasis in therapy.

What does forgiveness mean? It does not mean to ignore or to forget. The process of forgiveness involves recognizing, experiencing, and expressing the hurt and anger that a person has suffered at the hands of someone else. . . and then, letting go of these emotions, not so much for the sake of the other person, but for one's own sake. As one 35-year-old woman put it, "For years I've resented the fact that my parents favored my two brothers. When it came time to go to college, even though I was probably brighter than either of them, my father refused to pay the kind of tuition he was willing to pay for them and my mother went along with him. One of my brothers went to Stamford. I ended up at a local community college.

"I couldn't get going with my life until I got rid of my feeling of being mistreated in that way. It took a lot of work on my part. I had to get to understand what made my parents the way they were. I had to feel myself as a grown-up, someone able to shape my life on my own. I had to forgive them, and, in the process, free myself from the emotional slavery that my resentment had put me in."

Forgiveness does not have to lead to reconciliation. Sometimes the people one has to forgive are dead, and no reconciliation is possible. Sometimes they stand ready to inflict further injury, given half a chance, and for the sake of one's own health, must be avoided altogether. Sometimes there is an incompatibility of communication styles, lifestyles, and other values that make an ongoing relationship impossible. But just as often, forgiveness can set the stage for reconciliation with someone who has played or who continues to play a very important part in our lives. Without forgiveness, there can be no reconciliation; few intimate relationships can survive and grow that way.

Chapter 10

♦ ♦ ❖ ♦ ♦ ❖ ♦ ♦ ❖ ♦ ♦ ❖ ♦ ♦ ❖ ♦ ♦ ❖ ♦ ♦

Guilt

If aggressiveness has become a controversial quality in this culture, there is another quality equally as controversial and often ignored, one that is no less central to an understanding of depression in Western civilization: guilt.

The cultures in which people live shape the way they experience emotions; therefore, it is not surprising that certain emotions are experienced by individuals in some cultures but not in others. For example, the Western medical concept of depression—that it is a psychiatric syndrome characterized by specific affective, cognitive, behavioral, and somatic symptoms—may be unique to European and colonized North American cultures, since equivalent concepts of depression are not found among many non-European groups, such as Nigerians, Chinese, Canadian Eskimos, Japanese, and Malaysians. Even though they have no equivalent *terms* for depression, individuals within these cultures may still suffer from depressive disorders. However, the symptoms may be experienced, expressed, and responded to in distinct ways and attributed to different causes.

Some signs of depression are experienced cross-culturally. Many scholars who study symptoms of what we call "depression" in various cultures agree that certain symptoms of depression, such as feelings of guilt, self-deprecation, suicidal ideas, and feelings of despair, are often quite rare or even absent among non-European populations. Other symptoms, including disturbances of sleep, appetite, energy, body sensation, and motor functioning, seem to be more common.

One of the major symptoms of depression that is particularly common in the Western world is guilt. Guilt is not only a symptom of depression but also a cause of it; since guilt involves a loss of self-esteem, it can bring on depression—and depressed people can feel guilty about being depressed. The results of guilt can be devastating.

Whenever she felt unhappy, Emily Watts feared that she would lose her husband's love. She would ask him, again and again, whether he cared for her. At first he was reassuring. Later, as the same question continually resurfaced, he became impatient. She in turn would only feel more frightened of losing him.

She had spasms of irrational jealousy, and would search her husband's suits and wallet for evidence that he might be involved with another woman. When he went on business trips, she could not sleep at night. She pressured him repeatedly to quit his job and find one that did not require traveling. It never occurred to her that her fears were rooted in guilt, that her feeling of being unattractive and inadequate as a wife were a form of self-punishment, that her ultimate punishment would be the loss of the man she loved.

Why did Emily feel a need to be punished, and in this way? This was her second marriage. She had become involved with her present husband while she was still married to her first. Her first marriage had been problematic from the beginning; at 19, she had run away from home and married a young man she hardly knew. He subsequently began to drink heavily, and several times, in an angry stupor, he beat her up. He was never able to hold a job for more than a few months, usually getting fired after an argument with the supervisor. But because of her conviction that marriage should be a permanent contract, she persisted for 3 years in trying to make it work.

When she began her affair, she experienced a great deal of guilt over it. As it went on, she suppressed her guilt, telling herself that she had a perfect right to find some kind of closeness and happiness. Six months after she left her first husband, he committed suicide. Emily was torn between knowing that she had not directly caused his death and feeling that if she had stayed with him longer he might still be alive.

She did not call her feeling "guilt." Yet she did feel intensely responsible for what had happened to him. She told no one of her conflict. Gradually, she became depressed and developed the fear that her new husband, with whom she had been very happy, would eventually leave her.

In the course of professional counseling, Emily Watts saw for the first time the connection between her depression and the fear and guilt she had felt during her first marriage. "I thought that the best thing to do was to try to push it all out of my mind. I never talked about what happened to anyone. I can see I was wrong. It never occurred to me that I would feel so terribly responsible for something I had so little control over."

Even when feelings of guilt are not the cause of depression, guilt is easily provoked when someone is feeling despondent. A 32-year-old foreman lost his job suddenly, and a few months later his wife deserted him. His assumption—an unwarranted one—was that he had caused both these misfortunes. "If I had only treated her differently, she wouldn't have left me. And my job—if only I'd put in extra hours, they wouldn't have let me go." The fact was that his wife had never loved him. She had married him on the rebound from a love affair in which she had been rejected, and had found him lacking in what she "expected of a husband" from the earliest days of their marriage. As for his job, his employers had dismissed him only because they had lost several important contracts and could no longer afford to keep him on the payroll.

Unable to gain perspective on either event, he persisted in blaming himself: at times his vulnerability to feeling guilty went beyond reasonable limits. "Last week, at the new job, someone stole fifty dollars from one of the lockers. I know it's crazy, but when the company police started looking into it, I felt as if I had done it.

When I got rid of that weird idea, I thought I would be accused of it anyway."

There is a difference between depressed states that stem from guilt and those that are unrelated to feelings of guilt. Psychiatrist Peter F. Regan III demonstrated that depressed patients with a significant degree of guilt do not respond well to biological treatment. By contrast, depressed patients in whom guilt is not significant usually improve rapidly when biological treatments are used. Guilt will reinforce the tenacity of depression. It often propels people to go on repeating the behavior pattern engendering the guilt until they have come to terms with it.

Certain depressed alcoholics exemplify this point. A 51-year-old woman began therapy because of loneliness and feelings of despair that had plagued her for the two years subsequent to her husband's untimely death. She had also been using alcohol to take the edge off her depression, and had formed a habit of drinking nearly a fifth of Vodka every day.

Efforts on her own and through Alcoholics Anonymous to end her drinking proved unsuccessful. In fact, the more she focused on her drinking problem, the guiltier she felt and the more she drank. Through psychotherapy and with the aid of antidepressant medication, her depression gradually lifted. But her drinking continued until she was able to see how the anguish of the guilt itself was setting her up to drink again. Once she had forfeited her tendency to blame herself, she reentered Alcoholics Anonymous and eventually eliminated her drinking altogether.

Psychological theory points to a powerful superego as part of the personality structure of the individual who becomes depressed. Formed in childhood, the superego has two major components. The first is a sense of right and wrong, commonly called conscience. When conscience is violated, when people feel that they have transgressed their basic values—or someone else's values they think should be theirs—the result is guilt. The second component is self-concept. When people feel that they are pretty much the kind of people they want to be, they can be reasonably content. The greater the distance between what they are and what they feel they ought to be, the greater their sense of failure. At times, the superego can be so highly developed that the standards people expect to meet are impossibly high.

The superego is not the same as conscience; the former contains a strong emotional element, while the latter is a more intellectual awareness of one's value system. W. H. Auden, defining this difference in his book *A Certain World*, wrote:

> The superego speaks loudly and either in imperatives or interjections—"DO THIS! DON'T DO THAT! BRAVO! YOU SON OF A BITCH!" Conscience speaks softly and in the interrogative—"Do you really think so? Is that really true?"
>
> To say that their voices are different does not mean, of course, that they never coincide; indeed in a perfect society they would always coincide. . . .
>
> The limitation of the superego as a guide to conduct is that, since it is a social creation, it is only effective so long as social conditions remain unchanged; if they change, it doesn't know what to say. At home, the Spartans did not use money; consequently, when they travelled to countries that did, they were helpless to resist the temptations of money, and it was said in the ancient world that a Spartan could always be bribed.

Guilt-makers

Unlike the Spartan away from home, depressed people have a tendency to feel guilty, which makes them particularly vulnerable to those who know how to control them by activating their guilt. Because they often suffer from the assumption that they are somehow in the wrong, they are easily convinced that they are at fault in any situation, regardless of the facts.

A 39-year-old woman consulted a psychiatrist because she had been feeling hopeless and suicidal off and on for several months. "My husband said there was something wrong with me. We have terrible fights. He told me I was wrecking our marriage and if I didn't straighten out he'd have to leave me."

Over the next few sessions, the following impression of her husband emerged: rigid, opinionated, a man who demanded a high level of performance from himself and who was unceasingly critical of his wife. At one time or another he accused her of not being a competent housekeeper, of failing to discipline the children adequately, of not entertaining enough, of being uninterested in him sexually. When she would become upset and cry, he would accuse her of being emotionally unstable. "Is he right? Am I a complete failure? Am I all these awful things he says I am?"

The psychiatrist insisted on meeting her husband to get a clearer picture of the interaction. During the entire visit her husband acted more as though he were a colleague of the doctor's rather than the husband of the patient. "What can we do for her, doctor? She's too sensitive. Of course I think highly of her—I love her. She really seems very depressed. Do you think she's seriously ill? There's a history of mental illness in her family, you know. Or perhaps she didn't tell you." He denied that he had done or said anything that could have been upsetting to her. "There's nothing wrong with me. I don't have to come to see you or anyone else." And he declined to make another appointment.

Within 2 months, the patient reported that her husband was now angrily complaining about the length and cost of her therapy. He had also claimed that he was in regular contact with her therapist for "progress reports," which he was not. He dropped remarks like "Your doctor told me you're not doing enough to help yourself." His antagonism to her treatment appeared just as the patient herself was recovering some of her self-esteem and becoming better able to fend off his criticism of her.

Guilt-makers are not always so blatant in such efforts to make a husband, a wife, parent, child, or co-worker feel dreadful about himself or herself. Frequently the interaction occurs in a much subtler fashion. "Look how unhappy you are making your mother feel," "Why can't you be more grateful for all we've done for you?" and similar remarks made at the right moment, in the right tone of voice and with the right nonverbal backup, are often enough to keep slightly depressed people subject to the will and control of guilt-makers. Such maneuvering can sometimes be so subtle that some therapists have resorted to videotaping families to show them the destructive quality in their communication patterns.

What motivates guilt-makers? Most of the time they are totally unaware of their effect on others, since the motivation for that effect is buried too many layers below their awareness. Sometimes guilt-makers are sadistic, deriving a certain amount of pleasure from making their victims squirm. Sometimes making others feel guilty is a way of discharging their own guilt, which may originate from problems into which they have little or no insight. Finding someone else to blame relieves them temporarily of their own tension and distress. Sometimes their behavior is rooted in envy and competitiveness: by making other people feel incompetent and guilty, they can then feel more capable themselves. Sometimes the goal of their behavior is simply to control.

Guilt-makers rarely come to the therapist's office except to vindicate themselves. As a rule, they have too little insight. As long as they have someone to blame and control, they can protect themselves more or less effectively against experiencing depression. It is their victims who often end up depressed, feeling "I can never do anything right," and "It's all my fault."

Resolving Guilt

Guilt, of and by itself, is not abnormal even when it leads to depression. The ability to experience and recognize appropriate guilt and the cultivation of effective ways of coping with guilt have always been considered necessary attributes of the healthy personality. Guilt is an important mechanism for protecting people against becoming involved in behavior that is injurious to themselves or to others. When guilt is denied, or when people cannot recognize it or do not know what they ought to feel guilty about, they are likely to enter into situations that compromise their self-esteem. They may not realize how much they are hurting themselves until they become acutely depressed. Linking their depression to their guilt and then finding a way of resolving the guilt are fundamental parts of their recovery.

"I've lost my enthusiasm for everything," said a 46-year-old salesman. "For the past 2 years nothing has worked out right. I put off making calls and I've lost customers as a result. On weekends when I'm home, I'm too tired to spend any time with the kids. My wife and I hardly talk to each other. When we do, it often ends up in a fight." As he explored the sources of his unhappiness in therapy, he revealed that he had been having an affair with the secretary of one of his customers for nearly 2 years. "That couldn't be getting me down. As a matter of fact, it's the one pleasure I have, getting into bed with her once or twice a month. Besides, what's so unusual about that? Everyone plays around."

It took several months before he could convince himself that, regardless of what others did or did not do, for him the sexual involvement was stirring up guilt. His behavior contrasted with his upbringing. He had attended religious schools as a child and, until his early twenties, had been deeply involved in church activities. He had not had intercourse with anyone before marrying his wife.

He had abided by the strict, demanding codes of his fundamentalist background until other demands in his life, particularly in business, forced him to make compromises. He began whittling away at his ingrained values. He took a drink from time to time. He arranged for occasional kickbacks. He padded his expense account here and there. "Everyone's doing it. If you don't you can't survive." He ignored occasional twinges of guilt. By the time he was in his middle thirties he looked on religion as "a real handicap to making it." Until he began his affair, his home life had been relatively placid. After that, largely as a product of his unrecognized guilt, he turned it into a battleground.

"Just what do I do with this guilt now that I recognize it?" he asked. "I'm certainly not going back to the way I thought 20 years ago." He was confronted with two options: either to modify his value system as far as fidelity in marriage was concerned or end his affair and try to improve his life at home. He chose to end the affair. But it was not an easy choice to make. He was incredulous that, surrounded as he was by sexual permissiveness, he could still feel more comfortable with his original set of values.

Cultural Values

This culture is replete with confusing and contradictory values. Consider the reactions to the decision of the Supreme Court on the legality of abortion. There are those who hold that life begins at the moment of conception and that abortion is murder. Others feel that there are good medical and psychological reasons to perform abortions selectively. Still others feel that male legislators have no right to determine arbitrarily what a woman can or cannot do with her own body. Certain groups insist that all hospital facilities should be made available for abortion procedures even if owned and operated by religious groups opposed to abortion.

Everything that has brought cultures and people into more immediate contact with one another—from television to jet planes-—confronts the individual with a mass of available and contradictory options in the way of values. As a result it becomes difficult to know what to feel guilty about. This in turn leads to a Novocain effect: a numbing of one's personal sense of responsibility.

What a contrast to the world of Freud! The early analysts worked out their theories in a period of relatively static values. They were able to study individuals against the background of stable environmental influences. They could help patients by releasing their egos from the constrictions placed on them by stern, severe superegos without the patients then having to live in a world like ours, which does not differentiate between neurotic guilt and real guilt and which often cannot distinguish self-actualizing people from sociopaths.

"There is something seriously immobilizing in this society," commented a university president. "Between the blurring of values on the one hand and the massive bureaucracies on the other, you have to be sociopathic at times to get anything done. Otherwise, you just get frustrated and bogged down."

Traditional sociopaths are unconcerned with the needs or rights of others. They seek their own ends exclusively, often by exploiting and using people. They are unfamiliar with feelings of guilt. The vice-president of a large film production company, in an effort to be humorous, told the following story to his wife's psychiatrist, whom he visited only after she had made a serious suicide attempt.

"We were in Los Angeles for a couple of days, a business trip, contracts to take care of. Wanted to show some of our customers a good time. Got this girl, pretty, blond, mentally slow. Promised her a part in one of our pictures if she'd give us a gang bang. So she did, one after another. It was really something–and was she surprised afterward when we told her to get lost!"

This executive was sociopathic. In everyday life, others saw him as a dynamic, energetic, and clever businessman who knew how to make money. To have the sociopath as a cultural hero is not only confusing, it's dangerous. Millions of people have lost the sense of guilt and, along with it, the normal protective function that guilt serves. Often they can regain it only when an acute depression forces them to come to terms with their suppression of conscience.

Guilt is not always coexistent with depression, but it strongly determines the quality of the depression when it is present. For many, coping with depression means putting themselves back in touch with legitimate feelings of guilt.

There is also an urgent need for our society to clarify basic values by which its members can live. As Rabbi Roland B. Gittelsohn stated at a conference on Moral Values in Psychoanalysis:

> In physical medicine, the doctor treating the patient recognizes that there are certain physical laws of nature and of human nature, such as the laws involving nutrition, exercise, and so on. While the doctor understands these laws as absolutes, as inherent in and characteristic of nature, he also knows that they are relative in the sense of being applied to the specific patient and the specific situation; they will not apply in precisely the same way to every individual. . . .
>
> Isn't the same thing true of moral values and moral laws?. . . there are certain moral values and laws [within a culture] in conformity to which alone true health and happiness are possible.

Chapter 11

♦ ♦ ❖ ♦ ♦ ❖ ♦ ♦ ❖ ♦ ♦ ❖ ♦ ♦ ❖ ♦ ♦ ❖ ♦ ♦

Success Is a Risk

Depression has often been referred to as an "illness of success." It is frequently at the very point when physicians have established their successful practices, businessmen become executive vice-presidents of their companies, and inventors finally win their patent suits, that their lives do a somersault and depression sweeps in.

The Peter Principle maintained that many people are promoted one step beyond their capacity, after which they stabilize at that level of incompetence. There is an alternative to this concept. Promotion can bring on a depression, and the depression then passes for ineffectiveness. When people attain the very goals they have been seeking, the risk of his becoming depressed rises sharply.

Success often brings major changes—social, economic, and sometimes geographic—plus greater responsibilities and pressures. Many individuals, because of a deeply rooted sense of guilt, feel unconsciously that they do not deserve what they have achieved, and turn about to undermine and destroy it. For everyone, the attainment of a major goal in life activates a reassessment of personal worth and direction.

To the extent that our society is still upwardly mobile, being successful and having some external evidence of one's worth is a vital need. It is closely tied to self-esteem. Whether the goal consists of a higher position in a corporation, a larger income, the completion of a thesis or book, becoming a proficient athlete or winning a political contest, there is always a reinforcement of self-esteem in the achievement, and some degree of self-recrimination in not making it.

Paradoxically, the more dependent a person's view of himself or herself is on external evidence of accomplishment, the less satisfying such achievements will be. An ambitious research scientist described his struggle with ambition in this way. "From the time I was a small child, I felt driven to do well. My parents pushed me in school. If I didn't get straight A's in everything, I felt frightened, hopeless, even at 10 or 11. I graduated from college *summa cum laude*. You'd think that would be enough to quiet my self-doubts. But not at all. I wondered whether I would do well in graduate school. I was concerned about whether I would do any research that would be worth doing. And even when I was given one of the highest honors in science 30 years later, I felt that I didn't really deserve it, that the work for which I was being given such recognition was something I had fallen into accidentally."

Even though the "I" within each of us defies measurement, most people search in one place or another for ways to translate self-worth into inches, yards, and feet. Every society has its own measuring stick. Using money as a guide to determine personal worth is a traditional one. In his *Anatomy of Melancholy* (1621), Robert Burton wrote:

> In a word, every man for his own ends. Our *summum bonum* is commodity, and the goddess we adore *Dea Moneta*, Queen Money, to whom we daily offer sacrifices, which steers our hearts, hands, affections, all: that most powerful goddess, by whom we are reared,depressed, elevated, esteemed, the sole commandress of our actions for which we pray, run, ride, go, come, labor and contend as fishes for a crumb that falleth into the water. It is not worth, virtue, wisdom, valour, learning, honesty, religion, or any sufficiency for which we respected but money, greatness, office, honour, authority.

The close relationship in our culture between money and self-esteem is only too evident. It is not uncommon for people to have a sense of well-being only when they have a certain amount of cash in their savings account. It is possible to watch the moods of certain individuals fluctuate with the ups and downs of the securities market. Because personal financial problems are often so real and immediate, it is often difficult in therapy to point out the powerful emotional element people have introduced into their perception of money, even though it may have little to do with the facts of the case.

Many successful men and women have been able to confirm themselves in their work—not through a confirmation of self-worth, but rather through a confirmation of talent and ability. A close look at the evolution of their lives shows a logical relationship between what they are doing now and the interests and natural inclinations they demonstrated in childhood and adolescence. A very successful businessman who thrives on his responsibilities recalled organizing a group of teenagers in high school to provide a service of doing chores around people's homes. He served as the agent and took a fee for locating the job and the worker and putting the two together. Thirty years later, he was skillfully doing the same type of work for a computer programming company he had organized. A well-known writer recalled that her urge to write could be traced back as early as 9, when she created her own drawings to illustrate her stories for children, and again at 12, when she published a neighborhood newspaper that she typed, duplicated, and sold from house to house.

Obviously, there are many practical reasons that prevent people from doing the kind of work for which they are best suited. However, when people *do* have some choice, if they lose sight of the importance of pursuing interests in harmony with their personality, they run the risk of forfeiting fulfillment. There are also forceful, though subtle, social pressures that cause discontent even in those who have found a satisfying place for themselves. A 52-year-old housewife who came to therapy because she was depressed complained of a growing loss of self-respect. "I try to be a good wife and mother. But my husband's a busy man and my three children are grown and gone. I have friend and we go shopping together. Twice a week I work as a volunteer at a nursing home. I take care of the house. I cook the meals. I like to cook.

"I worked as a secretary for years, until the children came. I didn't really enjoy that, although we needed the extra money. If I went to work now, what I earned would be taxed on top of my husband's salary, but I feel that if I don't go to work, I'm losing out on something."

In the course of her therapy, it became apparent that she had never had any special career interests. In fact, as a child and teenager she had always daydreamed of having a home of her own, of a husband and children. Her dreams were quite elaborate and detailed: collecting recipes, making covers for the couch and chairs, baking, tending to flowers in her garden, sitting down after dinner in the evenings and sharing with her family their activities of the day. "That's what I always wanted. Now that I have it, why don't I enjoy it?"

Slowly and insidiously over the years she had become conditioned to believe that housework was demeaning, that there was something wrong with her if she admitted to herself that she enjoyed the day-to-day activities of being a wife and mother and had absolutely no desire to return to the world of business.

People commonly exchange their real feelings for feelings they are supposed to have. A successful physician complained that at the end of every day he arrived home in a state of exhaustion, barely able to participate in family life or reaction. "It's the terrible pressure I work under. I spend all day with patients, from 8 a.m. until 7 in the evening. You can't carry the weight of responsibilities I do and expect to be cheerful and energetic at the end of the day. And there's no way I can cut back."

There were two basic fallacies in this patient's thinking. The first was that as a physician he could not refuse to take patients referred to him, even though he might have referred them to other doctors when he was too busy. The second was his concept of work—that it was supposed to be hard and in some way unpleasant. Moreover, he had lost his own identity as a person in the role he had assumed as a physician. Envisioning the ideal doctor as conservative, thoughtful, quiet, and undemonstrative, he had thwarted his own tendency to be cheerful, spontaneous, humorous, and emotional—even in his personal life—in order to fit the image. As he began to realize in therapy that he really enjoyed his work and liked his patients, that he could see his life as a continuum rather than sharply divided into compartments, and that he did not have to hide himself behind a mask of formality at all times, his energy level increased. The days passed more quickly, and he was no longer so tired in the evenings. He had unlabeled his life experiences, no longer calling them "work" and "play," and found that he could move from moment to moment without the extra burden of subconsciously defining each moment in terms of its appropriate category.

Many people who have achieved success have done so at a price, sacrificing something of value—family relationships and friendships, for instance—along the way. Once they have reached the goals they have set for themselves, they may suddenly become painfully aware of what they have missed. The depression they experience can afford them a chance to restore balance to their lives.

Grace Laszlo was 49 when she became depressed. An outstanding commercial designer, the creator of prizewinning automobiles, soda-pop bottles, and typewriter cases, she gradually, over a 6-month period, lost interest in her work. She put things off, withdrew, and avoided social engagements. She had two important projects she could not begin. "I can't get going," she complained. "In spite of everything, I'm a failure."

From her early teens, Grace had demonstrated a special talent in art and had applied herself intensively to its development. She found a great deal of gratification in her work. As she became more recognized, she began to feel alienated from her parents and sisters. Her father, a clerk in a grocery store, and her mother, a secretary, had encouraged her to go to art school and wanted her to be successful. After she started moving in more sophisticated circles, she began to feel embarrassed about her parents' manners and appearance, hating herself at the same time for her embarrassment. When she won an important art prize, she waited to invite them to the presentation until the last minute; feeling unwanted, they declined to come.

Grace also discovered that in spite of her success, she was not getting what she hoped success would bring: popularity and friendship. Because of her dedication to work in high school and college, and the fact that she had to work part-time to pay her expenses, she had led a somewhat isolated existence. She was lonely, but rarely thought about her loneliness. Moreover, she felt that she was different from many of the teenagers in school. "I was ambitious. Most of them seemed to be willing to settle for a lot less in life than I was. I wasn't disliked, but then I wasn't liked either. I figured that one day, when I made it, I'd have plenty of friends."

Her success did bring many people into her world, but rather than caring about her as a person, most of them, as she sadly realized, were there to use her. For some, she meant money. For others, she meant contact with a celebrity. She did not know how to form close personal relationships; even when she married, she selected a man who had been drawn to her not as a person, but by his image of her as a stylish and prominent artist. The marriage reduced itself to arguments and jealousies; it lasted only 4 years and was childless. The loneliness that Grace had suppressed in her teens now swept in on her in full force. Her basic human need for closeness had not, and could not, be fulfilled through her achievements. The success that had separated her from her parents, now aging, filled her with guilt. She felt betrayed by her own efforts. "I'm really a failure. I wish sometimes that I had never had any talent. It has cost me too much."

One of the elements that make success so costly is the highly competitive climate that surrounds successful people. It encourages loneliness and makes it difficult for them to find anyone with whom they can share their problems. A sales executive described his predicament in these terms: "When I was having a lot of difficulty at home—my wife was unhappy and we used to have one argument after another, ending in threats of divorce—there just wasn't anyone I could talk to. At work I had what I would call working friends, but I wasn't going to talk to them. We had a veneer of camaraderie, but under the surface there was always the jockeying for better position. Besides, in business you're not supposed to have problems. Everyone does—but if you admit it or show it, you get tagged as unstable. It's a competitive ploy. . . . And having no one to share feelings with, everything became magnified in my mind. I couldn't get rid of things that kept bothering me or get any perspective. I just kept feeling more and more hopeless about things at home, and about my life in general."

Success is likely to stir up a kind of sadness because the achievement of a goal almost always involves an ending. Graduation from school, for most people a point of completion, commonly evokes a sense of loss. Finding the "right" man or woman and getting married, sending the last child off to school, and finishing a project all convey at one and the same time a point of success and an ending. The feeling "It is over" and the question "Where do I go from here?" combine to activate depression and a reconsideration of self-worth.

When Edith Green married at 22, she knew that Henry had no money and that they would have to live simply. She was quite prepared to put up with some deprivations while he finished his graduate work in architecture. They delayed having children for 3 years, while she worked as an administrative assistant at the university. After graduation he obtained a good position with a large firm in New York. A year later their first child was born.

Young architects are not well paid, so Edith took a part-time job as a bookkeeper. They lived in a one-bedroom apartment, and the baby slept in the living room. "This won't go on forever," she thought, "in a few years we'll be ready to enjoy life." In the summer they went to Jones Beach; in the winter they would share a bottle of chianti and pizza with friends. Occasionally they visited her parents in Florida. They went to the movies twice a month; otherwise, they usually watched television or played chess in the evening. Edith and Henry were "waiting."

On his thirty-ninth birthday, Henry was made a partner. His work had become well recognized. Now earning almost two hundred thousand dollars a year, it was time for Henry and Edith and their two children, both in school, to move out of the city to a suburb. Within a few months after moving to their new home, Edith began to experience a great deal of fear of going out of the house. She slept poorly at night. She was reluctant to meet any new people in the neighborhood. She put off decorating. Edith and Henry began to argue frequently, about nothing important. "What's happening?" she asked herself, worried and frightened.

For the first time, Edith Green was faced with the necessity of living with herself and her family without the preoccupation of not having enough money, enough room, enough time. A whole segment of her life was over and with it went the many pleasures she and Henry had shared, unnoticed since their joint focus had been on the "day when we make it." The moment they had both looked forward to for 15 years had come, and neither of them was prepared for it.

Depression, as it often does, deadened Edith's sense of enthusiasm as well as her sexual interest in Henry, and she began to wonder if she really loved him. It was a question she hadn't asked herself for years. Was she a good mother? Could she meet the social demands of their new neighbors? Would her children be able to adapt to the change in schools? Now that there was no longer any need for her to change diapers or rush off to her bookkeeping job or provide a young architect with encouragement, there seemed to be no need for her at all.

The husbands and wives of successful executives frequently become victims of success. They often get depressed or resort to alcoholism or a variety of other unhealthy behaviors. Their children openly rebel, rejecting the model of hard work and achievement they have been offered in favor of dropping out to "do their own thing." "I can't bear the guilt for my parents' unhappiness," said one adolescent girl. "Mother drinks too much and Dad is tired and irritable whenever he's home. He travels a lot. I've tried to speak with them, but they just won't listen. They have everything they ever seemed to want: a beautiful house I don't care if I never see again, their club, their friends. Dad's a top executive with an automobile company. But all their work hasn't made them happy. I think they were happier when they didn't have so much. They don't seem able to face themselves. I know it's not my fault, but I feel it is, somehow. That's why I can't afford to think about it any more. I don't know what kind of life I want, but I certainly don't want theirs!"

In the process of questioning the status symbols of society and the competitiveness in which their parents have immersed themselves, many young people, floundering in search of goals, have rejected those of their parents and have forced their parents to reconsider the definition of success. Describing such a confrontation with his 20-year-old son, a depressed business executive made this comment: "At first I was angry at him about his attitudes toward school. He was almost arrogant about what he thought should be taught and what shouldn't be taught, instead of realizing that teachers with a lot more experience than he had were making those decisions. But all my anger did was to make things worse. He just stopped talking with me about his ideas. I had wanted him to go into a profession, law or medicine. He kept throwing out all kinds of crazy ideas. He wanted to be a chef one day, run a farm the next. The more I tried to straighten him out, the more difficult he became. Finally I gave up trying. It was as if his refusal to listen to me implied that I was a failure, as if all the efforts I had made to become something—my father was a manual laborer—had been for nothing."

Whether it is set off by conflicts with children or by some other event, depression commonly occurs at the point at which people have reached the goals toward which they have been striving. It is then that they must reconsider who they are, what their lives are about, and where they will go from there.

Chapter 12

◆ ◆ ❖ ◆ ◆ ❖ ◆ ◆ ❖ ◆ ◆ ❖ ◆ ◆ ❖ ◆ ◆ ❖ ◆ ◆

Dependency: A Delicate Balance

The feeling of helplessness that accompanies depression is frightening. In severe moments of depression, a person may not be able to carry out ordinary tasks that could normally be done with ease. One woman, leaving her divorce lawyer's office, had to ask his secretary to accompany her to a subway she had been riding for 10 years. A high school teacher with years of experience found that he could not prepare his lectures or correct quizzes because his concentration was so impaired.

Helplessness deepens a depressed mood, often forcing people to become very dependent on those around them. Needing replaces wanting. The business executive who, in better spirits, felt that he had many options open to him should his job become unsatisfactory, now feels, being depressed, that if he loses it, he could never find another one. A depressed young woman is convinced that her current boyfriend is the only one who will ever fulfill her romantic expectations, and dreads the possibility of his rejecting her.

One of the reasons depression increases feelings of helplessness and dependency is the frequent damming up of anger and rage. The more dependent people become, the angrier they become under the surface as they struggle against their helplessness. Since they have trouble liberating their anger and being aggressive, the mounting rage intensifies their helplessness. Psychiatrists often observe a progressive increase in energy and self-confidence among depressed patients as anger is expressed and aggression released. "I started out in therapy unable to do anything," said one patient. "I couldn't concentrate. I couldn't communicate my ideas effectively. I couldn't get anything done. Over a period of weeks this formless rage came out in bits and pieces. I would clench my fists and pound on the arms of the chair. Every time I went through this, I felt more and more freed from an inner constriction, and more self-confident."

Feelings of helplessness are easily activated when dependency needs are especially strong. This is often a basis for depression. A common trigger for depression is loss. The more deeply dependent individuals have been on the person or things they have lost, the more depressed they will become.

Co-dependency

In more intense dependency situations, the lines separating the two people involved can actually blur. Such an interdependency is natural in infancy, when 3-month-old babies have yet to distinguish between themselves and their mothers as independent entities. A certain vestige of this confusion remains in most people, and may be reactivated in the experience of love. "I cannot live without you" may be a token of the depth and sincerity of the feeling one person has for another; or it may be meant literally, in the sense that the ego strength of one requires the constant love and approval of the other. It is as if there is something lacking in the personality that can be complete only when another person provides the missing ego link.

Such intense involvement is characteristic of what has come to be known as co-dependency. Co-dependency is commonly seen in persons whose lives are intertwined with alcohol and drug abuse by others in their family. Such individuals are caught in frustrating and futile efforts to fill the insatiable needs of these habituated and addicted persons—a trap from which they are often unable to escape without enormous guilt. In some ways, their own identities seem dependent on this bondage. A similar condition is seen among Adult Children of Alcoholics. The inevitable outcome for the co-dependent is depression.

The vulnerability of people whose sense of self depends on someone else is at once apparent. In order to maintain that relationship, they will often go to great lengths, subjecting themselves to all sorts of abuse and controlling behavior on the part of the person on whom they are dependent, in return for the security of thinking that the other person will "always be there." And if that person withdraws or rejects them, it is not just the loss of a close and meaningful relationship they must deal with, but the disruption of a system that has become essential for maintaining their sense of identity and wholeness.

"I was really hung up on Peter," said one young woman. "When I was with him I felt great. The rest of my life had meaning only because of him. When he would go away on a business trip or to visit a relative, I felt lost, lonely. I knew he loved me. But I needed constant reassurance of his love. I couldn't sleep. I ached all over. I was terrified that one day he might leave me.

"And one day he did. Not suddenly. He just kind of moved farther and farther away from me. I felt a terrible despair. I was convinced I would never find anybody else I could love that way. I needed him. I couldn't go on living without him. One night, after he abruptly hung up on me on the phone, I took an overdose. Without Peter, I was nothing, no one."

Fear of Dependency

The kind of dependency that involves a loss of self is extreme. The average person is to varying degrees dependent on people and things in his or her world. How he or she will handle his or her dependency needs is determined in childhood. Erik Erikson emphasizes that one of the first qualities children must develop in relation to their environment is trust—a trust born out of predictability. It is based on the clarity of the verbal and nonverbal messages that their families delivered to them. A great deal of insecurity in infants' environment, particularly when that insecurity is rooted in anxiety and ambivalence toward them by their mothers, creates a core feeling that "nothing and no one can ever really be trusted."

Such a lack of trust breeds serious difficulties that affect normal dependency needs. Instead of being able to allow themselves to need others and still set limits on that need, adults who emerge from such an environment will usually veer to one extreme or the other, either searching for the unattainable complete fulfillment of the dependency needs that were not met or rejecting any and all opportunities for healthy dependency, adopting a philosophy that "everyone must stand on his or her own two feet at all times."

Martin Shreiner was 49 when he had his first heart attack. Until then he had always been a stubbornly energetic man. As sales manager for a large manufacturing company he often worked nights and weekends, and traveled extensively to see customers. It never occurred to him to delegate significant responsibilities to any of his key assistants, most of whom were eminently reliable. "If I don't do it myself," he maintained, "it never gets done right."

Martin's physician advised him to make certain changes in his way of handling things if he wanted to remain in good health: to set aside some time to rest each day, to rely on others in his department to perform the tasks that did not require his judgment or experience. Because of his unrecognized fear and deep reluctance to depend on anyone other than himself, he denied the relevance of the doctor's recommendations. Within a year, he was hospitalized for a second coronary.

The ability to accept some degree of dependency determines the extreme to which people can accept and deal with physical illness as well as with emotional problems. Those who have a vested interest in denying the presence of ordinary dependency needs are especially threatened when they cannot influence and control circumstances around them. When such individuals become depressed, the feelings of helplessness can snowball. The initial slowing up and concentration impairment may not in itself be severe, but their reaction to not being able to stay in charge of themselves and their feeling that they are losing control can rapidly aggravate the depressed mood; at times it can reach panic proportions.

Many people are confused about the concept of independence, believing that it implies complete freedom from any dependency needs. Genuine self-reliance requires a reasonable appreciation of the fact that no matter how effective and self-confident people are, there are going to be times and situations when they must depend on someone else. An excessive need for independence prevents many people from reaching out for professional or personal guidance when they need it.

Alice Donnard was so afraid of being dependent on others that when, at her husband's insistence, she made her first visit to a therapist, she could not sit down for more than 5 minutes at a time. "I think better when I'm standing," she said. "I like to walk around when I'm talking." She insisted on leaving the interview before her time was up and informed the therapist that she would have to call him to make another appointment. When she did call, she engaged him in an interminable discussion over what times were mutually convenient to each of them.

Her husband had asked her to consult a marriage counselor with him because he had been finding their life together bewildering and depressing. She had been alternately angry and critical, affectionate and giving, during the little over a year she and Philip had been married.

Alice had found the 3 years of their dating relationship pleasant and compatible at all levels; however, once married, she could not cope with her feelings of being committed to and dependent on Philip. She established a rigid schedule for the responsibilities of their life together. "Everything in our marriage should be on a fifty-fifty basis," she outlined. "We will visit your family one weekend a month, and mine one weekend a month." Philip went along with her wishes. His first glimpse of the underlying problem came one night when they were making love. "I feel as if we are one person," he said softly. She replied: "Let's get something straight. I don't like that oneness business. We're two separate individuals. Besides, I think you've been getting too dependent on me."

He felt put off. The more he tried to clarify his idea that two people in love have a mutual need for each other that cannot be measured mathematically, the more she insisted that his dependency on her was abnormal. Hurt and angry, he began to strike back. Several times over the following months he screamed at her, "If you don't like the way things are going, pack your bags and get out." At other times, feeling more and more hopeless, he begged, "I need you, Alice. I want you. I don't understand why you always have to put down the idea of sharing."

Alice was afraid of sharing. Throughout a life of insecurity she had learned to count only on herself. When she was 4, both her parents had been killed in an automobile crash. She and her two brothers were shifted about among several aunts and uncles. By the time she was 16 she was an extremely self-contained and independent girl, admired by her friends and respected by her teachers not only for academic excellence, but also for working after school and in the summers to support herself. When she met Philip, she was working as a supervisor for the telephone company, where she made decisions easily and felt on top of her responsibilities.

As long as Alice remained aloof from any but the most superficial relationships with men she felt fine. She tended to date boys who were intellectually beneath her, and she always remained in command of the relationship. Only once before meeting her husband had she become involved with a man toward whom she felt a strong romantic and sexual attraction. Her ambivalence activated, she struggled back and forth between needing him and fearing his rejection, rebelling against the relationship and denying its significance. In the end, she abruptly stopped seeing him.

When she decided to marry at 34, it was not only because she felt that it was time for her to marry; she thought that she had found a man she could trust, who would respect her need for independence and, at the same time, give her the love and support she wanted. Unfortunately, she had underestimated the degree to which her need for independence clashed with any lasting commitment to a man. She had not considered how her inability to either lean on her husband to some degree or permit him to lean on her would produce a serious imbalance in their relationship and turn his otherwise normal dependency needs into a frantic and helpless bid for her love.

Dependency in Marriage

The majority of conflicts between married couples involve confusion over the meaning of dependency. This confusion is reinforced by traditional, though outmoded, assumptions that dependency is a sex-related characteristic. Women are supposed to be dependent. Men are denied the right to be dependent. Initiative and self-determination are unfeminine. Needing someone is unmasculine. Although the educational efforts of the women's liberation movement have done much to help change some misconceptions about femininity, there remains a deeply ingrained dogma that masculinity implies a kind of strength that precludes moments of helplessness.

In some cases, a steady shift in the balance of dependency between husband and wife takes place as the years go by; in others, one-sided or mutual dependency needs may be unusually strong to begin with. For such people, the closeness in marriage or in any love relationship forms a breeding ground for becoming so dependent that a loss of individuality can result. "I've lost interest in doing anything without my husband," said a 29-year-old woman who had been married less than 6 months. "I used to play tennis, see a lot of my friends, go to films by myself. Before we got married I quit my job to stay home and take care of decorating the house. But now I don't want to do anything. I haven't called a girlfriend in months. I'm tired all the time. I watch television during the day, but mostly I wait for Burt to come home. He likes to play golf on weekends. I hate that. I feel so lonely when he's not around." With him she felt alive and energetic. Without him she felt unmotivated, aimless. As long as she had been emotionally uninvolved with anyone, she was unaware of her potential for becoming so dependent.

Dependency in the Workplace

The same kind of excessive dependency can be seen in work situations. Bill Follet had been conditioned by his upbringing to be very dependent, at first on the approval of his teachers, and later on the approval of his supervisors at work. He was a claims manager for a large insurance company. His immediate supervisor was a vice-president of the company, a volatile and demanding man who valued Bill's reliability but, at the same time, was frequently critical of him. On several occasions he even blocked Bill's transfer to a better position within the company so as not to be bothered with finding a replacement. Bill's moods fluctuated and were strongly influenced by his boss's moods. Although he was indignant when he learned that he had lost out on several promotions because of his boss's interference, he continued to work at his job and still depended very much on the occasional word of praise he would glean from time to time. He sometimes thought of leaving the company, but never found the time or energy to look for another job. "I just don't seem to be able to let go of it," he observed. "It's as if I have no other choice."

Extreme dependency will cause a loss of self-confidence and with it chronic depression. Dependency has a way of feeding on itself. The more Bill Follet obtained the stingy recognition of his superiors, the more his appetite for any recognition increased.

Dependency in Hospitalization

People who have been hospitalized for long periods of time—whether for physical or emotional problems—often lose the sense of competence with which they previously dealt with life. Recent efforts to shorten the hospital stay of patients with emotional disorders have been based on the observation that long-term hospitalization aggravates the sense of helplessness originally activated by their fear and depression. After months away from the demands of their ordinary life, people may gradually become so adapted to a less demanding routine that they lose confidence in their ability to cope with everyday matters. Day-to-day life outside the hospital becomes unreal. They focus more and more on the details of hospital living. The first visit out is often dreaded. "Can I make it? Will I fall apart? Do I really want to go out?" In spite of the deprivations that exist in institutional living, it is as if they must be weaned away from it in order to stand on their own again.

A similar treatment problem can be seen in caring for the aged. As long as they are in familiar surroundings, able to cope with the demands of daily life, elderly people can usually function well. An unexpected physical illness that forces them into a hospital or a nursing home often leads to a rapid deterioration in their ability to handle their own affairs. They become very dependent on the nurses for many things they had previously looked after themselves. If such a condition of enforced dependency continues for too long a time, many will find it impossible to ever return to a reasonable level of self-sufficiency.

The Power of Dependency

Extricating oneself from a dependent position is bound to be painful. People can become as habituated to a person or a job as they can to a drug. The withdrawal symptoms can be just as severe.

Complicating the picture is the fact that helplessness can itself be a position of strength. A considerable amount of unhealthy gain can be derived from being dependent. When being helpless becomes its own reward and the dependent people realize the full reaches of their influence, they can dominate a situation simply by doing nothing at all. Any group—particularly a family—can be immobilized by this maneuver. "My mother-in-law has us all in a bind," said one man. "She won't drive a car—says she can't. She doesn't help my wife with the housework—says she doesn't feel strong enough to. She won't do anything to find an apartment of her own—says that she couldn't bear the loneliness of living by herself. She's been in our home for 6 years. She's only 57. She came to live with us when my father-in-law died. Every time we make a move to get her out, she gets conveniently sick. It never proves to be anything serious, just enough to keep us from doing anything. She runs our home, without lifting a finger."

People who use helplessness to control usually require a collaborator, someone who encourages their dependency and derives some gratification from it—or who at least does not appreciate the nature of the interdependent system. Any effort to restore a healthy sense of independence in such people will involve a change in the attitudes of those who, unwittingly or in the service of their own needs, may have been encouraging the persistence of their helplessness.

Dependency and Depression in Life Transitions

The very points in life at which dependency needs are most likely to be a major source of conflict are points at which depression is likely to occur—adolescence, for example. The adolescent is engaged in a classic struggle between wanting independence from the family and wanting the security of knowing that the family is still there in case anything goes wrong. As Robert Frost wrote:

> Home is the place where, when you have to go there,
> They have to take you in. . . .

Parents who fail to appreciate the delicate balance of needs within teenagers—how their overconfidence collides with their fear of failure and their susceptibility to depression—can seriously compromise their growing sense of self-reliance.

"All the time my dad communicates his lack of confidence in me," said one 16-year-old boy. "He's always putting me down. Compares me with guys who are more athletic. Compares me with the brains in school. Every time I make a mistake, even a small one, like the time I took the wrong train to the country and he had to wait an extra 20 minutes at the station, he bawls me out. I depend on what he thinks of me, more than I want to. He doesn't seem to realize that."

Retirement is also a time for dependency and depression. "I never realized how much I needed to work. It's been difficult to get readjusted. After 30 years with one company, going to the same office, seeing the same friends, you get into a routine. Then, all of a sudden, it's over. Pulled out from under you. The children are gone. There's just my wife and me. The one thing we can count on is getting older."

Chapter 13

♦ ♦ ❖ ♦ ♦ ❖ ♦ ♦ ❖ ♦ ♦ ❖ ♦ ♦ ❖ ♦ ♦ ❖ ♦ ♦

Adolescence: The Vulnerable Years

Frank Matthews lay in his bed, staring up at the ceiling. Everything in his room seemed so much smaller: the desk with the thin, adjustable lamp where he usually sat to do his homework; the bookcases that still held his copy of *Where the Wild Things Are, The Boys' King Arthur* next to it, and next to that, *Jane Eyre*, which he had just completed for assigned summer reading. The back of his legs ached. He sat up suddenly and rubbed the toes of his right foot as they stiffened, gripped by a painful cramp, the kind his father had told him were growing pains. He felt tears well up in his eyes.

Frank was 13. He wanted desperately to grow up and be 21, to have his own sports car, to be sought after by beautiful women, to have money in his pocket, to be free to come and go as he pleased. Only 8 years away! But 8 years, added to his father's age, 49, and his mother's, 45, would make his parents really old. They already seemed tired a lot of the time. The older he became, the closer they would be to dying. He began to sob, but then, quickly, he stopped. Boys don't cry, he swore to himself. He turned on his MP3 player. His favorite rock group drowned out his thoughts, and he fell asleep before the piece was finished.

Adolescents are especially vulnerable to feelings of depression. One of the major shifts in life takes place as they move from being children to being adults. Once primarily dependent and seemingly free of cares, little people excited by a trip to McDonald's or the local amusement park, they have suddenly become taller, tougher. They are focused around what mom and dad refer to as goals. They sense sexual stirrings, struggle to be independent, are eager to spend more time with friends than family. They want to be accepted, automatically, desperately, by the kids at school or by others who sneer at school and all that school stands for.

It is a time for grief, usually unrecognized, commonly concealed behind awkward self-consciousness. It is a time when all that went before—learning that one is a separate and distinct entity from one's mother, playing hide and seek with the children next door, gingerly letting go of a parent's hand and walking into the huge room filled with tiny desks and smelling of chalk, mastering language and arithmetic and how to win and how to lose—pays off as the teenager sheds the cocoon of home and assumes greater command over his or her own life. It is a time of ultimate confusion.

It should come as no surprise that adolescents are especially vulnerable to depression. Episodes of depression are an inherent part of the disruption and emotional reintegration they will be experiencing for at least 7 years, from 13 to 20. This is especially true in a culture that has obscured many of the traditional signposts that youngsters growing up in other times depended upon to guide them along the way—expecting a good deal of responsibility from them, offering them a structure of sound values within which to grow, and holding out definite promise for a future place in the world for them to occupy.

Coming of Age in a Troubled Society

Growing up in our present society can indeed be dangerous to a teenager's health and to his or her life. The rising incidence of suicide and suicide attempts among children and adolescents gives stark testimony to the hopelessness and pain so many of them endure.

Child and adolescent psychiatrists attribute this tragic state of affairs to the dehumanization of society and to the fragmentation of family life. Human beings have become statistics in bureaucrats' computers and targets of incessant marketing campaigns, even as psychologist Erich Fromm, years ago, predicted would occur. Conscientious parents realize they have only a limited period of time within which to communicate values to live by before their adolescent children become exposed to a world that seems to operate with a philosophy of "anything goes."

As the distance between life at home and life away from home has become enormously enlarged, they find it exceedingly difficult to set and enforce limits on their children's behavior; however, every adolescent needs to be provided with defined expectations and reliable structure during these tumultuous years. The influence of the family is further diminished by teenagers' susceptibility to the standards and values of their own age group. At the same time, educators have largely abdicated any responsibility for character development and behavioral control, because of indifference, lack of adequate skills, and, in some situations, legal constraints.

Teenagers who kill themselves do not do so just because they live in a troubled society. There are always intimate, personal reasons as well. One may attempt suicide, successfully or not, out of a naïve curiosity to experience death without really intending to stop living. Another may be trying to frighten someone, get his or her attention, or get back at him or her in anger. Still another may be running away, from hurt, rage, guilt, or despair. Some have undoubtedly been the victims of child abuse.

A Transition from Behavior to Insight

A key element in understanding the unique problem of depression in adolescence is the fact that this transition period is characterized by a shift from dealing with conflicts by means of behavior to dealing with them by means of intellectual and emotional insight. Because this change is still incomplete, depression in teenagers expresses itself quite differently than in adults. Moodiness and moments of disillusionment, tears and tension can occur. But depressed adolescents are far more likely to show their distress in ways that make it very difficult to recognize that they are, in fact, experiencing depression. Depression is commonly reflected in behavioral difficulties, particularly one set of symptoms that recur, again and again, such as stealing, drug abuse, bed-wetting, or underachievement.

Frank Matthews' parents were divorced when he was 15. On the surface, he seemed to show no emotional reactions to what was happening. For months, he could hear them moving about and arguing in the middle of the night. He heard his mother accuse his father of having another woman and his father's vigorous denials in response. When they finally sat him down to tell him they were separating and that he would be living with his mother and would see his father on weekends, they asked Frank how he felt about things. He muttered, "That's your business, not mine."

Until this event, Frank had resisted the pressure of his friends to try drugs. Now he began to experiment with marijuana, and within a few months, he was using it several times a week. He had previously been obtaining B+ grades in school, but now his marks fell to C and below. Concerned, his mother and father agreed to take him out to dinner one evening and talk with him about what they perceived to be his problems. In usual teenage fashion, he denied having anything to discuss with them. At one point, when his mother asked him whether he was troubled by the fact that his father was living with another woman, he replied, "What do I know about it? I'm only a kid, right?"

With great reluctance, he agreed to consult a psychiatrist. During the first visit, he said little, answering questions in as few words as possible. During the second visit, the psychiatrist, having discovered that Frank had enjoyed playing baseball and had several favorite rock music groups, devoted the entire hour to talking with him about sports and concerts; Frank immediately reported this to his father, who, enraged, called the doctor to complain that he wasn't paying good money to have his son just sit there and waste time going on about things that didn't matter. The psychiatrist's effort to explain to him that, in treating teenagers, it was essential to develop a relationship of trust and interest before exploring more sensitive issues fell on deaf ears. Frank's treatment was abruptly terminated. But it was resumed again when Frank's mother, unable to get him to go to school or even leave his room for several days, insisted.

Knowing full well how important involvement of the family is in the treatment of teenagers and, at the same time, quite aware of the need to assure the patient of the strict confidentiality of what is talked over together, the doctor suggested that Frank's parents come to his next session with him, to have a chance to meet the therapist and to enable the doctor to obtain a better feeling for what might be going on between them and Frank. "It doesn't matter to me," Frank predictably replied. "Whatever you say."

As the three of them sat there with the psychiatrist, the tension among them was evident. Frank's mother cried as she expressed her concern over her son's problems. His father stiffly reiterated his belief that all that Frank needed was more discipline. Frank said little until, prodded several times by the therapist, he suddenly stood up and screamed, "I want to live my own life, not your life! All I've been doing for the past year is worrying about you!" He asked his mother, "Don't you think I hear you up until two or three in the morning, smoking cigarettes and crying? And you"—he looked at his father—"don't you think I get mad when you take me out to lunch with that woman and that's the only time I see you, with her?"

"He has a point," the therapist said to Frank's slightly stunned parents. "Mind you, failing in school is no way for him to deal with his feelings. . . taking it out on himself. That's something Frank and I have to work out, so he can take more charge of his own life. But it does sound as though a few adjustments are in order."

In the course of several more sessions with Frank alone during which he expressed himself with much more freedom and spontaneity, it became apparent that he was being impaired by a number of depressive symptoms: waking up early in the morning, then falling asleep again and oversleeping and being late for school; fatigue; difficulty concentrating on his studies and being unable to complete his homework assignments on time; isolating himself from friends; and still using marijuana occasionally to give him a "lift."

"Let's try something," the psychiatrist suggested. "I'd like to give you some medicine, an antidepressant. It's not habit-forming. It doesn't give you a fake high... a lot better than pot. In a few weeks, you'll have more energy and you'll probably be getting your work done a lot faster."

Unlike many adolescents, Frank complied with this suggestion and, indeed, within a month, reported that he was feeling more cheerful and able to perform better. In fact, he had decided to try out for the varsity baseball team, having not played in over a year.

Denial in Parents

Unfortunately, the resolution of depression in adolescents does not always have the happy outcome that Frank Matthews experienced. Many families are intensely reluctant to arrange for professional care for teenagers, even when the evidence of disturbance is irrefutable. Some do not wish to relinquish their real or imagined control over their children. Others are engaged in a form of psychological child abuse; one father, whose son had committed suicide 2 weeks earlier, sent chills through a friend who was offering his sympathies by remarking, "I'm over it. You can't go on grieving forever." Still others are actually living out their own wishes and frustrations through the erratic and often self-destructive behavior of a child. As one mother defended her adolescent daughter's sexual promiscuity to a teacher who had recommended professional care, "There's nothing wrong with my little girl! Just because she's pretty and has a lot of boyfriends, the other girls are jealous of her. I know what it's like to be 15. When I was 15, I was lonely. My father wouldn't let me go out on dates at all. I'm not going to ruin my daughter's chances. I want her to be happy."

Many adults are skilled at denying the obvious. Some years ago, during a consultation with a community board exploring the issue of drug abuse in a small, upper-middle-class town, I was amazed to listen to parents and teachers alike insisting that there was no real drug problem at all. The police, the hospital authorities, and the teenagers themselves knew firsthand that there was and described it in detail. Nonetheless, plans for any preventive program were vetoed.

Adolescents are no more eager to seek help than many of their parents are to have them do so. As they see it, turning to a professional compromises their newly gained independence. Then, too, how would their friends treat them if they found out? And, of course, the stigma associated with seeing a therapist is far greater in their own minds than in those of adults. Their perspective is by nature limited; since a loss of perspective is one of the cardinal aspects of depression, the depressed teenager occupies a very precarious position, to say the least.

What Parents Can Do To Help

There are several steps adults can take to help adolescents weather crises more successfully and, if and when depressed, help them find suitable professional help and guidance, thus reducing the risk of chronic disability, academic failure, drug and alcohol abuse, injudicious sexual involvements and their consequences, inadequate formation of a sense of self, and the terrible risk of suicide.

Pay Attention

First, be alert to signs and signals of depression as they occur in adolescents. The mood is sometimes obvious; teenagers may look and act depressed—sullen, sad, tired, sleepless or oversleeping, withdrawn. They may voice feelings of boredom, hopelessness, self-recrimination, lack of self-confidence, even a wish to die (which should never be ignored). More often, however, the mood is concealed within self-defeating behavior patterns. Their school work declines. They do not want to involve themselves in activities that once gave them pleasure. Angry outbursts, belligerence, extreme defiance, and repeated episodes of getting into trouble may mask the underlying problem. It's also important to anticipate depressive episodes when events warranting such a reaction occur: parental divorce, the death of a family member, breaking up with a girlfriend or boyfriend, significant setbacks and disappointments in school, rejection by friends. Remember that being depressed in and of itself is not an abnormal condition. Adolescents should be approached with understanding, not automatically assumed to be unstable. If, however, aberrant behavior persists for an unreasonable length of time, the need for professional intervention is clear.

Communicate

Second, keep open all lines of communication. Of course, the roots of good communication are established during the years of childhood in the give-and-take of instruction, love, and play. But even though adolescents want more privacy as they move away from the family center, their connection to home can remain a powerful influence in their lives if they are surrounded by family members who care, respect their individuality, express interest in their current activities and concerns, and enable them to turn to their families when they feel, from time to time, overwhelmed or in need of guidance.

Ironically, many American parents have gone to an extreme in their efforts to avoid "interfering" with the lives of their adolescent children. People view the lovable, autocratic parent portrayed in the famous play *Life with Father* as a quaint, but obsolete, period piece. Today's parents often do not seem to know how to combine a sense of equality and respect for teenagers with a willingness to exert their authority and offer them wisdom and direction. Parenting has become polarized. At one extreme, certain parents brutalize their children; at the other, parents demonstrate outrageous permissiveness and a compulsive eagerness to see their children, always and above all, happy. It is as if they have forgotten the fact that they presumably have the benefit of having lived on this planet a somewhat longer span of time than their offspring and hence possess a vision of life that they should responsibly share with them.

Help Them Discover New Heroes and Role Models

Help adolescents find new heroes on whom to model their lives. Some will be remote: novelists whose books they have enjoyed but whose photographs they might not even recognize, film directors, Nobel prize winners, and Olympic competitors.

Some are near at hand: a teacher, a coach, a pastor, a boy scout or girl scout leader, a friend of the family, the father or mother of a pal. Not only must they be physically present; they must be there emotionally for the adolescent, conscious of the importance they may play in his or her growing up, ready to serve as advisor, confidant, mentor. They must do all they can to build an atmosphere in which young people can experience hope and the desire to fill their future lives with meaning.

Insist on Treatment

Most critically, parents must confront their responsibility for their children's health, both mental and physical. Depression is, after all, an illness, and parents must not ignore it or assume it will resolve itself given enough time. Depression can and should be treated to decrease the chances that it will interfere with a child's future well-being.

In 2005, after a series of studies, the US Food and Drug Administration required drug manufacturers to update the labeling of all antidepressants to caution that taking antidepressants may increase suicidal thoughts and actions among children and adolescents in the first few weeks of treatment. This should not, however, be taken to mean that depressed adolescents are not candidates for antidepressants. In fact, a 2007 review of the previous decade's pediatric trials concluded that the benefits of antidepressant medication outweigh their risks, even in people under 25.

Nonetheless, adolescents should see a doctor experienced in treating depression in younger patients, and their treatment should be under careful supervision. Currently, only fluoxetine (Prozac) is approved by the FDA for use in patients under the age of 18. Once treatment begins, parents should seek prompt medical advice if an adolescent develops nervousness, agitation, sleeplessness, irritability, mood instability, or suicidal thoughts, or if these behaviors worsen instead of improving.

Chapter 14

♦ ♦ ❖ ♦ ♦ ❖ ♦ ♦ ❖ ♦ ♦ ❖ ♦ ♦ ❖ ♦ ♦ ❖ ♦ ♦

Depression and the Elderly

"Loose quicksilver in a nest of cracks"

Orson Welles' classic film *The Magnificent Ambersons* was adapted from Booth Tarkington's novel. It's the story of a wealthy, prominent, closely-knit family, living in a small, Midwestern city at the turn of the century. George Miniver Amberson, spoiled, self-willed, announces that his chief ambition in life is to be a "yachtsman" at one of the gala parties held at the family's grand Victorian mansion. George proceeds to sabotage the relationship between his widowed mother, Isabelle, and an old beau, who is a widower. When Isabelle dies, George and his aunt Fanny are left penniless, and are forced to sell their home and move to a boarding house. His uncle, George Amberson, takes a job abroad at an American consulate. In a deeply moving scene, George and his uncle say good-bye to each other for what both know will be the last time. His uncle says, "Life and money both behave like loose quicksilver in a nest of cracks. And when they're gone, we can't tell where—or what the devil we did with 'em."

Life is indeed like loose quicksilver in a nest of cracks. The older you are, the faster time passes. Rich or poor, loss piles on loss. Episodes of grief and depression become the rule, not the exception. As one successful lawyer put it: "Forty was a troublesome milestone. But I got through it fine. Fifty was a breeze. But sixty—that was something else again. Six years later, I'm still recovering from the shock. I mean, suddenly, I know time is running out.

"I've started to play this unpleasant numbers game. Sixty-five minus fifteen is fifty. Only yesterday. Sixty-five plus fifteen is. . . eighty!

"I'm an active person, professionally, in my personal life. I've got a great family, one of the lucky ones you might say. I love my work. There are so many things I still want to do. Travel. I haven't been to a tenth of the places in the world I want to go to. Write a book, maybe, like all those other lawyers. Grandchildren.

"Last summer this guy I'm playing tennis with tells me I have to apply for Medicare. I mean, the government doesn't just give it to you automatically. You actually have to apply for it and best to do it a couple of months before you're sixty-five. So now I'm on Medicare and I've started to wake up at four in the morning and can't get back to sleep so easily, and these waves of sadness sweep over me when I least expect them. It's crazy. Seems like my wife and I are going to an awful lot of funerals lately. I don't like this one bit."

Aging and Depression

The incidence of clinical depression in men and women over age 65 is estimated to be about 8 percent. However, as many of 20–35 percent of elderly patients with medical illness are reported to be clinically depressed. White males over 65 have a suicide rate four times that of the national average.

In older people, depression is often manifested not so much as an obvious change in mood and behavior but rather as a variety of physical complaints which do not fit any recognizable pattern and are commonly associated with inexplicable physical pain. Older people who are depressed often have trouble sleeping, eat little and lose weight, complain of concentration difficulties, seem at times inattentive and unmotivated, and frequently have trouble remembering things. Suicidal thinking is certainly a sign of depression, and in elderly patients—contrary to what many believe—seldom occurs without the presence of depression.

But these very signs and symptoms are also prevalent among patients with chronic, debilitating physical illness. So it often requires expert assessment to determine whether a particular patient is suffering with clinical depression or with something else, such as Alzheimer's Disease, a fatal illness usually associated with extreme memory loss, profound deterioration of mental functioning, and a tragic downhill course. Depression in an elderly patient is sometimes a red flag warning of an early dementing illness. But older people who appear forgetful, are unable to get things done, and are withdrawn and apathetic may be suffering primarily from clinical depression; when they are, these deficits usually improve when the depression is alleviated by medication and psychotherapy.

Elaine Goldman's children noticed a change in her behavior about a year after her husband, Ira, died. Elaine, 68, had always been a very active woman. After her three children were grown, she went back to work as a part-time bookkeeper, gave a day a week to the local hospital taking magazines and books to patients, and took up bridge. But after Ira collapsed in the lobby of their apartment house and died within minutes of a ruptured aortic aneurysm, Elaine gradually relinquished one activity after another. She ended up spending most of her time alone at home, in bed, staring at the television, aimlessly shifting clothes and other belongings from one closet or bureau to another. She would often take dirty dishes out of the dishwasher and put them away on the kitchen shelves. Sometimes she'd turn the laundry machine on to cycle with nothing in it. Once, the superintendent of the building found some of her silver-plated flatware stacked next to the incinerator. He returned it to her and informed Elaine's oldest daughter, Susan, about her mother's odd behavior.

Susan and her two sisters had had numerous opportunities to observe their mother's forgetfulness and episodes of bewilderment. They were convinced that she was moving steadily into a state of dementia from which she would never recover. Their family physician was convinced as well. They began to consider that Elaine would be better off in a nursing home. But first, they decided to have her examined in the psychiatric unit of the hospital where she had once worked as a volunteer.

The doctors and nursing staff observed that Elaine's memory difficulties and her confusional episodes closely paralleled periods of depression. When she did not appear to be especially depressed, her mental abilities were much better. Her doctor did a Mini-Mental State Exam on her; she was not able to remember any of the three items she was asked about after 3 minutes, but asked again after 15 minutes, she could remember all three. This suggested depression rather than dementia.

Now convinced that Elaine was depressed, her psychiatrist started her on an antidepressant. She also visited her every day for half an hour. As Elaine became better able to converse, the psychiatrist spoke with her about many of the common problems facing older people—grief over her husband's death, the importance of maintaining her independence and as much control over her life as she could, reestablishing a sense of usefulness and purpose. She stressed the many good things that had happened to her throughout the years and especially the warm and supportive relationship she enjoyed with her daughters.

To everyone's surprise and delight—most of all Elaine's—she was home again in 8 weeks, not quite the woman she had been years ago, but well enough to live on her own, resume some of her activities, see her friends, enjoy her grandchildren. Susan gave her a brown and white kitten to keep her company.

Aging and Health

With age, health is a number one issue. People can no longer just shrug off a sharp pain in the chest as indigestion, as they might have done in their twenties, or a tight, vise-like sensation starting in the left shoulder and radiating down to the wrist as a result of too much exercise. Mammography and prostate antigen blood tests tend to take precedence over sex and stock market tips as topics of conversations.

Ed Baldwin was one of the fortunate ones. Ed and his wife, Marilyn, had just returned from a week's vacation in Naples, Florida, when his doctor phoned to tell him that the results of the blood tests that he had had done just before going away were in. "Everything looks pretty good, Ed," his doctor said, "except for the prostate level. Your PSA level is higher than it sought to be. I think we'd better arrange for a consultation with a urologist. Now, don't panic. It may be nothing. But best to be on the safe side."

The specialist put an instrument that looked like a miniature rocket up Ed's rectum. He did a sonogram, outlining the shape and dimensions of his prostate. "Looks okay," the doctor commented. Then Ed felt about eight sharp, stinging pricks as small tweezers sprang out from the rocket to obtain tissue samples for biopsy. "Call me Tuesday," the doctor told Ed. "I'll have the results for you then."

"It was the worst weekend I can remember in years," Ed later told a psychiatrist who he visited several times after his surgery. "He did the biopsy on Friday. All I could think about was an old pal, Jack Ramsay, who had prostate cancer 10 years ago. They operated on him and got it in time. But that was the end of Jack's sex life. Not that it matters when compared with what could have happened to Jack if they didn't get it in time.

"I read the obituaries in Saturday's paper. Almost never read obituaries before. And there they were, two obituaries of men who had died of prostate cancer, and both of them my age.

"I felt utterly helpless. Saturday night, Sunday, Monday, I couldn't have gotten more than four hours sleep each night. I couldn't concentrate on anything. My wife tried to be reassuring, but it didn't seem to make much of a difference. Sunday afternoon we went to a movie. It was a blur. I couldn't concentrate. We left before it was over. I could see in my mind everything I cared about slipping away. My life, I mean. My wife. My kids. All gone.

"Tuesday came. The doctor said he'd call me between ten and eleven. I was riveted to the phone. When eleven-thirty came and went, I didn't know what to do, so I called him. He said he was just about to call me. I thought I heard him sigh. "It's a neoplasm," he said flatly. I asked him what that meant. "A malignancy," he said. A chill rushed through me. I was shaking. I could hardly speak.

"Cancer?" I asked. He didn't answer me directly. He just said: "Come in this afternoon and let's talk about it."

"Then a strange thing happened. The doctor was sitting there, behind his desk, telling me that I'd have to have a CAT scan and maybe x-rays of the long bones of my body and that if things look all right—meaning it looked like the cancer hadn't spread from the prostate gland itself—he'd schedule me for surgery, unless I preferred radiation which he probably wouldn't recommend for me. I couldn't believe myself, but I actually started to feel better, and I know it was because for the first time in days I was feeling back in control of my life. Sure, I'd have to have surgery, but it was at least doing something, attacking the damned tumor and taking it out. I looked at him straight on: "When can we get the show on the road?"

"The tests, right away. If surgery, not for a few weeks, because of the bleeding with the biopsy." Then, almost as an afterthought, he added: "There's a new way of doing the operation. Chances are good that we can save your sexual sensation and potency."

Ed Baldwin's prostate cancer had not spread beyond the prostate capsule. His outlook for survival appeared excellent. He would not need radiation or any further treatment following surgery. But he would be followed carefully for years.

Ed had never been seriously ill before in his life. For the first time, he had been put rudely in touch with his own mortality. About 2 months after he returned to work, he began to feel a sense of persistent sadness, worse in the morning, gradually clearing up by noon. He slept fitfully. He felt he was not as mentally sharp as usual. He felt less interested in things that had previously sparked his enthusiasm. When he began to have fleeting thoughts of suicide—ideas that had never occurred to him before—he decided to consult a psychiatrist.

"What you're experiencing is depression. And why not, under the circumstances," the psychiatrist reassured him. "You're smart to come and talk with someone at the point in your life. This kind of situation is bound to stir up a lot of things. Even a short period of therapy can be extremely helpful. And if you get stuck in this mood, we can always consider an antidepressant later on, to restore your physiological resilience."

Ed's depressive symptoms abated without medication during a dozen psychotherapy sessions. It has now been 4 years since his operation. He continues to enjoy good health and an active life. Recognizing and dealing constructively with his depression not only prevented him from becoming trapped in chronic depression, but, as excellent studies bear out, will most likely improve his chances of staying in good physical health as well.

Depression and Cardiovascular Disease

There is a startling connection between clinical depression and cardiovascular disease. For instance, in one study people with a history of clinical depression who were followed over a 14 year period were 4 times more likely to suffer heart attacks than the non-depressed group with whom they were compared. Moreover, heart disease patients who were also clinically depressed were four times more likely to die within 6 months than those who were not. Cognitive difficulties and depression occur in nearly 50% of patients within a week following coronary artery bypass surgery. Dr. Donald R. Frey, in the *American Family Physician*, cited a study by T. P. Guck and colleagues in which they showed that patients recovering from heart attacks who were also clinically depressed were 3.5 times more likely to have subsequent adverse cardiac events than those who were not. He wrote: "It is particularly important to diagnose and treat depression in patients who have had a myocardial infarction because there is an association with progression of the disease. . . . [Moreover] Prior to a patient's first myocardial infarction, depression appears to be a risk factor for the development of heart disease. . . . early aggressive treatment of depression may play a significant role in the primary prevention of heart disease."

No one can be sure what accounts for this interrelationship between clinical depression and cardiovascular disease. Perhaps the increase in stress hormones and stimulation of the sympathetic nervous system that accompanies depression is a contributing factor. The deposition of calcium in the coronary arteries is considered to be an early sign of atheroscelrosis—the process whereby fatty plaques accumulate on the vessel walls, eventually blocking blood flow and resulting in damage to the heart. In one study, investigators reported that men with Type A personality who also manifested strong anger and hostility were significantly more likely to have higher levels of calcium in their coronary arteries. Such a finding is consistent with that of the author (F. Flach) and colleagues who showed a rise in serum calcium, increased calcium excretion, and a shift of body calcium from bone to soft tissues in untreated clinically depressed patients. This process was reversed with treatment and recovery. However, there would be every reason to assume that the calcium deposited in soft tissues, including the coronary vascular system, would remain there indefinitely, facilitating the formation of plaques and increasing the risk for heart disease.

Regular exercise is strongly recommended by physicians as part of any cardiac health program. Interestingly, regular exercise also helps ameliorate depression.

Depression after a Stroke

Clinical depression occurs in 30–50 percent of patients who have survived a stroke. A most intriguing aspect of depression in this context is that it appears to be closely associated with the location of the brain lesion that has resulted from the clogging of a blood vessel or hemorrhage into brain tissue. The frequency of depression is much higher in those patients whose left frontal region of the brain has been affected. Of course, depression can be seen in patients with lesions elsewhere as well. When depressed stroke patients are not treated for depression they show considerably less physical improvement over the 2-year period following the initial illness.

Post-stroke depression generally responds to treatment with appropriate antidepressants. The psychological and cognitive features of the depression are alleviated; patients participate in rehabilitation more actively, and their physical functioning improves much more substantially.

Side Effects in Older Adults Who Take Antidepressants

In older patients, antidepressants must be used with great care, since a number of these have side effects to which the elderly are especially vulnerable: orthostatic hypotension, for example, and anticholinergic complications such as dry mouth, constipation, and blurring of vision. The newer SSRIs, such as fluoxetine and sertraline, which seem to possess fewer such side effects, are rapidly becoming the preferred antidepressants in older people. The high incidence of other medical problems, including heart disease, and differences in how the body handles drugs—such as the rate at which various medications are metabolized and excreted—calls for careful assessment before starting medications and regular scrutiny throughout their administration.

Moreover, because older people are often taking other medicines as well, the interactions between antidepressants and these drugs must be well understood and diligently monitored. Using antidepressants, however, does not take the place of attending to the psychological and environmental concerns in the lives of elderly depressed people.

Coping Creativity with Losses and Changes

"As you sow, so shall you reap" the Bible says. These words hold true throughout our lives. The strengths and resiliences to deal with losses and changes of growing old evolve from a person's youngest years. To reach 70 with a solid support system in place, it is important to cultivate and cherish family relationships and friendships during all the decades that come before. It's also wise to start your own Individual Retirement Account as early as possible, so that your money can grow tax-free and be there for you when social security alone may not be enough to meet your everyday needs.

Alicia and John Anderson sold their home in Pittsburgh, Pennsylvania, where they had lived for 30 years, and moved to St. Petersburg, Florida. They had dreams of playing golf and sitting on the terrace of their apartment at the end of each day to watch the sun set over the Gulf of Mexico.

But Alicia and John had failed to do their homework. Neither of them was a very outgoing person, so making new friends wasn't easy. John had seriously underestimated what it would cost them to buy a condominium with the proceeds from the sale of their house in Pittsburgh. They never spent more than a week every few years in Florida. When faced with day after day of relentless sunlight and heat, they found themselves spending most of their time indoors and their air-conditioning bills soared.

The Andersons had three married children. Their two daughters lived in the Pittsburgh area; their son lived in Boston. Naturally, they had hoped that their children and grandchildren would visit them regularly. But by the end of their first year in Florida, only their son had visited once, alone, for just 3 days. It was too expensive for Alicia and John to make more than one annual trek north.

For much of his life, John had managed a small men's clothing store. He liked his work. He enjoyed the regular contact with his customers whom he had grown to know well over the years. He could have gone on working there as long as he had wanted to. Breaking away had not been easy. Now, he had little else to do but read the papers, shop for groceries, and watch television. His dream of playing golf proved more costly than he could afford. Insidiously, a gloominess and irritability enveloped him. Faced with her husband's mounting depression, Alicia began to feel that their white-walled, orange-roofed apartment, which overlooked dry, brown, parched ground and was clustered among a hundred other apartments indistinguishable from theirs, had become a prison.

On her insistence, John consulted a psychiatrist who gave him an antidepressant and referred him to a counselor for therapy. Over the next few weeks, he seemed a little better, but not much. When he began to complain of a variety of aches and pains for which the physician at the local health center could find no explanation, Alicia had had enough.

"We've toughed this out long enough, John. I can't take it anymore. We are going home!" She spoke in a tone that John had long since learned invited no disagreement.

Within 3 months after they moved back to a pleasant garden apartment in a Pittsburgh suburb, John's depression had vanished altogether, although he remained slightly embarrassed about what he had been through. Depression, for the Andersons, had not only been a critical signal that they had made a serious misjudgment in moving to Florida. It was the spark that set them in motion, overcoming inertia and any humiliation, forcing them to admit their mistake, correct it, and return to the place where they could spend the rest of their years cradled in the familiar.

A 72-year-old grain broker put it this way: "I knew where I wanted to retire when I was 40. On the Shrewsbury River, near Red Bank, New Jersey, only an hour from the town where I had spent all my life. So, when I was 40, I bought a piece of land right on the river—you could afford to buy waterfront property in those days. It was overgrown with trees and shrubs and you had to push your way through the thickets and brush to get down to the river. We used to go down there a dozen times a year and stand on that ground and I'd imagine the kind of house I'd build there when I didn't have to commute to New York every day. By the time we did build, 6 years ago, my wife and I felt we were moving to a place where we had also spent most of our lives."

Growing old doesn't have to be dismal and unhappy. It can be as fulfilling a time in life as any other, if one knows how to deal with the changes age brings and the moments of depression that such changes induce. "Move a little slower" is a line in a Frank Sinatra song. Why not move a little slower? Why not take the time to consider and reconsider what life is all about? To paraphrase T. S. Eliot, you arrive where you started and "know the place for the first time."

Chapter 15

♦ ♦ ❖ ♦ ♦ ❖ ♦ ♦ ❖ ♦ ♦ ❖ ♦ ♦ ❖ ♦ ♦ ❖ ♦ ♦

Depressogenic Environments

There is a constant interaction between every human being and his or her environment. This interaction is always in a state of flux. When something happens in a person's environment, he or she reacts to it. This, in turn, produces a response from the environment to which he or she will again respond.

Considerable variation exists with regard to what degree people are susceptible to external influences. Some are highly sensitive to what goes on around them; others are not. For those who are, the environment can have a profound effect on mood. Their world may regularly confirm a healthy sense of self-esteem, allow for the expression of feelings, and provide them with an atmosphere of hope. On the other hand, if their environment provides no ego support, prevents them from becoming self-reliant, repeatedly stirs up hostility and at the same time blocks its release, provokes unnecessary guilt, or causes them to feel lonely and rejected, it can be called depressogenic. Such an environment will provoke moods of depression in the majority of people who inhabit it.

Consider, in its simplest terms, the impact of a sarcastic remark. It is essentially a put-down. To what extent will it hurt the person toward whom it is directed? It depends on how much he or she relies for self-esteem on the opinion of the person who made the remark and how repeatedly he or she is exposed to such attacks. Consider the following dialogue:

> HUSBAND: I'll be about an hour late for dinner tonight. I have to meet Bob for drinks to talk about my life insurance policy.
>
> WIFE: Go ahead. Have a good time without me. It doesn't matter what time you come home.
>
> HUSBAND: (*feeling slightly wounded and agitated*): It does matter. But this is the only time we can get together. It's important. We're not going to have a ball. We're going over things that have to do with our financial security—yours as well as mine. (Thinking to himself, "What have I done wrong now?")

The provocation here is the husband's announcement that he will be late for dinner. His wife's reaction is sarcastic. It is designed to hurt, to make him feel guilty. It succeeds because he loves her and is concerned about her feelings and how she regards him. If he has had a long-standing problem in apportioning his time, her reaction may well be warranted. On the other hand, if she is hypersensitive to being rejected, or competitive and essentially envious of his opportunity to spend an hour with a friend and business associate, her response is skewed—that is, based more on her own needs than on the reality of a situation. In that event, she is contributing to a depressogenic climate in her home.

Depressogenic Environments and Self-Esteem

A depressogenic environment fails to provide people with adequate support for their self-esteem—and often, in fact, actively undermines it—or repeatedly activates emotions and conflicts that susceptible individuals cannot handle without becoming depressed.

The effect of such an environment may be mild or severe, depending on the intensity and persistence of the depressogenic factors.

Unless people are already depressed, it is usually possible for them to overlook or respond with brief anger to provocations from people who matter little to them. But being attacked by someone whose love and respect are valued highly can generate feelings of hurt, guilt, or helplessness that can have a considerable impact. This is especially true when criticism does not focus on the person, but consists instead of irrelevant and denigrating comments about his or her character. When a parent corrects a child by saying: "Stop that! You're going to break it!" the effect on the child is quite different from that produced by an exclamation such as "Stop that! How can you be so *dumb!*" Adults too often interact with one another—verbally and nonverbally—in ways reminiscent of parent-child relationships, going after egos instead of issues.

Every human being depends to some degree on the way they are perceived by those they trust. One's self-perception can either be validated or confused. A compliment from a superior at work can confirm that one has been doing a good job. Being passed over for a deserved promotion, or being promptly criticized for mistakes and barely recognized for excellent performance, will generate in most people a mixture of hurt, resentment, and doubt about their own abilities—which can lead to depression. To be on the receiving end of an "I'm O.K., you're not O.K." interaction in a marriage will shatter anyone's sense of self-worth, unless they are so insulated and unresponsive that the critical and depreciatory communications fail to reach them.

If the evaluations delivered to people from those close to them are confused and distorted, they will predictably have a detrimental effect on the recipient's self-image. Questions thrown out more as accusations—"Why are you always so angry?" "Why are you so selfish and unappreciative?" "Why aren't you a better wife?"—will produce an inner state of confusion and doubt in the person to whom they are directed. Even when there is a grain of truth in them, they are more likely to provoke defensiveness than insight. When they are untrue and unsubstantiated and more reflective of the inner conflicts and distorted perceptions of the one who is criticizing than of the behavior of the one being criticized, they can seriously threaten the recipient's sense of identity.

A depressogenic environment is made up of thousands of verbal and nonverbal exchanges that take place daily and that stir up in the vulnerable individual a loss of self-esteem, guilt, inexpressible anger, and a chronic sense of not being understood. The following conversation between a father and his son illustrates the process of inducing guilt:

> FATHER: Why couldn't you come by to see us last weekend?
>
> SON: Mary and I had to take the children to a picnic. I thought I told you about it.
>
> FATHER: I don't recall. You don't seem to spend as much time with your mother and me as you did.
>
> SON: (*slightly annoyed*): We're here today. Besides, we spent a week with you last month, most of my vacation.
>
> FATHER: Somehow I feel like you're a stranger. I'm not getting any younger. Your mother gets very upset when you can't come.

If his son had really been avoiding him, the father in this example would probably have had a just cause to be critical. As it happens, his son, daughter-in-law, and grandchildren had been spending one or two weekends each month with him. What he basically resented was the complete economic and personal independence his children had attained. He needed the control he had once held over his family, and now most of it was gone. He himself was depressed, but because he would not acknowledge it, his reaction took the form of making them feel guilty, as if they had rejected him. This did not detract from his loneliness and his genuine wish to see them, but it did provoke a sense of guilt in them and create a depressogenic atmosphere in his home.

Depressogenic for Some, Not for Others

Within a home or an organization, an environment which is depressogenic for one person may not be for another. A young lawyer was repeatedly frustrated and depressed as long as he worked for a large and tightly organized firm. He had no clients of his own. All his work was meticulously checked. He was anxious for greater responsibility, but knew it would be years away.

He had been an outstanding student in college and had not required the reassurance of grades to bolster his self-esteem. He was also a "self-starter," and found it difficult to operate within the rigid lines of the law firm. After a period of discouragement punctuated by heated arguments with his immediate supervisor, he quit and found another position in a smaller and less prestigious firm, where the lines of command were not so stringently drawn and he had immediate access to any senior member. He was encouraged to take on as much responsibility as he could handle, and he approached his work with renewed hope and enthusiasm.

Even as a rigidly structured organization may be more depressogenic for a self-actualizing individual, a more loosely organized group may be depressogenic for someone who requires a high degree of order to feel secure and function most effectively: "I just couldn't get my bearings in the last job I had. I was never sure what was expected of me. There wasn't much feedback and I was left pretty much on my own." Two years after graduation, this young scientist had obtained a good position with a well-known company in which every individual was given a good deal of freedom and responsibility. He was extremely dependent on the opinions of others. When left to his own devices, he would work 10 and 12 hours a day, perfectionistically, never knowing how to set limits on his efforts. In his job, he became increasingly unsure of himself and afraid that he would be fired for doing incompetent work.

Finally he decided that it would be better for him to find a more structured situation. He obtained a job teaching at a graduate school, where, being better able to define his responsibilities and his place within the organization, he felt quite comfortable and did extremely well in his work.

Depressogenic for All

Some environments, however, are basically depressogenic to practically everyone who lives or works within them. If, for example, the texture of an organization becomes too complex and constricted, as within many bureaucracies, the net effect can be stifling both for those who work in the organization and for those who have to deal with it.

Individual judgment gives way to forms and procedures. As the workers adapt more and more successfully to the system, they lose their decision-making abilities and flexibility vanishes. Constructive action is replaced by compulsiveness, by a series of delays and Kafka-like levels through which each and every item must pass, whether it takes weeks, months, or years.

The lack of responsiveness within such an environment has such a subtly depressing quality that it can conceal from those within it their own inner sense of depression. "I didn't know I was depressed all those years—not until I retired," said one company employee. "Everyone else seemed to be in the same boat. I thought it was just the normal way to be."

Depression is Contagious

One of the characteristics of certain depressogenic environments is that they are comprised largely of people who themselves are caught up in states of chronic depression, often without realizing it, and often as a result of conflicts that originate in their personal lives and are carried over into work. Frequently, the more energetic and independent people leave. Those who remain exude an air of futility that seems appropriate to the setting, and continually reinforce each other's depression.

For depression is contagious. Nurses and doctors who work with depressed patients in psychiatric hospitals often leave at the end of the day exhausted and wondering about their own lives.

Surrounded for hours by patients who complain about their unhappiness, who resist efforts to reassure and encourage them, and who stubbornly refuse to socialize with others or attend recreational activities, the staff members often find themselves taking on the pessimism and hopelessness to which they are exposed. This can occur even though they are professionally trained and realize that the ultimate prognosis for many of these patients is excellent.

Depressed people, in other words, help create their own depressogenic environments. "I love Karl. I really do. But unless you can do something to help him, doctor, I don't know how much more I can take," a 43-year-old woman remarked, describing the effect that living with her depressed husband had been having on her. "I'm normally a cheerful person. I think that a solution can be found to almost any problem. But during the last year, Karl has been so pessimistic and moody that I'm beginning to get that way myself. We can't ever make plans. It's as if there isn't any future. He drains me."

Within any group—a family, a business, a government—the most important figures who influence the psychological quality of the environment are those at the top. In business, it is the chief executive officer and his immediate associates. In a religious order, it is the superior. In the home, it is the parent, or parents, who exert the strongest influence in setting the tone of the environment. Every group takes its character to a significant degree from its leadership. If the leadership is depressogenic, the environment will be as well.

Harold Mills was appointed executive vice-president of a major chemical company at the age of 47. An engineer by profession, he had little management experience. Now he had been recruited to run an organization with thousands of employees.

Mills, unaware of his lack of executive aptitude, thought of himself as a good leader and rejected the suggestion that he might spend a few months at an advanced management training program. He was by nature an extremely distrustful and sensitive person—sensitive to his own feelings but not to those of others. Slow in making decisions, he liked to think about issues for a long time before committing himself. He was often unaware of, and unresponsive to, the needs of those beneath him.

He preferred to keep a firm control over everything that happened in the company. He did not want any individual to become so prominent or so powerful that he might jeopardize his command. Although slow to respond to ordinary suggestions or requests, and offering little or no support to the more energetic or creative members of his group, he was still extremely vulnerable to being forced to comply with demands made by senior executives in positions of strength. If, for example, the vice-president in charge of sales, who had a long history of excellent customer relationships, demanded a larger staff and budget and offered his resignation as an alternative if his request was denied, Mills would grant the money, however reluctantly. By contrast, if an innovative plan to develop new business leads was presented to him in an open and constructive way, he would sit on it for weeks and sometimes months. If he finally gave the go-ahead, he would often fail to back the strategy at key moments.

His tendency to withdraw, except when he was bludgeoned into action, caused a serious vacuum in leadership. This was further aggravated by his need to divide and conquer. He played one lieutenant against another, the research and development group against the sales executives, the board of directors against his own hand-selected staff. His purpose: to maintain control. The result: a seriously depressogenic environment.

When Harold Mills arrived at the company, it was comprised of half a dozen bright and energetic leaders in various positions. One of them, anticipating trouble, quit as soon as he learned who was taking over. During the next 3 years, key members of the company gradually resigned, one after another, to find other places where they could work effectively.

One executive in particular experienced a serious depression before he could bring himself to relocate. Although skeptical, Ed Fosse had been willing to give the new chief executive officer a chance. Six months after Harold Mills's arrival, Ed presented him with an important blueprint for restructuring the marketing approach for one of their most important products. Mills sat on the plan for 3 months and, when questioned, would reply, "I'll get to it as soon as I can." Subsequently, Ed began to receive increasingly confused and mixed messages from Mills's office. First he was told his budget for the coming year would be reduced because of smaller profit margins. Then he was sent a note commending him on a report he had given before a meeting of the board.

At a small conference of executives he made a mildly critical remark indicating his annoyance at the delay in hearing from Mills about his marketing plan. Three weeks later, he was called into Mills's office, where he was confronted with his remarks. "Ed, I understand that you're seriously critical of the way I run this outfit," said the boss. "If you don't like it here, you can certainly leave. Your work is, frankly, not that impressive anyway."

One month later, Ed received a commentary on his plan. Harold remarked that it was good, but added that the timing for such an approach was poor. Ed's response to this event was frustration and self-doubt. Losing perspective into his initial evaluation of Harold, he began to feel that he was losing his own touch, that perhaps his work had indeed fallen off. He became worried and agitated, found it hard to sleep at night, and, at moments, felt as if his career were coming to an end. He had worked for this company for over 10 years, and until now had never considered going elsewhere.

The causal factors for his depressive response were evident. Normally a sensitive person, he deserved some recognition for his work from those in authority. Had Mills come right out and told him that he wasn't going to support his work, he could have handled this overt rejection firmly and definitively. But Mills didn't do that. Instead, what he communicated added up to such ambivalent messages as: "We want to keep you here, but we're not going to give you any support" and "I'm not interested in your gripes and criticisms, but if you exert enough pressure—threaten and berate me—I might just give in to your requests."

Finally, there was Mills's pathological need to maintain control at all times, even at the expense of the company's growth. To ensure such control, he instinctively demoralized his subordinates. Four years later, after a disastrous profit-loss statement, the board of directors asked for Mills's resignation. By then the key positions in the firm were occupied only by executives whose own personality quirks allowed them to survive in, and at times flourish within, the depressogenic nature of the environment he had created.

How People Make Family Members Depressed

The principles involved in the creation of a depressogenic environment are similar whether an organization is large, such as a corporation, or small, such as a family. The most commonly employed tactics used to induce depression within families include:

1. Keeping an individual from finding some degree of independence, while one or several members of the family maintain control.

2. Stirring up separation anxiety; that is, encouraging a dependency that convinces the more dependent member that he or she cannot possibly survive without their emotional support.

3. Delivering ambivalent messages that undermine self-esteem and at the same time block legitimate self-defense, such as "I love you, in spite of the kind of person you are."

4. Repeatedly provoking guilt by making a family member feel responsible, regardless of the facts.

5. Misinterpreting intentions and motives so that the more insecure member begins to doubt his or her own perceptions, even though they are more accurate.

6. Contaminating family interactions with a competitiveness that stems from envy and jealousy.

7. Providing a monotonous, unstimulating environment that resists any effort to introduce humor, spontaneity, and joy.

8. Refusing to permit any open show of emotion, particularly assertiveness and appropriate displays ofanger.

9. Using a chronic state of depression to express anger indirectly, making other members feel helpless, guilty, and confused in the process.

10. Blocking open and direct communication.

In the past few decades, therapists have become more aware of the importance of dealing with the entire family rather than limiting therapy to the person who is declared the "patient." In the earlier psychoanalytic approach to therapy there was an assumption that once the depressed individual recovered, he or she would be able to cope with any but the most destructive environmental conditions. It became obvious, however, that many patients would reach a plateau of improvement from which they could not move on. This was at first interpreted as "resistance." But now it is clear that members of some patients' families may have a vested interest in keeping them from pulling out of their depression. In such cases, therapists often attempt to involve the families in the therapeutic experience for the purpose of modifying depressogenic elements in the home. Sometimes patients, with new insights, can succeed in altering the attitudes of other family members by themselves. At other times, such a complete breakdown in communication within families takes place that patients have no choice but to remove themselves from their families.

In their book *The Intimate Enemy,* George Bach and Peter Wyden, describing various destructive ways of channeling hostility between married partners, have called attention to a particular sadistic ploy that they term *gaslighting*. Gaslighting, which involves chipping away at the victims' perceptions of themselves and their surroundings, is a term derived from the classic film *Gaslight*, in which Ingrid Bergman played a young bride being driven out of her mind by her husband. Among other fiendish maneuvers, Charles Boyer, as her husband, kept turning the lights up and down, but denied that they were changing. His wife was torn between accepting her own perception of the fact that the lights were flickering and his insistence that they were not. Although Boyer's intentions—thwarted, fortunately, by the arrival of Joseph Cotten—were more sinister, variations on this theme seen in everyday life generally lead to depression in the victims.

In the following example, an adolescent girl's depression could be accounted for by her mother's use of modified gaslighting techniques. "I haven't any confidence in myself," she said. "I don't feel attractive. I'm all right as a student, but nothing special. I don't know what I want to do with my life. I don't mind that—I'm only 17. What really gets to me is that I can't think about myself in a constructive way. I'm too busy thinking about the way in which my mother looks at me.

"She calls me fat and stupid. And then, when I cry, she asks me what I'm upset about. I got angry at her a few times. She acted really hurt, as if I had done something awful. She accused me of being ungrateful for all she had done for me.

"Done for me? What? I wanted to go away to college. We could afford it. I could get some state aid. She was against it. When I came home late a few times from a dance, she called me a whore and a slut. It makes you not care any more. I can't please her. I can't please myself.

"I don't get any support from my dad. He's quiet, and he never speaks up for himself. Mom told me that she would have left him a year or two after they were married but she couldn't for my sake. Whenever I try to talk with him about anything serious, he pushes me away. I feel awful about him. He seems like such a tragic figure. I can't understand why he stayed with her. She treats him as if he were nothing, less than nothing."

Rigid, self-centered, guilt-inducing, domineering, this girl's mother was the key influence in the character of the family. She had succeeded, over a period of years, in encouraging her husband to withdraw into his own private world, while repeatedly demoralizing her daughter. Her unconscious motives: competition, to express her envy of her daughter's youthfulness and attractiveness; control, to keep her daughter from becoming independent of her; and denial, to focus attention on the problems and difficulties of other family members and keep criticism away from herself. Her husband had long since entered a chronic depression. Her daughter, acutely depressed in her attempt to break away from her mother's influence, had sought counseling to help her in her efforts toward independence.

B. F. Skinner once pointed out that gamblers seem to violate what he calls "the law of effect": they continue to gamble even though their net reward is negative. In other words, the player wins often enough to continue playing in spite of the fact that he or she loses frequently and—because the odds are stacked against him or her—will lose in the end. Skinner attributed this phenomenon to the influence of what he called a variable-ratio schedule of reinforcement. A similar process can be seen in human relationships. "I love you" can be communicated in word and action just often enough to keep the other person caught in the relationship, even though he or she is repeatedly subjected to indifference and at times contempt and will, like the gambler, lose in the end. In the game of dating, one of the most effective ways to force the more involved person to be "hung up" is to activate his or her anxiety by the conditioning effect of such on-again, off-again messages.

One young woman described her dating experience as follows: "I can't get him out of my mind. One weekend he takes me to Nassau and tells me I'm his life. The next week he disappears completely for 10 days, and when he comes back he acts as though I'm just another date. He even tells me about other girls he takes out. But whenever I build up the energy to break it off, he comes on strong again, telling me that someday, somehow, we'll live together. Sometimes I just want to die. I can't think of any other way to get rid of him."

The fact that a situation or an environment is depressogenic may not become apparent until it changes in some significant way. When changes are extensive—when a tightly structured environment begins to come apart—the conflict between the old way of doing things and the new produces confusion. The more strongly conditioned that people have been to the previous structure, the more likely they are to experience depression in trying to adapt to the new one.

When any organization undergoes a major change—even when there is hope of restructuring it on a new and more effective level—some of its members who have been chronically depressed may become aware of it for the first time; others may become depressed in response to the change itself. For either group of people, such a disruption offers each individual a real opportunity to resolve his or her own emotional conflicts and learn from depression, and also to work together with others to build environments that will not be depressogenic.

Chapter 16

♦ ♦ ❖ ♦ ♦ ❖ ♦ ♦ ❖ ♦ ♦ ❖ ♦ ♦ ❖ ♦ ♦ ❖ ♦ ♦

Living with Someone Who Is Depressed

Diana Brent wondered why she had not heard a thing from her close friend Laurie in nearly 2 months. At first, she assumed that Laurie was too busy to return her calls. As the weeks passed, Diana began to wonder whether she might have done something to offend Laurie, but could not come up with anything in particular. A feeling of hurt gradually gave way to annoyance: "At least she could call me." Finally, feeling quite rejected, she came to the conclusion that she had simply lost a good friend for no apparent reason.

What Diana did not know, because Laurie failed to tell her, was that Laurie was depressed. Being depressed, she had withdrawn from her friends, not wanting to see anyone, not wanting to impose her mood and unhappiness on them. She also did not want them to engage in a futile and irritating attempt to "cheer her up."

Because withdrawal—not wanting to be with people and not wanting to communicate with them when they are around—is a common sign of being depressed, the "other person" frequently feels that the depressed individual is pushing him or her away. "My wife just isn't the same," commented one man. "When I try to talk to her about business, or friends, or redecorating the house, I not only get no enthusiasm, I sometimes don't get any response at all, or at best a monosyllabic one. For weeks now she's shown no affection toward me. When I bring it up, she just apologizes and says that she'll try to do better. When I ask her what's wrong, I get nowhere. And when I ask her whether I've done anything to upset her, she says no, but she acts as if I have. The net result of all this is that I'm getting pulled down. I feel terribly responsible, but I don't know what for."

The first assumption many people make when living with, or relating to, a depressed person is that somehow they are responsible for the depressed person's unhappiness. The guilt that accompanies this assumption often makes people want to avoid the depressed person. Feeling guilty, especially when it is difficult to understand why, makes such an individual feel uneasy and irritable with the depressed person who stirs it up. One therapist, when asked whether working with depressed patients made him uncomfortable or impatient, replied, "Less than it might, because I can have more perspective than the person's family; I *know* I haven't been the cause of their unhappiness."

The likelihood of feeling rejected or guilty is greater when there seems to be no reason for depressed people to be depressed. When there is a well-defined and easily recognized cause for the unhappiness, neither unhappy people nor those around them need to puzzle over what is happening. But when depression follows a presumably happy event—the birth of a child, a significant promotion at work, or a move to a new home—the apparent lack of connection between the two is confusing, leaving everyone to wonder who and what are responsible.

It is not unusual for people who have never been depressed to underestimate both the pain depressed people experience and the length of time the depression may last. "Pull yourself together, Helen. Your mother's been dead for over 3 months"; "How can you say our marriage is terrible when we've had 8 really great years?"; and "I just don't understand how you can be so discouraged about your appearance that you don't want to go anywhere." Comments such as these, expressed in a perplexed and angry way, are common responses to depressed people when those near them lack any insight into the nature and causes of the mood. People who have never experienced depression or deny it in themselves tend to be impatient with the depressed person. It is an impatience caused partly by the slowness and indecisiveness that go along with being depressed and the persistence with which depression hangs on. It is an impatience that is a response to the underlying anger and hostility often lurking behind the depression.

When someone is anxious, it is likely to stir up the anxiety of those around him or her. When someone is depressed, it is likely to have a depressive effect on those around him or her. Therefore, those who would like to be helpful to depressed people frequently find themselves unable to be empathetic because of the feeling of futility they may have when in contact with them. Of course, this only serves to reinforce depressed people's feeling of hopelessness and their conviction that they are rejected and misunderstood.

It is especially difficult for advocates of the supremacy of will power to understand or cope with someone who is depressed. Such people mistakenly assume that "you are what you choose to be" and see a deliberateness in depressed people's attitudes and behavior that they find intolerable and provocative. Psychiatrist Lawrence Kubie once defined will power as the energy required to overcome a neurotic block such as a phobic or compulsive fear. For the depressed individual, will power implies the energy required just to go on with daily life, attending to various tasks, seeing people, communicating, in spite of the underlying urge to withdraw. But for those who have never been depressed and who honestly believe that both mood and self-esteem are a matter of forcing oneself to feel cheerful, depression seems a most mysterious and contrary process indeed.

One mildly depressed woman was having difficulty falling asleep at night and would wake up an hour or so early in the morning. During the day she was exhausted. "It's your own fault that you're tired during the day," reasoned her husband. "You have to *make* yourself go to bed earlier and lie there until you get to sleep. I get angry with you because you're just not trying." The more he admonished her to correct her sleep difficulty, the more trouble she had getting to sleep at all, and bedtime became for her a time to be dreaded.

How one reacts to depressed individuals obviously depends on the form the depression takes and the response of depressed people to their mood. It is frustrating when someone will not or cannot take steps to help himself or herself. "My daughter is having awful problems in her marriage," said the elderly woman. "Her husband has found someone else. She knows about it. But neither of them wants a divorce. My daughter is miserable. She cries all the time. I want to help her, but she won't let me. I suggested she talk with a psychiatrist. She said no, she didn't need to. Besides, she's afraid he might tell her to pack her bags and leave. She doesn't want to do that. I can't tell you how upset and helpless I feel." Since this woman had undergone episodes of depression at various times throughout her life, she was not angry or impatient with her daughter. What she did feel was frustration: "I know she needs professional help, and basically she does too, but she just won't do anything about it."

The most difficult type of depression to be in contact with is not the most dramatic, but the most indirect. It is when people themselves do not recognize their depression, or seek to solve their conflicts through behavior such as the excessive use of alcohol, or blame everything and everyone for their misery and unhappiness to the extent that those around them will find it hard to empathize and difficult to help. By contrast, when people experience depression clearly and directly, and can understand to some degree why they are down, it is much easier to reach out to them. Rollo May, in his book *Paulus*, wrote about the depressive episodes that Paul Tillich experienced: "His depressions never made the rest of us depressed because they were open. . . . If we admit our depression openly and freely, those around us get from it an experience of freedom rather than the depression itself."

The more intense kinds of depressive reactions can be frightening. "My husband slept only 2 or 3 hours a night," said a 34-year-old woman. "In spite of this he went to work and put in a full day. By the time he came home, he was wiped out. He often went into the bedroom, closed the door, and cried. I could hear him. If I went in to talk to him, he would accept my comfort for awhile, but sooner or later he would get up from the bed and pace around restlessly. He wouldn't watch television or read. He never talked about suicide, but he seemed so upset. I was terrified that he might do something to himself. He said he wouldn't. He said such ideas had never entered his mind. But I just couldn't understand why he was so upset.

"I've been down myself, but I usually know why, and it rarely lasts more than a day or so. With him, it kept going on for weeks. I couldn't stop being afraid until, with therapy, he started to show some improvement. And even now, 6 months later, if he gets up during the night or seems a little preoccupied, I become frightened. I have to learn to trust all over again."

One's reaction to depressed people is strongly influenced by some of the specific conflicts that are caused by, or contribute to, their depression, such as dependency. "Almost from the beginning of our marriage, Neil wanted to be with me all the time when he wasn't at work," commented his wife. "At first it was romantic. But now, 2 years later, it's stifling. He used to have a lot of interests. He used to seem independent and decisive—the kind of man I wanted. But now it's like having a second child around the house. I have to make whatever plans there are. He spends hours in front of the television set. I get the distinct feeling that he needs me in an unhealthy way—that if anything happened to me he'd fall apart. It's an awful responsibility. It literally turns me off. I love him and I need him, but not this way."

A loss of sexual desire is another example. It is not unusual for depressed people, whatever their age, to lose sexual interest. This can easily be misinterpreted by their spouses or by anyone else with whom they have been sexually intimate as a sexual rejection. "My husband hasn't made love to me in months. We used to have a good sexual relationship. Now I wonder if he's found someone else. For a while I kept pushing him about it, and then the more we tried, the less he could do. I wish I knew what was wrong."

How one reacts to depressed people is also influenced by one's own personality. It is easier to understand what depressed people are going through if one has experienced some measure of depression oneself. People who are afraid of their own emotions will be especially stirred up by another person's depression. The husband of one depressed woman was so frightened of feeling depressed himself that he found it necessary to separate from his wife until she started therapy. "Being around her scared me, I don't know why. I couldn't say or do anything to comfort her. I was tongue-tied. I finally had to leave for awhile. I was only making her worse by losing my temper. She realized it had nothing to do with my love for her. I just couldn't handle it."

Each person's sensitivity to taking the blame on himself or herself varies, and those who are most inclined to feel "it's my fault" will also be the most likely to assume the responsibility for depressed people's unhappiness. The difficulty a person has in accepting criticism and anger will also affect his or her attitude. During recovery, the depressed person will feel freer to express his or her anger appropriately and to be more aggressive. If people who live with the person find it hard to cope with this change because of their own difficulty in handling anger, three things can happen: they may try to get the depressed person to suppress his or her emotions again, they may enter into open conflict with the depressed person, or they may become depressed themselves.

The father of one 16-year-old boy described how, as his son pulled out of a depression, there were outbursts of anger that the family found hard to handle: "Bill was always a good boy . . . did well in school . . . was fun to have around. He never gave us any grief. Then, when he was 15, he became sullen and morose. Something was bothering him, but he wouldn't tell us what. His work fell off in school, and he began skipping classes. He wouldn't see any of his friends. On the advice of our family doctor, we took him for some counseling. After a few weeks he began to have outbursts of anger at his mother and me. We weren't used to it. He accused us of interfering with his independence, of keeping him from growing up. At other times, he would just be mad because something went wrong—dinner was later than he expected or a trip that he planned had to be canceled.

"It was like having a stranger in the house. Worse yet, it was painful because we didn't know what to do. What he said hurt our feelings, especially mine. Also, I was brought up not to express any disrespect toward my parents, and sometimes I came down hard on him. Now I can see that he had to go through that phase. Getting out the anger was part of breaking away from us and getting out of his depression."

Guidelines for Relating to a Depressed Person

Changing the way in which close relatives, friends, and co-workers relate to depressed people is part of helping them recover from their depression with insight. Certain important principles are involved:

1. *Understand that the depressed person really hurts.* Regardless of whether the circumstances seem to justify the extent of their reaction, their distress is real and not feigned. Depression has been called a tactic to manipulate and control others. It is not. While it is true that people who tend to be manipulative use depression for that purpose, depression, in and of itself, is not a ploy unless the personality of the depressed individual is already constructed that way. Even when the depression is an expression of anger or represents a plea for understanding, it still hurts. Any effort to suggest that a depressed person's moods are false will clearly reinforce his or her sense of alienation and rejection.

2. *Empathize, rather than sympathize, with the depressed person.* To feel sorry for them only reinforces their feeling of hopelessness and confirms their lowered sense of self-esteem. It may also make them feel more helpless and dependent.

3. *Don't confront the depressed person with unbearable truths.* A 42-year-old man decided to clear the air in his marriage by admitting to his wife that he had been having an affair. His wife had been somewhat depressed for several months following her father's death. Not heeding her mood, he relieved his own guilt by his confession—a

highly dubious tactic under any circumstance—and thereby triggered a suicide attempt. When controversial issues are to be discussed effectively, it is usually best to wait until the individual is no longer depressed.

4. *Provide hope realistically.* Offering reassurance to the depressed person—telling him or her that everything will be all right—is important, but must be done judiciously. At that moment, the person does not feel that everything will be all right. Although in need of encouragement, he or she is not likely to trust it. Moreover, if any real dangers exist—financial difficulties, the threat of divorce, a child's illness—the person does not want the dangers denied. Pretending that there is nothing wrong when something is very wrong is hardly the way to offer reassurance.

   One woman, to help her depressed husband feel better, found herself telling him that she loved him and "would stay with him forever," even though she had been regularly consulting a counselor for months to help her cope with what she considered to be a basically poor marriage. The reassurance did not work because, in spite of it, he was picking up all kinds of nonverbal messages from her that contradicted what she said.

5. *If you offer reassurance, base it on a fact.* The depressed person—whether in that mood for a day, a week, or a month—has lost perspective. When depressed, he or she feels as if things have always been the way they are, even though he or she knows it isn't true.

A man who had been a fine father, a good husband, and a successful businessman felt, while he was depressed, that he had failed on all three counts. His wife, seeing that he had no appreciation of himself as he really was, found ways and means to gently remind him of how much he meant to her and the children. Intuitively, she did so quietly, repeatedly, without overdoing it, often by dropping a reassuring remark here and there, which he heard, even though he did not immediately respond. Therapists know that the tenacity of depression often works against reassurance, and that too great an emphasis on the positive aspects of their patients' personalities and lives will only drive them further into depression, as if they must prove to themselves that things are hopeless and that they are without worth.

The extent to which one becomes involved in trying to help depressed people depends upon the nature of their relationship. Obviously, it would be imprudent for casual friends to take a major responsibility for helping someone cope with depression. They can make it clear that they are available. They can be supportive. But they should not push beyond the limits set by the nature of the relationship itself.

For a close friend or relative, however, the responsibility is greater. "It isn't just that I want to do something for him—I have to," said the wife of a man who had been experiencing depressive moods for nearly 3 years. Finally, on the advice of a friend, she consulted a psychiatrist. "I feel foolish being here," she remarked. "I don't really know what you can do to help."

The psychiatrist was able to outline a strategy for her to persuade her husband to start treatment; he suggested that she encourage her husband to overcome any embarrassment he might feel about taking such a step. The psychiatrist was also able to help her reshape her thinking about her husband's depression. "I had begun to think he didn't care about me anymore. I couldn't help regarding his anxiety as a kind of weakness. I thought our marriage was falling apart. Now I can see that all these things were the result and not the root cause of his depression. You've given me hope."

The depressed person's family plays a vital role in hastening his or her recovery. By understanding the nature of depression and offering the person the support he or she needs, the family can help him or her work through the depression. Together, they can evolve a sounder system of relationships.

Chapter 17

◆ ◆ ❖ ◆ ◆ ❖ ◆ ◆ ❖ ◆ ◆ ❖ ◆ ◆ ❖ ◆ ◆ ❖ ◆ ◆

Breakthroughs in the Biology of Depression

In recent years, much of the significant research into the causes of depression has focused on its biological aspects. The most popular and fertile field of research has been based on the hypothesis that depression is associated with inadequate levels of brain chemicals called neurotransmitters.

The brain contains millions of nerves that talk to each other. The point where one nerve ends and the next begins is a tiny space called a synaptic cleft. Neurotransmitters facilitate the transfer of information at these conjunctions. Some theorize that depression is associated with inadequate neurotransmitter levels within the brain, and that various antidepressants work by increasing the levels of these neurotransmitters, particularly serotonin and/or norepinephrine. Recently, research has also linked depression to two other neurotransmitters, dopamine and glutamate, as well.

Although changes in neurotransmitter levels certainly affect depression, it is likely that changes in neurotransmitter levels are the tip of an iceberg, reflecting many complex biological interactions that take place in the central nervous system when a person is under stress, and perhaps as closely related to one's reaction to stress as to depression per se.

Although the average person need not follow the innumerable details, it may be helpful and reassuring to know that a growing body of evidence shows that depression and resilience are, in fact, at least partly based in biology.

Brain Imaging

One of the most exciting developments increasing our understanding of the connections between brain function and behavior is the emerging field of brain imaging, which indicates the location and amount of biochemical activity in various parts of the brain. In addition to proving that depression does indeed manifest itself in physical ways, it holds the promise of being able to pinpoint exactly where biology goes awry, and by extension, how to direct research in order to correct it.

Brain imaging first emerged in the 1990s with Positron Emission Tomography, or PET, which made it possible for the first time to take sequential, three-dimensional pictures of the brain in action. PET scans measure oxygen and blood sugar levels, resulting in vividly colorful images ranging from yellow and orange in a normally functioning brain to dark green in one in which activity is greatly reduced. Among certain depressed patients, dark green was prominent, suggesting a reduction in global glucose metabolism. These images were the first visible evidence of depression's biological roots.

Today, other forms of brain imaging, including Computed Axial Tomography (CT), Magnetic Resonance Imaging (MRI), and Single Photon Emission Computed Tomography (SPECT), are adding to a rapidly growing stream of data about brain structure and brain function. From studies of blood flow to research into neurotransmitter levels, brain imaging is revealing new details about the differences between the brains of people who are depressed and those who are not.

One interesting finding, for example, is that in people with depression, the part of the brain called the ventromedial cortex is much smaller and less active than normal. This part of the brain allows people to switch from one mood to another, and is critical to the ability to experience pleasure and positive reinforcement. Other recent research shows that people with depression have less activity in the prefrontal cortex, the part of the brain that regulates emotion and inhibits inappropriate and incapacitating emotions. This may be one reason why they feel and express negative emotions more often and more intensely. Similarly, brain imaging suggests that certain parts of the brain connected to the ability to focus on the outside world work more slowly in people with depression, which could explain in part why depressed people have trouble shifting their focus away from their own thoughts and toward their surroundings.

Brain scans of depressed patients also show left-right brain asymmetry, suggesting that left brain activities, such as intellectual processes, are greater than imaginative or pictorial activity, which is normally associated with the right brain. The imbalance seems to correct itself when the depressed state goes away.

Greater understanding of the brain's inner workings holds great promise for new forms of treatment. In 2005, for example, neurosurgeons discovered that they could create a fast, dramatic improvement in severe and previously treatment-resistant depression through a technique called deep brain stimulation, in which a tiny pacemaker-like device provides continuous electrical stimulation to a particular area of the brain. At this point, however, the technique remains experimental, as it is still unclear how or why it works.

Brain imaging has also led to the observation that brain activity increases when both eyes are closed, more so than when only hearing is eliminated or when both eyes and ears are closed. Moreover, as visual stimuli are administered in more complex forms, higher glucose metabolic activity can be seen in the occipital cortex, where focal vision—the aspect of vision required for the identification of objects as opposed to their location in space—is registered.

The eye is one of the main pathways for information processing from the outer world to the brain. My own research has dealt with the adequacy of visual information processing in a variety of normal and pathological emotional states. Among chronically depressed patients, I have noted a significant degree of perceptual dysfunction. First, the eye movements involved in convergence (coming together to see things more closely, as required in reading) and divergence (moving apart to see things in a broader context of farther away) are either too small or too great.

Moreover, the ability to fuse the perceptions arriving via each eye into a single image in the brain appears to be weakened, and a loss of depth perception in the chronically depressed person reduces everything to a two-dimensional field. It is interesting to note that in experiments using hypnosis to suggest a loss of depth perception—and subsequently a return of depth perception—irritability, tension, and depression appeared in the subjects when the three-dimensional field was flattened out. A return of a sense of well-being, and even, at times, euphoria, resulted when depth was restored. Because it is possible, by means of lenses and special exercises, to restore depth perception, improve fusion, and induce greater control over both convergent and divergent eye movements, the use of visual training, with or without lenses that enlarge or reduce the amount of space that an individual must deal with around him or her, should indeed become a routine addition to the treatment of the chronically depressed person.

Hormones

Hormones are chemical substances produced in glands, such as the thyroid gland or the adrenal glands, which travel in the bloodstream to carry vital messages to various parts of our bodies. *Cortisol,* for example, is a hormone produced in the adrenal cortex, a gland located near the kidneys, which is stimulated by stress and readies the body to respond effectively when challenged.

The Dexamethasone Suppression Test (DMST) is a simple, clinically useful procedure to determine the operational integrity of the hypothalamic-pituitary mechanism, located near and in contract with the brain. This axis, as it is called, releases ACTH into the bloodstream to stimulate the production of the stress hormone cortisol. Predictably, under stress, human beings release cortisol; transient, modest increases in this hormone can be detected in the bloodstream at such times, and when the stressful period passes, these levels should return to normal.

Certain depressed individuals, however, seem to show a much higher than normal level of cortisol. When they are given dexamethasone—a compound that, in normal subjects, lowers the level of blood cortisol—they fail to show the expected response.

The DMST itself consists of determining the baseline blood cortisol levels by taking two or three blood samples on the day before the test itself. Then a small amount of dexamethasone is given at night; on the next day, the blood levels are determined again. People who are not depressed show very low plasma cortisol levels in these second-day samples; by contrast, depressed patients, particularly those who have physical signs and symptoms such as a poor appetite, substantial weight loss, and severe insomnia with early morning awakening, and who present, overall, the look and feel of serious depression, fail to show such a reduction in circulating cortisol.

Of course, many questions remained unanswered. Is this abnormal finding related primarily to depression or to the stress of being depressed? Or is it related to some biological force (or lack thereof) that explains not so much why the patient is depressed but rather why he or she tenaciously clings to the depression, unable to shift back into gear and recover from the mood spontaneously and in a reasonable period of time? It would appear as though the mechanisms that normally limit the degree of one's psychological reaction to stress, and, later on, shut them off, aren't working in certain depressed patients, shifting an otherwise acute depressive state into a more intense and chronic one.

From a clinical perspective, the DMST is of limited value in assessing a person's clinical condition. The depressed patients who show a positive response, confirming the diagnosis, are usually those whose clinical pictures shout of depression anyway. The decision to use antidepressant medications in conjunction with psychotherapy is usually made on clinical grounds. On rare occasions, when a physician is considering a more serious approach to treatment, such as electric convulsive treatments, the DMST may provide a piece of information that can help him or her make decisions and recommendations.

Other research has implicated the *thyroid* hormone as a possible culprit in the etiology of chronic depression. The pituitary gland near the brain releases a hormone called the thyrotropin-stimulating hormone (TRH); this, in turn, activates one called the thyroid-stimulating hormone (TSH) which stimulates the production of the hormone thyroxin in the thyroid gland. Thyroxine plays a very important role in the response of our bodies to stress; it increases alertness and accelerates physiological activity at many levels. To evaluate this chain of reactions, a relatively simple procedure has been devised. Inject a specific amount of TRH. Then take blood samples every 15 minutes for 45 minutes. In a healthy person, TRH should stimulate the production of TSH, and this increase should be reflected in elevated levels of TSH in the blood.

However, in a number of conditions including chronic depression (especially intense chronic depression that is accompanied by suicidal tendencies), this response is inadequate or is not seen at all. TRH fails to stimulate TSH as if should. About 25 percent of clinically depressed patients show this deficiency.

Is this test useful? In everyday practice, probably not. However, as with the DMST, it highlights a biological factor that may be very important in chronically depressed individuals: feedback failure. Imagine stress, registering in the brain, switching on an alerting, problem-solving, perhaps even lifesaving reaction. The body must respond by increasing the amount of cortisol and thyroid hormone, resulting in heightened consciousness and a greater readiness to deal with whatever challenge has been posed. Among chronically depressed patients, too much cortisol has been produced and the system cannot be turned off; moreover, the thyroid system fails to respond to the warning light.

Somehow or other, these influences must be put back into shape, and this may be a factor in how the antidepressant drugs work. This may explain why, in certain patients, adding small doses of thyroid hormone to antidepressant medication can make the difference between success or failure in treatment. Of special interest is the fact that this blunting in the TSH response to TRH can be seen among depressed individuals after they have recovered, suggesting that, rather than being directly related to any specific episode of depression, this thyroid dysfunction reflects a vulnerability in the hormonal system that constitutes an impairment in a person's overall ability to adapt to stress.

Psychiatrist Peter Whybrow has extended research in hormone function to a broad spectrum of behavior—particularly the relationship between sexual drives, which are commonly reduced during states of depression, and stress, which triggers depression and is also reinforced by the distress the depressed person experiences. The *stress hormones* called corticosteroids, such as cortisol, are produced in the adrenal cortex, located near the kidney. When one's car feels as though it is out of control, when one's husband or wife suddenly announces that he or she wants out of the marriage, when a child is seriously injured, rising to the occasion and dealing with the challenge requires the body to produce more cortisol.

In the last decade, further research has suggested that elevated levels of cortisol are somehow connected to unusually high levels of corticotropin-releasing factor (CRF), a hormone that triggers the sequence of events that release other stress hormones. Studies have found that depressed people have increased concentrations of CRF in their spinal fluid and that they have a higher than average number of CRF-producing brain cells. CRF-blocking drugs are in development, and one clinical trial improved the symptoms of depression in a small group of patients.

There is a daily rhythm to cortisol production, as there is to many other bodily functions. It is one of the so-called circadian (daily) rhythms designed by nature to give order and coherence to the complex functions of our bodies, synchronize them internally, and enable the whole organism to adapt to the periodically changing external environment. The normal span of an external day is 24 hours; most of us have adjusted to this cycle. However, if the periodical signals of the environment are experimentally excluded, our real, internal circadian periodicity has proved to be slight but significantly longer, ranging from 24½–25½ hours.

Following the dictates of this rhythm, the highest blood level of cortisol in someone who is not depressed occurs in the early morning, the lowest level around midnight. However, among a number of individuals who are clinically depressed, the cortisol levels are generally higher throughout the entire cycle and the normal circadian rhythm is obscured.

So, in addition to the hormone influences on depression, the issue of rhythms has been implicated as well. *The daily sleep-waking cycle is one of the most obvious reflections of circadian rhythm.* Insomnia is one of the most pronounced signs of depression. It is also one of the most painful, since people who are depressed are denied the respite from suffering that sleep provides.

The nature of sleep has been a major focus of research in depression. Sleep encephalography—brain waves determined during sleep—has demonstrated two types of insomnia among people who are depressed. The first involves a delay in falling asleep, probably due to tension and agitation; the second involves disturbed maintenance of sleep, early morning awakening, and changes affecting rapid eye movement (REM) sleep.

REM sleep is characterized by tumultuous brain activity accompanied by paralysis of the voluntary musculature. Breathing is irregular. Cerebral blood flow and brain temperature are elevated dramatically. The eyes dart back and forth, as though the sleeper were watching a tennis game, while the brain dreams. Depressed patients manifest a shortened REM latency, that is, a decrease in the number of minutes of sleep that pass prior to the onset of the first REM period; such patients also appear to experience a greater amount of REM sleep. Moreover, most of the REM sleep occurs during the first third of the night rather than the last part, as it normally should.

These changes in the character of sleep suggest that certain chronically depressed individuals may suffer from a disruption in the synchronization of their circadian rhythm, an interpretation that seems to be confirmed by a similar advance in the rhythm of cortisol production and body temperature seen among such patients. An experimental effort to restore synchronization involves planned sleep deprivation. In sleep laboratories, such as those established in a number of medical teaching centers, depressed patients have been systematically kept awake all night or part of the night during the REM phase of sleep, and this procedure seems to produce a temporary improvement in mood. It is interesting to note that tricyclic antidepressants (discussed at length in Chapter 7) suppress REM sleep. This could be one explanation for their efficacy. Patients receiving these medications often report diminished dreaming, with a rebound effect of intensive dreaming taking place for a short while after the drugs are stopped.

Mineral metabolism is also subject to circadian rhythms. During the 1950s and 1960s, my own studies demonstrated that depressed patients lost calcium from the body while depressed and retained it during and after their recovery. It was not clear whether the *calcium shifts* were of central importance in depression or primarily a reflection of other biochemical changes within the body. Theoretically, the calcium shifts might well be important, since calcium is a major regulator of central nervous system activity. Fluctuations in the amount of calcium at the cell membranes affect the flow of substances in and out of the cell; for example, the influx and efflux of sodium ions. In addition, calcium is a nervous system "sedative"; it reduces the excitability of the brain. Calcium metabolism is partially regulated by messages delivered via hormones. Reduced hormone production by the parathyroid gland leads to low blood levels of calcium; this, in turn, can induce hyperexcitability of the nervous system, which, if severe enough, can result in convulsions. Abnormally high parathyroid hormone production can elevate calcium levels to such a degree that mental confusion, coma, and even death may ensue.

Calcium metabolism is also influenced by stress hormones such as cortisol. Physiologist Hans Selye, in his description of stress responses, pointed out the importance of calcium when he stated that stress accelerates the aging process by activating the removal of calcium from bone and its deposition in soft tissues (where it does not belong). In fact, my subsequent studies showed that the calcium that was being retained in the bodies of patients who were recovering from episodes of depression was going to bone; by means of radioactive isotope calcium-47 we could track its movement. In the continual interchange of calcium that takes place within bone, and between bone and the rest of the body, the recovering patients revealed a decrease in the amount of calcium leaving bone and an increase in the amount of calcium being deposited in bone. At the same time there seemed to be a slight decrease in the amount of calcium circulating in the bloodstream. Many people have come to believe that vitamins, such as the vitamin B complex and especially vitamin B6, and minerals, such as calcium, magnesium, and zinc, make a positive contribution toward the body's ability to cope with stress. Runners, including marathon runners and those who just jog, have described a lifting of mood that can reach euphoric heights at times as a result of the physical exertion involved. Movement stimulates calcium retention; immobility induces calcium loss.

Several other studies also suggest that calcium metabolism may play a pivotal role in the biology of depression. Radiological studies show that depressed post-menopausal women have a significantly greater degree of diminished bone density as compared with non-depressed ones. Moreover, exercise, which is known to enhance calcium retention and its buildup in bone, has also been reported to alleviate depression. A very new diagnostic procedure, the helical (spiral) CAT scan, provides a way to measure the amount of calcium in the coronary arteries; the higher the level of calcium, the greater the risk of coronary artery occlusion, leading to angina and myocardial infarction. People with a history of clinical depression have a greater risk of heart disease, and one can easily entertain the possibility that one mechanism to explain this may be the deposition of calcium in coronary arteries during episodes of stress and depression, or over a long period of time in untreated, chronically depressed individuals. Although some evidence suggests that calcium itself may not produce life-threatening arterial obstruction—plaque does—knowledge about its relationship to plaque and coronary disease is still quite rudimentary.

Seasonal Affective Disorder is a form of depression with a decidedly seasonal flavor: worse in the fall and winter, during the dark months of the year, and better—even to the point of feeling "great"—during the brighter spring and summer months. When depressed, such individuals tend to oversleep, overeat, gain weight, and feel very lethargic. As doctors Frederick M. Jacobsen and Norman E. Rosenthal have shown, such people can be helped by treatment with light. Regular exposure for anywhere from 2–6 hours a day to 2500 lux of full spectrum light seems to induce improvement within a few days; this light treatment must be maintained during darker seasons in order to prevent recurrences of depression.

With remarkable advances in genetic research and the hope of exciting new treatment for a variety of illnesses that may have a *genetic component*, research in this aspect of depression has received new impetus. The risk for depression in first-degree relatives (children, brothers, sisters) of patients with major clinical depression is three times as great as that for the general population; for those of patients with bipolar (manic-depressive) conditions, it is somewhere between two and six times greater. What remains a mystery is whether this genetic link is specific to depression or, instead, indicates a biological deficit in the physiological resilience required to manage the disruption-reintegration cycle that stress induces. The latter explanation seems more likely.

However, the importance of such biological features does not preclude equal consideration of psychological and environmental elements. For it remains essential to view the human being as a whole—mind, body, inner world, outer world, acting, reacting, interacting, creating.

Chapter 18

♦ ♦ ❖ ♦ ♦ ❖ ♦ ♦ ❖ ♦ ♦ ❖ ♦ ♦ ❖ ♦ ♦ ❖ ♦ ♦

The Anatomy of Melancholia

Even though the majority of people who experience depression do not become severely depressed, some do. There are times when depression is clearly a medical problem and warrants sound professional care. The manic-depressive reaction, the agitated depression, the paranoid form of depression, the state of severe panic that can overwhelm the depressed person—each of these conditions calls for rather specific psychotherapeutic and biological approaches to treatment, sometimes including hospitalization.

Over the past few decades, a number of professionals have advocated dismissing traditional diagnostic thinking and replacing it with concepts that envision depressed people as a part of an interactional system that encompasses other people in their environment. This attitude, which leads to a refusal to define the patient as "sick," has much to say in its favor. Diagnosis can easily become a form of labeling that can be misleading and compromising. Because of the forbidding quality of the term *mental illness* implicit in diagnostic concepts, many people who are depressed are afraid to acknowledge it and therefore do not take steps to get help when they need it.

The traditional approach whereby patients are singled out as being "sick" can lead to underestimating the extent to which they are indeed victims of others who may require their incapacitation in order to preserve their own equilibrium; their recovery may force a major reshuffling in personal relationships. Moreover, the labels themselves have an unfair impact on the outlook of improvement. Terms like *schizo-affective disorder* and *manic-depressive psychosis* convey an unwarranted impression of incurability, even though many patients with these diagnoses have excellent chances of recovery, especially since the advent of such biological treatments as antipsychotic medications, lithium, and various mood-stabilizing anticonvulsants. There is also a strong cultural bias to diagnosis. In England, for instance, the diagnosis of manic-depressive reaction has frequently been used for patients who in the United States would be diagnosed as schizophrenic.

Diagnostic concepts can also be misleading when they are misinterpreted to imply that people who do not fit into specific categories of emotional disorders—who do not manifest hallucinations, delusions, or serious changes in mood—are necessarily whole and intact. Nothing could be further from the truth.

Disorders of Personality—the narcissistic, the compulsive, the hysterical, and the passive-aggressive—are no less devastating than disorders that manifest themselves in profound disturbances of thinking, perception, or mood. Of course, since these disorders often go undetected, those around the people who suffer from the disorders often suffer much more than do the patients themselves. An intense need to control others, a proclivity for inducing guilt and dependency in others, a marked selfishness, and insensitivity are no less problematic than depression; in fact, they are often more so.

However, to deny that there is any such thing as mental illness shows a lack of common sense. At times such a denial can deprive a patient's family of some understanding of what they are going through. The father of an adolescent boy who had been hospitalized on and off for 3 years related this experience:

"When my son first became ill, he was only 13. He was depressed and attempted suicide. His behavior was strange, like mumbling incoherently to himself. I thought when he went into the hospital that he would be there only a few months. I did everything I could to cooperate with the doctors. I gave the social workers a complete history of my family. "When I visited my son, I tried to do everything they told me . . . let him get angry at me if he wanted . . . avoid talking about things that might be upsetting. My wife and I were riddled with guilt. The longer the illness went on, the guiltier we felt. I tried to find out what was wrong from the doctors, but they talked with me only in terms of family relationships. I assumed that they thought my son's illness was the product of problems between my wife and me, and that we had done something awful to him during his childhood. It was 2 years later that I was finally told by a consulting doctor that he was suffering from a form of schizophrenia. He explained to me what that meant. For the first time I realized that a lot of things had gone into my son's illness: chemistry, genetics, things that might have happened during the pregnancy over which we could have had no control. It was the first time we felt any relief from the terrible guilt."

The careful use of diagnosis provides a sound basis for medical treatment. Depression is not only a mood; it is also a diagnosis. For a select group of patients—the severely depressed and those with *manic-depressive reactions* (now called *bipolar disorders*)—the diagnosis is vitally important in studying the causes of the condition and bringing effective treatment to bear on it. For instance, *if depression is the only condition to be dealt with—unipolar depression or dysthymia—antidepressants such as the tricyclics or the selective serotonin reuptake inhibitors will be considered. If depression occurs within the context of bipolar disorder, lithium or the anticonvulsants carbamazepine or divalproex sodium are indicated.*

To maintain that there is no such thing as mental illness contradicts the fact that throughout history special groups of individuals have had symptoms that correspond to current concepts of the more severe mood disorders and the schizophrenias, whatever they may have been called at the time. In 1620 at the University of Basel in Switzerland, Fridericus Flacht, later to become official physician for the City of Worms, published his *Treatise on Melancholia*. He wrote:

> Depression is an alienation of the mind. . . . such men often [shed] tears without any cause; others [laugh] uproariously. One thinks the Heavens will fall; another thinks himself to be a clay vessel, hence he carefully avoids contact with men, lest he be broken. . . . Fear and sorrow [last] for a long time without an obvious cause. . . . [There are] other types of madness as Mania. . . those especially seized upon by Mania with the greatest boldness and rage do not hesitate to attack anything threatening. . . .
>
> Another [man] imagined his buttocks to be made of crystal and hence whatever he had to do, he carried out in a standing position, fearing that if he sat down the structure of his buttocks would disintegrate into a thousand fragments.

The early physicians did not distinguish between various types of mental disorders, but clumped them all under one label: melancholia. It was not until the latter part of the nineteenth century that clinicians began to differentiate more carefully between the various forms of mental illness. From the disorders called melancholia, the Swiss neurologist Eugen Bleuler extracted the group he termed *the schizophrenias*. His definition of schizophrenia was based on the presence of certain signs and symptoms that included: a serious disruption in the logical processes of thinking; a separation of the intellectual from the emotional processes, so that schizophrenic individuals might be thinking about sad and upsetting ideas with an external appearance of indifference; an autistic involvement in the people's own perception of reality, providing them with the ability to define their world according to their delusions; and a profound ambivalence in the way they experienced themselves and the outer world.

In severe states of elation and depression, known as the manic-depressive reaction, a close relationship exists between the mood and thought processes of the patient that is lacking in schizophrenic patients. In 1899, the German psychiatrist Emil Kraepelin established the diagnosis of manic-depressive psychosis, a disorder in which a change in mood was of primary importance; that is, where the thinking processes of patients were intact and the content of their thinking followed logically from the basic mood. If elated, the patients' exuberance affected their ideas, and their extravagant behavior stemmed from their spirits. If depressed, their preoccupation with morbid concerns reflected their hopelessness.

Kraepelin described the clinical signs of the manic-depressive reaction, including the predictability of its periodic quality. At certain seasons of the year, particularly spring and fall, such individuals would enter into episodes of elation or depression for no apparent reason. The rhythmic nature of the mood changes suggested that a biological clock within patients determined when and for what period of time their mood might remain altered. Kraepelin's description of manic-depressive patients is still valid, although more careful attention is now paid to distinguishing various types of mood disorders and *what was once called manic depressive illness is now referred to as bipolar disorder.* Subsequent research has indicated an important genetic influence on such mood disturbances, as well as metabolic changes that include a tendency for sodium to be retained within the cells of the nervous system during episodes of disturbance.

John Traynor was 47 when his father died. For a week or so after the funeral he seemed quieter, more withdrawn than usual. Then, without warning, he purchased a valuable painting from a gallery for $11,000, a price he could ill afford. A few weeks later, he began calling up his friends and neighbors, suggesting that they get together to form a committee that would raise several million dollars. The purpose: to rebuild the downtown section of the city in keeping with its nineteenth-century traditions. He also signed a pledge for fifty thousand dollars for the local community chest drive.

Neither his wife nor his attorney was able to deter him from his overactive behavior. Whenever they tried to speak with him he became enraged, threatening to divorce his wife and fire his lawyer. When his wife arrived home one afternoon to find him in the library with the telephone torn from its socket, screaming that someone had tapped his phone to learn about a new invention he had developed, she called the family doctor in a panic, and they arranged for him to be admitted to a psychiatric hospital.

Instead of entering a grief reaction after his father's death, Traynor had become elated, buoyant, boisterous, full of himself and full of grand schemes and ideas. He manifested a sharp sense of humor. He became easily enraged. At the height of his elation, he had become delusional. He was diagnosed as suffering from a manic-depressive (bipolar) reaction, a condition which affects about three or four people out of one thousand.

In the hospital, he was given antipsychotic medication. Within a few days his manic excitement began to subside. By the end of the second week, however, he was profoundly depressed and sat in his room, refusing to come out. He would not speak with the doctors or nurses. On one occasion, he attempted to hang himself on the closet door with his towel. Because of the life-threatening severity of his condition, he was given a series of eight electric convulsive treatments. He improved rapidly during the course of treatment and by the end showed no signs of either elation or depression.

He remained in good condition for 4 years. Sometimes he seemed a bit down, and at other times he was more energetic and active than usual. These swings seemed to have a rhythm about them, being more noticeable around the time of the anniversary of his first episode. Then, abruptly and without warning, he became deeply depressed despite the lack of apparent change in his life situation. He made a serious, impulsive suicide attempt, tying a stone around his waist and jumping into his swimming pool. He was hospitalized again.

This time he was given tricyclic antidepressants, which had begun to be used during the years subsequent to his previous illness. His depression slowly lifted. He remained in fairly even spirits for another few weeks; however, he gradually became euphoric, overtalkative and demanding. "I didn't intend to kill myself. Why should I when I have everything to live for? There is so much joy in the world. And I have found a way of feeling that joy. No, I won't tell you. It's a secret. You might find a way of taking it away from me."

By now he was very much elated and frankly delusional. The doctors started him on lithium and over the next two weeks his elation subsided. Within two months he was well enough to be discharged from the hospital. He has been receiving lithium for the last 8 years and has had no recurrence of either elation or depression.

John Traynor exemplifies the importance of diagnosis in determining the choice of biological treatment—in bipolar conditions such as his, using lithium and anticonvulsants like carbamazepine (Tegretol) and divalproex (Depakote). These medications are effective in reducing the manic phases of bipolar disorder; furthermore, they seem to prevent such patients from entering into recurrent episodes of elation or depression. However, they have no established effect in relieving depression in patients with unipolar depression, and even in those who are bipolar, antidepressants may be required (combined with a mood stabilizer, of course), to alleviate depression in the depressed phase of the illness.

As more information is obtained about bipolar illness and its treatment, several new insights emerge. The majority of psychiatrists in the United States today use divalproex in these patients. Lithium has become a second choice, because of various side effects such as impairment of cognition (thinking processes) and the risk of kidney damage. In treating acute mania, divalproex may be combined with one of the new, so-called atypical antipsychotic drugs, such as olanzapine (Zyprexa) or risperidone (Risperdal). These are not without their own set of potentially serious side-effects, such as obesity and glucose metabolism dysfunction (diabetic complications) with olanzapine and extra-pyramidal motor effects (restlessness, tremulousness, impaired coordination, akathesia) with risperidone. An anticonvulsant, lamotrigine (Lamictal), sometimes proves useful to manage those bipolar patients whose presenting symptoms are primarily depressive.

Electric Convulsive Therapy and Transcranial Magnetic Stimulation

John Traynor's case also illustrates the value of electric shock treatment in the management of especially severe or psychotic states of depression. Electric shock treatments were originally discovered by accident, when the Hungarian psychiatrist L. J. von Meduna attempted in 1935 to use convulsions in the treatment of schizophrenic patients. He believed that there was a low incidence of epilepsy among schizophrenic patients, and that epileptic patients rarely developed the symptoms of schizophrenia. This assumption, later disproved, led to his hypothesis that the induction of a series of grand mal convulsions, of the type characteristic of epilepsy, might have beneficial effects in schizophrenic patients. Although some improvement in the condition was noted, the fundamental change produced by the convulsions appeared to be in mood, whether depression or elation. Subsequent investigations with depressed patients clarified the impression that a series of about six shock treatments would dramatically eliminate the mood disorder.

Giving electric shock treatment is a relatively simple procedure. In a special treatment room, the patient receives anesthesia and muscle relaxants. Once asleep, he or she receives a sufficient amount of electrical current via two electrodes, one attached to each temple, to induce what is technically known as a grand mal seizure, which resembles an epileptic convulsion. There are, however, few, if any, bodily movements, since they are blocked by the use of the muscle relaxants given with the anesthesia. After the convulsion, which lasts less than a minute, the patient will sleep for an hour or more, and when he or she awakens, he or she will usually not recall anything of the treatment itself.

Curiously, the therapeutic effects of the electric shock treatments do not depend on the actual physical manifestations of the convulsion. By the same token, the electricity is not relevant either. Inhalants—gases that can be given to produce convulsions—have the same therapeutic effect. The procedure works somehow by lowering the seizure threshold of the central nervous system and by inducing an associated shift in the metabolic balance of minerals and biogenic amines within the cells and at the cell membranes.

Although antipsychotics, mood stabilizers, and various antidepressants have markedly reduced the need for electric shock treatments, a certain number of patients still respond more adequately to shock than to these drugs. Moreover, electric shock treatments work more quickly and with more guaranteed effectiveness. Therefore, they are still often used in patients who are intensely disturbed—for example, those who represent serious and immediate suicidal risks.

The rapid relief of symptoms by means of shock treatments, however, can discourage patient and doctor alike from exploring the psychological and environmental factors relevant to the depression. This often leaves patients unprotected against a future recurrence of their mood disturbance. To many, the procedure itself sounds "brutal," although the physical complications of shock treatments are fewer and less serious than those incurred in performing a routine appendectomy.

Most people are understandably reluctant to allow themselves to be helplessly wheeled into a treatment room where anesthesia will render them unconscious and a group of doctors and nurses will then perform a procedure that alters the chemical and electrical balance of their brains. As a result of doctors' aversion to giving the treatment as well as patients' aversion to receiving it, there undoubtedly have been many occasions when shock treatments should have been used, but were not.

Transcranial magnetic stimulation (rTMS) is a relatively new approach that seems to be as effective as ECT in the treatment of severe clinical depression and lacks the negative associations of the older treatment. rTMS involves passing an electrical current through a metal coil applied to the scalp to produce fluctuating magnetic pulses. The procedure is painless and appears to carry no significant side-effects. Unlike ECT, it is not accompanied by seizures, so no anesthesia is required. P. G. Janicak and his colleagues at the University of Chicago are among those who have been investigating rTMS, noting that it was just as effective as electric convulsive treatments in relieving clinical depression in severely ill patients.

Other Diagnostic Categories of Clinical Depression

Attempts to define various types of unipolar depression have been made. Some divided mood disorders into an exogenous type in which external events in the patient's life could be identified as triggering the reaction, and an endogenous type in which no such external changes could be easily detected. The former were said to be more psychogenic in origin, the latter more biologically determined. Such a distinction has not been validated and has limited clinical value. In fact, studies indicate that in the vast majority of patients with major depressive disorders of the unipolar type, stress factors do contribute significantly to the initiation of the depression.

Another category of depression that has been defined is *dysthymia*, a milder but more persistent form of depression that can last for years without ever reaching a crisis point. Dysthymia is characterized by years of low self-esteem, anxiety, lack of drive, pessimism, low moods, and negative thought patterns. Often such patients feel that "it's just the kind of person I am and the kind of world I live in, " and most of those around them tend to agree. In fact, such patients often respond to psychotherapy and antidepressants, especially the newer selective serotonin reuptake inhibitors (SSRIs). When a dysthymic patient becomes more gravely depressed and fulfills the DSM-IV criteria for a major depressive disorder, clinicians commonly refer to this development as "double depression."

Another attempt at definition included linking depression to certain times in the life cycle, such as "involutional melancholia" or "depression of the aging period." These distinctions were of little practical value, and, if anything, led to the misleading assumption that depression occurring during menopause, the male climacteric, or during the aging period was fundamentally different from depression appearing earlier in life.

A subgrouping that has proved clinically valuable, serving as an important clue to treatment, is the diagnosis of psychotic depression, which frequently—although not exclusively—takes the form of a paranoid depression. Anyone who is depressed will feel hypersensitive and easily rejected. If the lack of trust accompanying this sensitivity becomes sufficiently intense, the person may become paranoid, even delusional. In mild forms, the paranoid quality can be quite confusing to friends and relatives. "My wife has been accusing me of having an affair," said the husband of one depressed woman. "I can't get her off the subject. Of course, I haven't. I've never played around in 20 years of marriage. But, all of a sudden, she thinks I'm a son of a bitch. When I had to shorten our vacation from 10 days to a week this summer, she had a fit. Said I was doing it to hurt her; that I didn't love her any more, or if I did, that I didn't know how to care about anyone except myself."

In more severe forms, the paranoid element is quite evident. A 30-year-old engineer had an argument with one of his close friends one evening. The next day he was quite depressed and did not go to work. By that evening he began to imagine that his mail was being intercepted and that people were spying on him from a neighboring house. He couldn't sleep at all that night. By the next day he was so frightened and agitated that his wife had to call the family physician, who arranged to hospitalize him. On a regime of therapy that included phenothiazines and antidepressants, his paranoid delusions subsided within a few days. His underlying depression, however, became more pronounced, lasting for another 4 weeks before it finally began to lift.

The diagnosis—a depression with paranoid features—alerted the physician to the importance of adding major tranquilizers to the antidepressant treatment program in order to reduce the fear and agitation that were giving rise to his paranoid delusions, and without which the antidepressant alone would probably be ineffective.

With the rapid growth in biochemical approaches to treatment, diagnosis, accompanied by a careful evaluation of the emotions and symptoms of the depression, has an important place in psychiatry. It permits physicians to select more accurately the right treatment for the right patient at the right time as they attempt to relieve his or her distress and dysfunction and, at the same time, facilitate the process of psychotherapy.

Any discussion of depression must look at the powerful effects of alcohol on the central nervous system and the ways in which such effects can profoundly influence the experience of depression. Alcohol can both induce and aggravate depression; its abuse significantly increases the risk of suicide. If, after 3 or 4 weeks of sobriety, signs of depression abate, alcohol has probably been the main cause of the depressed state; if not, the patient is probably suffering from a clinical depression that requires specific treatment: psychotherapy with or without antidepressants, preferably selective serotonergic reuptake inhibitors (SSRIs). However, depressed patients with alcohol abuse problems are not likely to make significant strides toward recovery without abstaining completely from alcohol, usually with the help of a twelve-step program such as Alcoholics Anonymous.

The indisputable effectiveness of biological methods of treatment in many patients with mood disorders underscores the importance of searching actively for an understanding of biochemical changes in brain function that in some instances go along with being depressed, and in others may actually cause the depression.

Chapter 19

♦ ♦ ❖ ♦ ♦ ❖ ♦ ♦ ❖ ♦ ♦ ❖ ♦ ♦ ❖ ♦ ♦ ❖ ♦ ♦

Depression in Childhood

Cinderella. Snow White. Winnie the Pooh. Kermit the Frog, *The Wizard of Oz*. Barney the Purple Dinosaur. *Where the Wild Things Are*. Disneyland. Hide-and-seek, scooter tricks, and soccer games. Reading, writing, and 'rithmetic. Childhood is no time to be depressed.

Unfortunately, too often it is. Practically from the time they're born until they reach puberty, children can be sad and irritable, feel lost and hopeless, and become disinterested in the very activities they once enjoyed. Their confidence and self-esteem can be undermined. They can fail in school. They can even commit suicide.

Children are no more immune to life's tragedies than anyone else. In fact, they are particularly vulnerable—still small, in many ways helpless, naïve, lacking in experience and coping skills that adults have hopefully acquired. Parents can be cruel and abusive. Their heated arguments can frighten their children. They can be harsh and punitive, frightened and depressed. They can jump ship, abandoning everyone aboard. They get divorces, sometimes bloody ones. They can overprotect their children and make them too dependent. They can drink too much. They can abuse alcohol and drugs. They do get sick. They can die young. Under any one or more of such circumstances as these, children get depressed.

But as with adults, there is a difference between normal depression and clinical depression. "When grandpa died, everyone was very unhappy," a bright twelve-year-old girl described. "I would find dad in the library, just sitting there alone, staring into space, and he would jump when he heard me come into the room and make an effort to smile. I was very sad too, because I loved grandpa. I had a lot of good memories of times together. I'd lie in bed at night and sometimes cry myself to sleep. I didn't want to go to soccer practice, but I made myself go. My grades fell off, not much, but from straight As to a lot of Bs and B pluses. I kept wondering if there was a heaven and if grandpa was there and whether we'd all be together again some time. But as the months went by, I felt more myself again. I accepted the reality of his being gone, with God mom said, and I knew I had to get on with my own life. Dad seemed better too."

It is when being depressed lingers on and has an significant effect on a child's behavior that parents must start to consider clinical depression. This is also true when a child seems to be depressed in the absence of any apparent cause.

Manifestations of Depression in Children

Children manifest depression in some ways like adults and in other ways unique to children. The onset of clinical depression may be sudden or gradual, but it usually involves a *noticeable change in behavior.* A six-year-old boy is no longer interested in playing with his friends. He is sleeping terribly. He grows increasingly lethargic, and would spend all day Saturday in bed if his mother allowed it, which she doesn't. An eight-year-old girl is having an unusually difficult time studying and has become short-tempered and visibly sad at home. She gorges herself on cake and chocolate ice cream, and complains of stomach aches for which the pediatrician can find no physical explanation. She is restless and sometimes frankly agitated; her parents can hear her stomping around her room upstairs late into the night. Unbeknownst to any, she thinks about killing herself by taking a fistful of her mother's valiums.

While it is important not to read problems into the behavioral changes of normal, healthy youngsters, it is no less important to be ready to recognize when a child may be clinically depressed, what may be causing this change in mood, and what to do about it.

Eleven-year-old Benny had a rough time in the fifth grade. His grades fell from B plus to C minus, across the board. He'd never done well in math and history, but now he was doing poorly in all his studies. In school, his class participation was minimal and his teacher described his appearance as frankly morose. "It's not last year's Benny," she noted. At home he complained of hating school and of being stupid. He spent most of his time in his room with the door closed and was often late for dinner. On weekends he no longer went outside to join his friends to bike or play baseball. Once he ran away and got as far as the bus station downtown, but he couldn't think of anywhere to go so he just went home. Ordinarily a fairly well behaved and obliging youngster, he had become frequently irritable and argumentative.

His mother tried to get him to talk about whatever seemed to be troubling him. She got nowhere. His father thought he might be beginning puberty, but when he tried to broach the subject, Benny just stared at him with a look of disdain and abruptly walked away. His dad then took a more disciplined approach, telling his son that if he didn't get it together, be more polite and do better at school, he'd deprive him of privileges, like television and his weekly allowance. Benny didn't seem to care. At their wits end, they conferred with their pediatrician, who referred them to a child psychiatrist. So both parents went by themselves to see Dr. Will Handliss. On hearing the story, Dr. Handliss said he suspected that Benny was depressed and he set up an appointment to see him too.

At first, Dr. Handliss could find no trigger for Benny's depression. In fact, the boy himself said he didn't feel sad or down. "I don't feel anything," he described. "And I don't have anything to talk about." As is often the case, Dr. Handliss used a strategy of conversing with Benny about the kinds of topics in which a boy of eleven might be interested, like sports or special hobbies. The youngster's replies were brief, but he did reveal that he had lost interest in most of the activities he had once enjoyed. The diagnosis was confirmed. An uncle, his father's brother, had been treated for clinical depression; so had his maternal grandmother. The doctor considered a role for genetic influences and the option of using an antidepressant, but he decided to defer this decision until he had learned more about his patient and the family situation.

It took several more visits with the parents before they finally admitted that their marriage was in serious trouble. They had been alienated from one another for several years. Now they were considering divorce. It wasn't that they had open arguments that the children might overhear. Rather, they lived in an atmosphere of mutual coolness and a "need-to-know" style of communication.

"I never thought the children could be aware of our problems," his mother said. "We did our best to hide them."

"You really can't hide much from children," Dr. Hendliss noted. "They have incredible radar. Benny hasn't mentioned anything about this, but I am 90% sure he's aware of what's going on. Is this divorce business real . . . I mean, imminent?"

"Close enough," Benny's father said. "We've both spoken with lawyers. We've talked about terms of separation. I suppose it could happen in a month, more or less. Not that it's something I want," he added sadly . . .

His wife looked away to avoid his gaze.

"Well, if you are serious about this, I think you should be prepared to discuss it with Benny and find out what he's feeling about it. You know as well as I do that parents' splitting has a profound effect on the children. They get depressed. And if things aren't brought out in the open so that they can express some of their anger and grief and get rid of some of the guilt . . ."

"Guilt? Why would they feel guilty?" Benny's mother interrupted defensively.

"They just do. They feel that somehow it's their fault. And that adds to the depression they already experience when their whole world's coming apart. I think we should meet together with Benny and gently approach the subject. If I have your permission to do so, I can talk with him about it first. I know how to encourage him to voice his feelings and he will be more open to hearing you discuss it."

With the issues identified and being addressed with Benny, a slow but progressive improvement occurred in his demeanor and behavior. His grades improved. He once again took part in sports and other activities with his friends. And he found new ways to understand and express the sad and sometimes frightening feelings that he felt as his parents moved to live apart and officially end their marriage.

For many children, of course, treatment for clinical depression can be much more complicated. Parents' problems—such as alcoholism or pathological gambling—and psychiatric illnesses, such as adult schizophrenia, must often be directly addressed, since a child's disturbance is often a mirror for destructive interactions within the family. At other times, antidepressants may be indicated. As with any medical procedure, the risk-reward ratio must be kept in mind. Would a particular child's progress be better served by allowing him or her to struggle within the limitations imposed by chronic depression, relying entirely on his own and his parents' psychological therapy to do the job, or by giving him or her an antidepressant that would improve mood and enable him to function more effectively while other therapies are being carried on? This decision must be made collaboratively between doctor and parents, with the child being encouraged to cooperate in an informed way, mitigating the fear of stigma that both family and patient may experience.

The use of antidepressants in children, especially when prescribed by physicians not trained in psychiatry, presents a special risk. For many depressed children who are severely depressed or whose depression persists, there is definitely a place for antidepressants used in conjunction with individual and family psychotherapy. However, their use with children is still highly controversial. They have not been as widely subject to careful study in children as one might wish, in part because of ethical considerations. Currently, the FDA approves only fluoxetine (Prozac) for use in children, and then only in those older than age 8. While research to date indicates that antidepressants seem to cause no interference with normal growth and development, the FDA warns that they may cause an increased risk of suicidal thoughts and behavior in children in the early weeks of treatment. Children who take antidepressants must be carefully monitored.

Bipolar Illness in Children

Another particular concern in treating depressed children involves bipolar disorder (once known as manic depression). When it first appears in childhood, it often begins with a prolonged period of depression and irritability. The doctor must be doubly careful with diagnosis before prescribing medication, as common treatments for bipolar disorder will not help someone with depression, while antidepressants can trigger a manic episode in someone with bipolar disorder.

Bipolar illness (manic-depressive disorder) is usually thought of as an adult condition. In fact, in many cases the onset of the illness can be traced to childhood. Half of the adults suffering with bipolar disorder had their first episode before age 17. About 20% had their first episode between 10 and 14 years of age, and 10% had their first episode between ages 5 and 9.

The Child and Adolescent Bipolar Foundation estimates that more than one million children suffer with bipolar disorder in the United States. Genetic influences are strong. Nearly 80% of children with bipolar illness have a family history of bipolar disorder or of one or more parents who have had significant clinical depression and/or alcoholism.

Children with bipolar disorder manifest behavior difficulties that go beyond ordinary depression. Many of these may easily be explained away at first glance, since they are exaggerations of fairly common behavior patterns. Moreover, they must be considered in their totality, not as an isolated observation. Consider separation anxiety. Innumerable children seem anxious about leaving home to start school or homesick for a week the first time they go away to camp. But if they become seriously upset every time mother leaves them at home and cannot overcome fears of being away from home, this may be a warning sign of something—though by itself it does not necessarily indicate bipolarity. Add to this picture an explosive temper, rages and tantrums lasting hours whenever a child is told "no"; restlessness and over-activity alternating with periods of lethargy; distractibility and impulsive and risk-taking behaviors; low self-esteem and avoiding playmates because of a fear of social interactions; silliness and goofiness and grandiosity in thinking, alternating with periods of depression and withdrawal; and you should be giving serious thought to bipolar disorder. Other signs, less common, include bed-wetting, especially in boys; night terrors; learning disabilities, poor short-term memory, lack of organization, manipulative behavior, and lying. Even less common, but still quite suspect, are cruelty to animals and self-mutilation.

A child who is developing a bipolar disorder is truly a "handful" for his or her parents. Consider Nickie Kendall. One minute he is a smiling and loveable youngster, the next he is agitated and shouting angrily for half an hour. He is frequently stubborn and sometimes frankly negativistic, refusing to do what his parents ask or demand of him. Teachers have been complaining about Nicky's aggressive behavior since kindergarten, but he continues to achieve good grades and his parents incorrectly assume that his problems are the result of his being so intelligent. He never seems to miss a chance to embarrass his family and does not know what it is to apologize. Finally, in desperation, his teacher insists on a psychiatric consultation, and, after a thorough evaluation, the doctor starts Nicky on the mood stabilizing anticonvulsant divalproex (Depakote)—currently the preferred medication for bipolar disorder in both children and adults—bringing about a remarkable improvement in his condition.

If a child has bipolar illness, failure to diagnose and treat it quickly and effectively carries the serious complication of denying the child the opportunity to experience vital educational and interpersonal growth. It also bears a significantly increased risk of school failure, alcohol and drug abuse, and suicide. Of the group of drugs called mood stabilizers in bipolar disorder, two anticonvulsants have been approved for the control of childhood seizures, *carba-mazepine* (Tegretol) in children of any age, and *divalproex* (Depakote) in children over 2 years of age. Risperdone (risperdal) has been approved for short-term treatment of manic or mixed episodes of bipolar disorder in children and adolescents aged 10 to 17. Lithium has been approved for mood stabilization in children over 12. FDA approval implies that these drugs have been adequately tested for efficacy and side effects in the population group cited.

Every depressed child is unique, in his or her own way. In some ways, in Western countries, growing up is easier than it was a hundred years ago—physically, that is. But psychologically it is probably just as difficult if not more so. Two-parent homes and healthy, happy families are increasingly hard to find. It is sometimes hard to tell whether physical and sexual abuse of children is more widespread or just more visible. Many schools have failed at their missions, not just to educate but also to encourage the development of character and the skills and values necessary to cope with life's challenges. Many parents have lost sight of the genuine spirituality that once served as a beacon to enrich the souls of other generations.

Children are the future of humanity. In all too many instances, they deserve a good deal better than they are getting.

Chapter 20

◆ ◆ ❖ ◆ ◆ ❖ ◆ ◆ ❖ ◆ ◆ ❖ ◆ ◆ ❖ ◆ ◆ ❖ ◆ ◆

Depression in the Aftermath of Devastating Events: Post-traumatic Stress Disorder

Traumatic events—earthquakes, floods, automobile and airplane accidents, wars, acts of terrorism—can easily set off acute episodes of depression. This is especially true if such events are very intense or if they are prolonged, exposing people to serious and often life-threatening hardships from which there seems to be no obvious escape. Those who survive are expected to be relieved and grateful, determined to quickly put the entire experience well behind them. At least that's what the stiff-upper-lip philosophy teaches.

Of course, nothing could be further from the truth. Terrible personal traumas in childhood, such as physical and sexual abuse, leave lasting scars, as do combat experiences for many soldiers at the front. In the past, acute depressive episodes were often neither acknowledged and understood nor effectively dealt with. They went underground, becoming chronic and exerting a destructive influence on the intellectual, emotional, and interpersonal lives of those affected. "My dad is a very irritable person. He can lose his temper at the drop of a hat," one patient told his therapist. "Growing up I was scared of him. He never hit me, or anything like that, but the way he'd look at us kids when he was mad was enough to give us the shakes. He never slept well. We could hear him pacing around the house night after night. Mom would yell at him to come upstairs and go to bed, but that didn't do much good. When he was sixty-one he had his first heart attack—he's had two more since then—and had to stop working. Fortunately he's been tight-fisted most of his life and saved up enough to move to a retirement condo in Florida. My wife doesn't get on with him at all. She refuses to visit him, and even to let the children visit.

"Your father is old enough to have been in the Second World War," his therapist noted.

"In the marines. Okinawa. Iwo Jima. He has a drawer full of medals."

"So he could be suffering with long-term depression . . . I mean, Post-traumatic Stress Disorder . . . what used to be called 'battle fatigue', and before that 'shell shock'. Maybe, if your wife were informed about this, she could develop more tolerance for his difficult temperament. Too bad he couldn't have had some of the treatments we have available today."

Post-traumatic Stress Disorder

The year was 1992. Dr. Warren Thorpe, 44, married with two children and a very successful ophthalmology practice, hadn't slept well for months. Tossing and turning most of the night, he was lucky to get a total of three hours sleep. He'd lost his appetite for food and along with that about ten pounds. He felt too tired to go to his gym to work out. Around the house he was curt and irritable with his wife, Laurie. He stopped going to his son Martin's soccer games or helping his daughter Helen with her homework. Driving to work in the mornings, he often felt strangely apprehensive; his pulse would race and his heart pound vigorously for minutes at a time. Several times over a span of four weeks he had either postponed surgery or turned his cases over to one of his associates. Dr. Thorpe was falling apart. And as his hopelessness grew so too did his sense of helplessness and confusion. Something was wrong. That he knew. But as to the what and why of it, he did not have the foggiest notion.

A complete physical examination revealed nothing. His doctor suggested a psychiatrist. At another time, Warren would have found the recommendation absurd. He remembered psychiatry from his medical school days, when he had considered it so much double-speak. But now, he felt, he had very little choice.

As his psychiatrist carefully reviewed the history, he uncovered other times in Warren's life when he had experienced anxiety attacks, perhaps not as severe as now, but significant enough. Warren had handled these by pushing the feelings aside and getting on with his life. Finally, they had gone away.

"When was the very first time you felt this sense of dread?" his psychiatrist inquired.

Warren considered the question. "In medical school, the last year. I was agitated about where to go for internship and whether to be a family doctor or a specialist and, if so, what specialty to choose. I had a lot of trouble concentrating. I'd been an A student, but that last year I fell down to the middle of the class. I was having some difficulties in my personal life too . . . a girl I was dating called it off and I was upset by that."

"Have you ever been exposed to a serious traumatic event?

"Like what?"

"A serious traumatic event, one that threatened your life . . . or seeing someone killed . . . "

"I was in the Navy during Vietnam, but I didn't see action." Warren shrugged. "No accidents." He smiled wryly. "I was afraid I'd get shot once."

"Tell me about that."

"It was the spring, at the end of my third year at med school. I was in the city and I went into this liquor store to buy a bottle of wine to take with me to dinner with some friends. I was in the back of the store, behind a pile of boxes. You couldn't see me from the front or the counter where the owner was standing. Suddenly I heard loud voices and the ring of a cash register. Then the sound of a gun, two shots, and more yelling and then a door slamming shut.

I waited—it must have been four or five minutes but it felt like an hour—and when I didn't hear anything else, I peered out carefully from my hiding place. I didn't see anybody. So I came out and walked slowly to the counter and looked over it and there was the owner, a Chinese guy, lying on the floor, blood pouring out of his chest. I felt scared, but kept my wits and grabbed his phone and called the police and told them to send an ambulance."

"The timing is right," his doctor commented.

"Right for what?"

"This took place just before you started to have anxiety symptoms."

"You mean this had something to do with what happened to me in senior year? I don't think so. I wasn't the one shot. The owner recovered, by the way. Besides, I was going to be a doctor. I was used to the sight of blood."

"Not used to being killed."

"They didn't see me."

"The thought must have crossed your mind."

Warren looked thoughtful.

"And what about afterwards? Did you have any anxiety afterwards?"

"Of course. I dreamt about it a few times and in a couple of the dreams they did find me and were on the verge of shooting me when I woke up. And I'd get jumpy every time I went into a liquor store or even a grocery, so I avoided them as much as possible. But this settled down in a few months."

"You say you broke up with a girl the following fall. How did that happen?"

"I don't know. She accused me of becoming cold and distant, not the guy she used to know. Maybe she was right. I was having trouble concentrating on my studies and felt somehow . . ." Warren paused, searching for a word " . . . somehow numb, like things that mattered to me didn't matter as much."

As the interview proceeded, Warren's doctor ascertained that his patient continued to experience a sense of detachment from other people and to find it hard to express affection and love. He was often jumpy and nervous. "I can't let anything just go by. And for years after my internship, I'd jump every time the phone rang." He admitted to losing his temper easily over relatively small matters. While his hyper-alertness paid off in his work performance in the operating room, it had become a decided disadvantage in his personal relationships. "I catch every slight," he noted. "And I've been very jealous of my wife at times."

"And have you been depressed?"

"Yes. Sometimes."

"I think you are experiencing a depression now," the psychiatrist said calmly. "But it's really a form of Post-traumatic Stress Disorder."

"PTSD? I thought that's what you got if you were a front-line combat veteran."

"PTSD can result from any event that seriously threatens you . . . in your case, that shooting."

"But that was nearly twenty years ago."

"It begins somewhere. Sometimes the reaction clears up. A lot of the time it goes chronic. What's remarkable is how well you've done in spite of it."

"And here I was thinking that I was getting into a mid-life crisis."

"Maybe that too. In our next sessions, we'll try find out what may have stirred up these old scars at this time. For now I want to start you on an antidepressant, sertraline (Zoloft). It's a selective serotonin reuptake inhibitor, increases the amount of serotonin at the synapse. These drugs, as you know, have been shown to be effective against depression. I've used them in other diagnostic situations, including PTSD, with good results. Maybe someday they'll test them out and get approval for this too."

"Off-label prescribing, doc?" Warren said amusedly, using a phrase that was meant to remind the psychiatrist that they were both doctors.

Regular use of sertraline and ongoing psychotherapy led to a marked improvement in Warren's condition in several months. He was advised to continue in therapy to improve his interpersonal relationships and general coping abilities. His doctor also recommended that he plan to continue sertraline indefinitely, or at least until some very fundamental changes had occurred within him.

Depression and PTSD

What does PTSD have to do with ordinary depression or clinical depression? In the diagnostic manual it is a different diagnosis, classified as an anxiety disorder with its own special characteristics. However, a review of the long list of signs and symptoms that are part of the diagnosis of PTSD immediately reveals a strong resemblance to those of clinical depression. Furthermore, depression itself, along with guilt, obsessive thinking, and sexual dysfunction, are common to patients with either or both diagnoses. So too are anniversary reactions, feelings of estrangement, a marked diminution in interests and participation in activities that once were important sources of satisfaction, as well as helplessness and hopelessness about the future.

To qualify for a specific diagnosis of Post-traumatic Stress Disorder a person must have been exposed to a traumatic event in which he or she experienced, witnessed, or was confronted with a situation involving actual or threatened death or serious injury to oneself or others. The emotional response must consist of intense fear, helplessness, and/or horror. Anyone who survived or even witnessed first-hand the attacks on the World Trade Center in New York on September 11, 2001 would easily meet these requirements.

But there's more. Details of the traumatic event must be persistently or recurrently *re-experienced* in one or more of the following ways:

- Recurrent, intrusive distressing recollections or dreams of the event
- Acting or feeling as if the traumatic event were recurring, such as a sense of reliving it or having flash-back experiences
- Intense psychological distress and/or physiological reactivity at exposure to internal or external cures that symbolize or resemble an aspect of the traumatic event

There must also be evidence of persistent *avoidance* of stimuli associated with the trauma and *numbing* of general responsiveness that was not present prior to the trauma, as indicated by three or more of the following:

- Efforts to avoid thoughts, feelings, or conversations associated with the trauma
- Efforts to avoid activities, places, or people that arouse recollections of the trauma
- Inability to recall an important aspect of the trauma
- Markedly diminished interest or participation in significant activities
- A feeling of detachment or estrangement from others
- A restricted range of affect (e.g. being unable to experience and demonstrate loving feelings)
- A sense of a foreshortened future (e.g. one does not expect to have a career, marriage, children, or a normal life)

Finally, there must be evidence of *increased* arousal, as shown in difficulty falling or staying asleep, irritability or outbursts of anger, problems concentrating, hyper-vigilance, or exaggerated startle responses.

Who Is at Risk?

When dangerous events are truly horrific, just about anyone can be at risk for developing Post-traumatic Stress Disorder. However, not everyone exposed to a seriously threatening situation develops PTSD. The more immediate and intense the threat—if one were actually inside the World Trade Center when the planes struck and escaped, or if a journalist covering the war in Iraq is traveling with a group of army rangers when one of their vehicles suddenly hits a roadside bomb—the risk is far greater than if either of these events were witnessed at some distance. In fact, the greater the distance, the lower the risk. Moreover, a number of individuals who display a higher level of pre-existing resilience may weather the worst of traumas successfully, recovering from the emotional and physical impact in a matter of weeks. Such people may manifest what is called acute stress disorder, which, in and of itself, does not predict whether they may go on to a true Post-traumatic Stress Disorder.

Why are some people more vulnerable? Lack of sufficient psychological, biological, and/or environmental resilience is one factor, and it is a common denominator of all other known factors. People with a history of clinical depression that may not have been adequately treated are at higher risk. So are men and women with a family history of anxiety. Particular life events have also been shown to increase risk, including a history of physical or sexual abuse, early separation from one's parents, being part of a dysfunctional family, and problems with alcohol and drug abuse. But when the dangerous events are truly horrific, just about anyone can be considered to be at risk.

Similarities between the Treatment of PTSD and Depression

The resemblance to clinical depression does not stop with the symptoms of PTSD. The differentiation between acute PTSD and chronic PTSD is very much like that between acute and chronic depression. Even as patients whose experience with depression becomes a chronic illness have a greater incidence of clinical depression in their families, so too the families of PTSD patients have a higher incidence of anxiety disorders. Both situations speak to genetic factors that may contribute to a predisposition to illness. More appropriately, this may be a predisposition to impaired biological resilience. A clue to this similarity is found in the action of serotonin-reuptake inhibiting drugs, such as sertraline. Sertraline, the drug that Warren Thorpe's doctor started him on in 1992 has, since then, been shown to be effective in PTSD as well as depression. In fact, these drugs have also been found to work in other psychiatric situations, such as in patients with a diagnosis of social phobia who persistently avoid social situations (allegedly for fear of embarrassment), and where there is also a high family incidence of anxiety disorders. *From a symptomatic vantage point, these conditions seem different; but if the same drugs alleviate each of them, they must have more in common than meets the eye.*

The psychotherapeutic treatments that have been "tested" for all three are similar as well—cognitive behavioral therapy and interpersonal therapy—although these may be modified according to the clinical picture. For example, in someone with depression the emphasis might be on the identification of negative self-concepts and their replacement with positive ones, whereas in PTSD and social phobia, progressive exposure and desensitization to anxiety-producing thoughts and situations may take center stage.

The management of the immediate responses to catastrophic events has largely consisted of interventions by trained crisis specialists. These professionals stand ready to be empathic and reassuring listeners for the traumatized. Sharing one's emotions with another human being can go a long way toward alleviating the fear, anger, and bewilderment that overwhelm so many of disaster's victims, rescuers, and observers. This may go a long way toward preventing or ameliorating Post-traumatic Stress Disorder.

And there is yet another approach to the healing that must take place after tragic events. When the teen-age boys and girls who had watched their classmates murdered and knew that their own lives were endangered in the Littleton, Colorado high school shootings were offered the services of crisis counselors, many of them refused, preferring instead to speak to the pastors of their respective churches. Here they hoped to find not only emotional comfort but also a way to make spiritual sense out of such an evil happening.

Chapter 21

Spirituality and Depression

Religion and Psychiatry

Psychiatrists have traditionally ignored the importance of patients' religious and spiritual lives in their work with them. They remained the true heirs of the legacy of Sigmund Freud who, in *Future of an Illusion* in 1927 wrote: "Religion would thus be the universal obsessional neurosis of humanity . . . it comprises a system of wishful illusions together with a disavowal of reality. . ." The notion of God, he believed, was entirely rooted in the projection of a powerful parental figure onto the universe to provide people with an explanation for their origins and existence and with a false sense of security as they placed their hopes and wishes in the hands of a powerful force with human attributes, who meted out punishments and offered solace and blessings to those who but asked. Carl Jung was one of the early psychiatrists to take issue with such ideas, but his influence remained overshadowed by that of Freud for decades.

In a 1971 study, Dr. Henry W. Sims and Dr. S. I. Spray reported that 40% of psychoanalysts and 26% of non-psychoanalytic psychiatrists who had been brought up with religious beliefs had subsequently become atheistic or agnostic. As recently as 1992, Dr.

Wendell Watters, a professor of psychiatry at a leading university, wrote in his book, *Deadly Doctrine*, "... Christian doctrine and teachings are incompatible with many of the components of sound mental health, notably self-esteem, self-actualization and mastery, good communications skills... and the establishment of supportive human networks." And in the year 2000, a random survey of members of the American Psychiatric Association revealed that 42% of them did not regard religion as important in their own lives, in contrast to 88% of the general population who did. Obviously many therapists and their patients saw the world and human behavior in very different ways; even if the subject of religious faith was never addressed, this difference had to significantly affect the doctor-patient relationship and the patient's treatment in subtle but meaningful ways.

To be sure, psychiatrists were well aware of the negative side of religion. They were appropriately prepared to recognize that many patients would incorporate religion into the structure of their illnesses: obsessive guilt, compulsive rituals, hallucinations and delusions rich with religious content. It was easy to spot individuals whose belief systems were extremely inflexible and whose intolerance led them to reject others who disagreed with them. Parents whose religious convictions kept them from getting needed medical assistance for very ill children and clergy who abused children were newspaper headlines. And professionals were cautioned—correctly so—not to use their unique positions of trust and influence to impose their own beliefs—or lack thereof—onto their patients.

But during the past decade, the picture has started to change. The importance of spiritual beliefs and experiences to matters of health in general and coping with emotional problems in particular has finally emerged into the light of day. The American Psychiatric Association has published a set of guidelines underscoring the usefulness of gathering information on the "religious or ideological orientation and belief of their patients so they may properly attend to them in the course of treatment." At the same time it wisely warns doctors not to "force a specific religious, antireligious, or ideological agenda on a particular patient."

With the financial help of the John Templeton Foundation, many medical schools have set up programs to educate students to value and assess the role faith may play in their patients' lives. The late Dr. David B. Larson was a leader in this area. Among his many contributions, he and his colleagues developed a set of simple, straightforward questions designed for professionals inquiring about a patient's religious attitudes. Physicians should do this assessment—or one like it—routinely.

1. Do you believe in God or a higher power?
2. What does your belief in God mean to you?
3. What religion do you practice/follow?
4. Do you presently practice your religion and, if so, how frequently?
5. How important is your religion or spirituality to you?
6. Which religion did your family practice when you were growing up?
7. How has your religion/spirituality shaped your life?
8. Have your religious/spiritual beliefs changed over time, and, if so, how?
9. Has your religion/spirituality helped you, and if so, how?
10. Has your religion/spirituality hurt you in any way, and, if so, how?

Studies of Religious Faith/Spirituality and Depression

With the acknowledgement that religious faith and spirituality have a bearing on mental and physical health, clinicians have begun to actively investigate what some of these connections may be, especially with regard to the effect of religiousness on the experience of depression. Many studies report a strongly positive correlation between religiousness and a greater degree of happiness, life satisfaction, and morale. Keeping in mind the distinction between depression and clinical depression—namely that depression itself is not the illness, but rather it becomes an illness when one is unable to experience it directly, keep it within appropriate limits, and recover from it in a reasonable amount of time—people with no religious affiliation appear to be more at risk for clinical depression than those who are religiously affiliated, a finding that is even more pronounced among African Americans. Studies indicate that people who are more religiously active have fewer depressive symptoms; the lack of organized religious activity increases the odds of experiencing significant clinical depression by 20–60%.

Religious involvement is inversely correlated with suicide ideation and behavior; this may be related to moral objections to suicide, as well as faith being a source of hope, self-esteem, and social support. As one 41-year-old man who had been hospitalized in a state of severe panic and depression described: "The first week I was there, I was on constant observation. An aide was assigned to watch me at all times, even when I was asleep. They were afraid I might do something to myself. I did think about suicide. Sometimes the urge was pretty strong. But I will always remember one day taking a shower and feeling the water running all over my body and having the sensation of two realities. Part of me felt utterly hopeless . . . no point in going on living. But just as powerfully, another part of me felt as though I was sharing in Christ's suffering and death, something spiritual and universal, and that when this anguish passed I would somehow be a better person for it. Killing myself was no longer an option. For the first time I felt a glimmer of real hope."

The high levels of hope and optimism, the willingness to forgive, and a greater freedom from hostility and resentment, enable many religious individuals to enjoy better health. Studies show religious people to have greater marital stability, a lower rate of drug and alcohol abuse, less delinquency and criminal activity, less anxiety, and better self-esteem. Myron Block, a 39-year-old marketing executive, had just lost his job. He went to his family physician for a physical exam. Afterwards he spoke with him about his situation. "Down about it? Sure. But down and out, never! Several of us were pink-slipped. We were all upset. My friend Charlie was particularly upset, and he still is. He feels absolutely worthless, over the hill, really depressed, too humiliated still to even go out and look for a new job. But it didn't affect me that way. My sense of worth comes from something a lot deeper. Even when things go very wrong, when maybe I've made some mistakes, it doesn't tear my self-esteem apart. I'm me. God made me and loves me and will be with me through thick and thin. I count. We all count. The rest—money, education, social position, and work—is important, but, in a way, it's window dressing. It's the soul that matters. For years, I've lit a candle every Friday night for my parents. I don't go to services at the temple as often as I should, but I say my prayers. I ask for God's help. And he gives it, in his own time and way, and when he does, I never forget to say 'thank you'."

Are studies indicating that religious people are less likely to become clinically depressed to be interpreted as meaning that true faith can prevent depression altogether, or conversely that becoming depressed points to a lack of genuine faith? Not at all. The experience of depression, following significant losses, is practically universal. If normal depression shifts into an illness, important elements are involved having little or nothing to do with a person's religious convictions, (e.g. neurobiological events.) For example, religious coping appears to mitigate the psychological or cognitive signs and symptoms of depression, such as feelings of hopelessness and futility, loneliness, or preoccupation with negative thoughts. However, it does not influence physical symptoms, such as appetite and weight loss, diminished sexual drive, impaired concentration, or insomnia, that often require treatment with antidepressant medications. Moreover, it seems that in situations in which a patient's distress is involved with family abuse, care-giving problems, or difficulties with children, the risk of depression actually increases with religiosity; perhaps this occurs because reality is in such stark contrast to such a person's ideals, and his or her readiness to assume responsibility and experience personal guilt when things don't go right.

Then too, there are times when depression attacks the very faith one has found so invaluable throughout life. Josephine Buscani, 47, and her husband, Tony, 53, had been married for twenty years when

Tony died. It was sudden and happened on Easter Sunday morning. The previous Wednesday he had complained of indigestion and fatigue. It was unlike Tony, who was stocky, muscular, and very strong. He never missed a day's work at the Volkswagen-Audi dealership where he was the chief mechanic. On Thursday he went to see his family doctor, who advised him to consult with a cardiologist. An appointment was set up for the following Monday. On Saturday he cut his lawn and trimmed the branches off several trees. He was in the bathroom, getting ready for Easter services at Church, when Josephine heard a loud thud. She ran to the bedroom. By the time she reached the bathroom, Tony was lying on the floor, gasping for breath. She ran to the phone and dialed 911. By the time she returned, he was dead.

Josephine couldn't cry at the funeral. Nor could she cry in the privacy of her own home. Days went by with very little sleep. She lost 15 pounds in a week. She didn't know whether to feel sad or angry that God had taken Tony away from her. Tony and she had been very religious. They attended Mass every weekend. She had professed a special devotion to the Blessed Mother. Tony favored St. Anthony, after whom he had been named. Their faith was deep and genuine. Now, Josephine felt betrayed. "I can't pray," she confided in her sister. "We always wanted children, but I couldn't have any, so we accepted that as God's will. Is that what I'm supposed to do now? Accept Tony's death as God's will? I can't. I won't!"

Several months passed. Josephine had long since gone back to her work as manager of a local supermarket, but she struggled to focus and had to make a real effort not to fly off the handle at her employees. She still slept poorly, and began to have chest and abdominal pains that her doctor told her were psychosomatic and for which he recommended a consultation with a psychiatrist. She hadn't been to church since Tony's funeral. She tried to pray, but couldn't. Several times she thought of calling up her pastor and talking with him, but it never happened. Finally, she went to see the psychiatrist who told her she was depressed and suggested some talk sessions and an antidepressant. Four weeks and seven visits after she began seeing the doctor, she felt that treatment was really having an effect. Not only did she feel better, she even felt hopeful. "I can make it. It will never be the same without Tony. But I have family and friends," she told her doctor. "I even have God," she added tentatively. "Anyway, I feel a little more like praying. "

Josephine began attending Sunday services again. On the first anniversary of Tony's death, she asked her pastor to remember him in a Mass. When she told him how close she had come to losing her faith forever, he nodded kindly and reassured her that her reaction was by no means unusual. "Almost isn't final," he said. "God works in mysterious ways. Maybe if you hadn't been so depressed you couldn't turn to Him, you wouldn't have seen a psychiatrist and you wouldn't have been given the medication that has obviously helped you so much."

Intrinsic vs. Extrinsic Religiousness

In a study reported by Braam, Beekman, and Deeg et al in 1997, people who indicated that strong religious faith was "not important" to them were three times more likely to *become* clinically depressed. If already clinically depressed, they were six times more likely to *stay* depressed. This is consistent with the observations of Dr. Harold G. Koenig and his colleagues at Duke University, who assessed a group of clinically depressed patients who were also suffering with various medical illnesses. The higher the patients' scores were on a test called the *Hoge Intrinsic Religiousness Scale*, the faster they recovered from cognitive and emotional symptoms of depression. To understand these observations, one must consider the difference between intrinsic and extrinsic religiousness, as originally defined by Gordon W. Allport and J. M. Ross in 1967.

The intrinsically religious person internalizes his other beliefs. He or she lives by them no matter what outside social pressures may come into play or what the consequences may be (keeping in mind that nobody is perfect all the time). The extrinsically religious person, on the other hand, uses religion in a more utilitarian and self-serving way, to get status or personal security, for self-justification, or for social interactions. In the vast majority of studies mentioned so far, it is intrinsic religiousness that makes the difference. It is reflected in both church attendance and in private prayer. The important thing is that it comes from the heart, representing a genuine faith in God and one's relationship with God that combines an appreciation of one's own power as well as God's. Moreover, the way one experiences God is quite relevant. Among those who believe that God is benevolent, the incidence of clinical depression is significantly lower than among those who think of God as primarily a punitive figure; the incidence is also higher among those who feel totally helpless to affect a distressing situation, believing that only outside forces can help and pleading desperately for God to intervene directly and at once.

Faith, Physical Health, and Longevity

Faith appears to be good for one's overall health. Cardiovascular illnesses are more frequently seen in depressed individuals; in patients with coronary ischemia, depression worsens the outcome, possibly due to alterations in platelet function and changes in autonomic tone. Depression is also associated with a higher mortality rate following acute myocardial infarction; for those patients who survive, the recovery process is often a more complicated one. Studies suggest that the recovery rate from medical and surgical procedures, from the repair of hip fractures to coronary bypass surgery, is faster among believers. Moreover, patients undergoing such treatments appear less likely to have serious complications or die.

W. J. Strawbridge and colleagues followed a group of men and women over a 28 year period and reported, in 1997, that those persons who attended religious services weekly or more were 25% less likely to die than non-attendees; for women, the beneficial effects were stronger than those associated with not smoking, and for men, stronger than those associated with regular exercise. In yet another study, R. A. Hummer and colleagues reported that attending religious services more than once a week added an average of 7 years to the life span of Caucasian men and women and 14 years to that of African Americans.

By Way of Explanation

So far, study after study makes a strong case for the importance of faith. Most of these studies have involved Christian men and women. Less is known about the effects of faith within other belief systems, but one may presume it to be no less beneficial. Nor can such investigations answer the ultimate question, which is: When you pray, is there someone up there listening and responding? Or is it purely a placebo effect, the age-old power of suggestion? Do people of faith and healthy people share certain common factors—better social support systems, more organized lives, better stress-coping mechanisms, or a more efficient immune system? Then too, suffering has traditionally been thought of as a necessary part of spiritual growth. But is this necessarily true? If therapy and medications are used to alleviate the suffering of being depressed, are some people in search of spiritual enrichment being denied such an opportunity by being made too comfortable? Or, on the other hand, may greater freedom from suffering enable a more rapid and even more meaningful acquisition of spiritual insight?

Then too, the very nature of faith may defy scientific scrutiny. After all, faith is a belief in things not seen—and, for that matter, not heard, felt, smelled, or tasted. To know something to be a fact means that whatever it may be can no longer be an object of faith.

One conclusion is evident: whatever the true nature of religiousness, it must rightly be considered an essential ingredient of resilience, vitally important for managing and overcoming clinical depression, and for preventing normal depression from becoming an illness.

Chapter 22

♦ ♦ ❖ ♦ ♦ ❖ ♦ ♦ ❖ ♦ ♦ ❖ ♦ ♦ ❖ ♦ ♦ ❖ ♦ ♦

The Best Healing Is Prevention

"The best healing," the official Physician for the City of Worms wrote in 1620 in reference to melancholia, "would be to work at foresight." However, the prevention of depression is much more complex than the prevention of other human ailments. It does not mean the elimination of sadness; all of us will experience some despondency at one time or another in our lives.

Prevention in medicine is twofold. Its simplest meaning is a system of health care that encourages people to recognize the need for professional help as soon as possible, to be motivated to seek it, and to have some assurance that the attention they receive is skilled and appropriate to their needs. In a broader context, prevention involves a set of scientific and behavioral strategies to assist recovered patients in their efforts to stay well. It also means educating the rest of the population on the nature of depression and how they may protect themselves against its consequences.

The aim of preventive efforts against depression is not the complete elimination of depression per se, *but of chronic depression and the traps that chronically depressed people are liable to construct.* Prevention involves experiencing depression directly rather than denying it and thus converting it into other physical, psychological, or behavioral channels. It means resolving, within people and their environments, conflicts that make them depressed when they needn't be. These goals must be incorporated into educational programs of various types to strengthen our abilities to cope effectively with life stresses; it is no longer practical to leave such learning to chance.

In order to facilitate early diagnosis and effective treatment, preventive efforts should strive to create an atmosphere in which people who are caught in depression know how and where to find capable professional help when they need it, and do so without delay and embarrassment. Unfortunately, *one of the most serious obstacles that prevents people from seeking help for depression continues to be the fear of the social and career consequences of being discovered consulting a psychiatrist for treatment.*

"I'd no more go into my boss and tell him I'm depressed than stick my head in a lion's mouth," said one corporate executive to his psychiatrist. "Please send the bill home and make it out as if my wife were the patient, not me. As for insurance, I have some, but I'm not going to apply for it. . . . I can't trust personnel. If word leaked out I'd be in real trouble. I'm up for a vice-presidency. There's no way I'd be promoted if they knew I was depressed.

"Funny. . . . You know, I'd rather have a heart condition, even though I suppose, from what you've told me I'll get over this and be better than I was before, and a heart problem can go on forever. I can imagine what would happen if I told my boss I had fast heartbeats and had to take a couple of weeks off for treatment. He'd say 'Fine! Take as much time off as you need. I hope you're in good hands. If you need the name of a specialist, let me know.' Then he'd reassure me that my job was safe. . . . But, within five minutes after I'd left his office having told him I was depressed, he'd be on the phone telling his boss about it, suggesting the vice-presidency be given to Charlie or Joe and that they find some easy niche for me when I came back if I came back—because, as everyone knows, I'd never be right again."

Even when one has acknowledged the need for help, the question remains: *where does one find a competent professional*? The family physician is often the first one consulted, particularly if depression is accompanied by a variety of physical symptoms. For many years, the lack of adequate training in psychiatry for the nonpsychiatric physician had been a stumbling block in the way of proper management of depressed patients. Many teaching programs failed to make psychiatry relevant to the everyday practice of medicine, and the budding physician was often left with the idea that psychiatry was either a specialty devoted to the treatment of the insane or a hodgepodge of theories founded on the observations of Freud and his small band of dedicated disciples. However, in the last 20 years, major efforts have been made in recent years to educate family physicians to recognize and treat depression, and many depressed patients have been quite successfully treated for their symptoms exclusively by their own physicians.

Ironically, these educational efforts may have been a bit too successful. *There is a rising trend among physicians to miss the presence of significant physical disease in patients who combine physical illness with depression.* Conditions such as cancer, diabetes, heart disease, thyroid disease, viral infections, and hepatitis, to mention a few, are often accompanied by some degree of depression. In one study, the family doctor, biased in favor of treating the obvious depression, failed to diagnose a concomitant physical ailment 33 percent of the time. Psychiatrists are reported to have missed the physical illness in nearly 50 percent of such cases.

As psychologists and social workers assume increased responsibility for the care of depressed patients in private practice and institutional settings, the risk of missing an underlying physical illness becomes even greater. In this same study, nonmedical professionals missed the diagnosis of physical disease in nearly 84 percent of depressed patients.

There is, in fact, such a vast array of people assembled to help others with personal and emotional problems nowadays that a "caveat emptor" situation has been created. It is often impossible to know how skillfully or poorly any professional will handle one's difficulties until well into a program of therapy. Skills differ. Experience differs—as do the theoretical bases of therapeutic strategies. The specific tactics differ as well, depending on the therapist's style, training, and talent.

Reducing the Risk of Recurrence

The second, more fundamental approach to prevention involves strategies to prevent people who have emerged from a period of chronic depression from slipping back into it again; such principles are the same as those required for all of us to deal with significant life changes and, when acutely depressed, keep us from becoming trapped in it.

For some patients, ongoing antidepressant drug therapy may be required, but it is no less important to modify value systems and patterns of behavior that predictably lead to personal difficulties. The person who is vulnerable to chronic depression often reveals a long-standing habit of procrastination and denial, of putting off dealing with situations that seem difficult or unpleasant. The person may not sit down quietly with his or her spouse to talk of ways to improve their sexual life or with a business partner to explore how to strengthen their working relationship. Critical issues are submerged, pushed underground, and ignored rather than being dealt with directly, as they arise.

Two personality traits in particular seem to produce a special vulnerability to chronic depression. The first is difficulty setting limits on oneself or others; that is, not knowing when and how to say "no." A 44-year-old physician, who nearly quit the practice of internal medicine during an episode of severe depression, was encouraged to reappraise how she had set herself up for depression and what steps she could take to modify her behavior in the future. One of her big problems was her inability to say no. Asked to take on more and more patients, she always concurred. Asked to assume more committee responsibilities at the hospital with which she was affiliated, she would automatically say yes. When patients who could have arranged to see her during regular office hours asked to be seen in late evenings or on weekends, she complied. Her brother, in need of money, had asked her for a loan of twenty thousand dollars; the patient gave it to her, even though, with two children in college, she could ill afford to do so. She never said no to her husband either, though she frequently failed to do many of the things she said she would do. She had neither the time nor the energy. Frustrated, angry, disillusioned, her husband had gone through a period of depression himself; when he recovered, he raised the issue of separation—it was not what he really wanted, but his suggestion was enough to combine with other pressures in the doctor's life to trigger her depression.

The second source of special vulnerability is a fragile sense of self-esteem and excessive dependence on the opinions and attitudes of others in order to maintain self-esteem. Anyone but the most ardent egotist will temporarily experience a loss of self-esteem when faced with failure or defeat. Depression itself is commonly accompanied by a diminished sense of self-worth. But a certain number of people are so dependent on external sources to bolster self-esteem that, when they are deprived of such input or, as is commonly the case, when they repeatedly read negative meanings into neutral comments or constructive criticism, they quickly slip into moods of depression. One way to reduce the negative impact of intrusive, self-deprecatory thoughts is to develop a conscious, systematic habit of quickly dismissing them and replacing them with positive ones.

There is, however, no more potent antidote for lowered self-esteem than the ability to look back over one's life and gain a fresh appraisal of the valuable things one has done, however small they may seem. This theme was the basis of Frank Capra's classic film *It's a Wonderful Life*. Jimmy Stewart plays George Bailey, who could never leave his hometown of Bedford Falls because he felt he had to preserve the building and loan association his father had founded against the chicanery of Mr. Potter, the local banker (played by Lionel Barrymore). George, threatened with the immediate collapse of everything he has devoted his life to protect, stands on a bridge on the outskirts of town, wishing he had never been born, and contemplating suicide. It is not a psychiatrist but an angel named Clarence who appears to him, and with great compassion, proceeds to show George what would have happened had he never lived.

In the angel's scenario, George's wife lives the life of a frightened, unhappy spinster. His brother, a Navy hero in the Second World War, drowns when he is 8 years old because George, never having lived, was not there to save him. His uncle Billie, who worked for George, is an alcoholic and ends up a permanent inmate at the local mental institution. Bedford Falls is renamed Pottersville. This vision restores George's sense of his own value and his will to live; he rushes home to all his friends and family who love and cherish him and who have gathered together to save him from his predicament.

If one is too young to have had such a past—or simply doesn't, for whatever reasons—there is always tomorrow. Although some people are driven to use perpetual activity to run away from confronting depression, one should never underrate achievement as a legitimate way to gain healthy self-respect.

Moreover, one should be prepared to use common sense measures to pull oneself rapidly out of ordinary down moods, diverting one's mind from topics of concern. Many people mistakenly believe that a person should focus on a problem until it is solved. If one's mood is slightly depressed, the temptation to dwell on it is even stronger, especially on thoughts that are the focus of depression, such as not enough money, rejection by friends, poor family relationships. Such concentration reinforces one's sense of helplessness and futility, whereas moving one's attention toward other activities—work, a game of tennis, a film—often serves to snap one right out of a mood that might otherwise cling and grow in its intensity.

A Contemporary and Viable Concept of Depression

Fundamental to all prevention is a concept of depression that is contemporary and viable. To hold up the hope that anyone can go through life without experiencing episodes of emotional disruption is to set the stage for bitter disappointment; yet that is precisely the philosophy by which many of the more affluent societies in the world today operate. This error has been reinforced by a medical model that implies that depression itself is an illness and that mental health implies freedom from emotional pain.

Throughout everyone's lifetime, periods of relative stability are interrupted by episodes of outright instability. The strength that enables one to transit these peaks and valleys successfully is called psychobiological resilience. One must have what is called ego strength; one must be capable of tolerating distress for reasonable periods of time, exchanging old visions of reality for new and better ones as emotional reintegration takes place. To do so, the biological systems involved in adaptation to stress must operate efficiently; if, for example, corticosteroid production increases under stress, such an increase should not be excessive, and the mechanisms that turn the system off automatically when the physiological need for the biological response has been met must be in place. A final component of resilience is a person's environment: it must be sufficiently supportive to allow a person to go through episodes of disruption without converting his or her distress and disorientation into hopelessness or panic, yet sufficiently flexible to encourage reorganization along meaningful, constructive lines. Drawing from the language and concepts of contemporary physics, Ivor Browne and Vincent Kenny wrote:

> Scientific developments have shown a symmetry-breaking process at all levels from elementary particles up to biology and ecology . . . with open systems [such as those human beings represent] we find what appears to be an active principle emerging in matter which is characterized by change, instability, and continual fluctuation.
>
> A bifurcation point is reached when fluctuations destabilize the current organization of the system. Issues of "being" and "becoming" are raised here in the context of the indeterminate nature of the "choice" of direction the system will take. The system may disintegrate into chaos [chronic depression and disability] or suddenly reorganize itself into a fresh, more differentiated, higher level of organization.

Acutely depressed individuals find themselves at such bifurcation points. They are confronted with serious, unavoidable risk, and there may be no way to predict what form reorganization will take or whether such reorganization will occur at all. "These processes," Browne and Kenny go on to state, "have direct applicability to human change processes and are readily illustrated with the framework of crisis theory."

Among mental health professionals, crisis intervention has

become a widespread approach to give people who are immediately overwhelmed by acute depression a chance to obtain rapid relief from fear and anguish and, at the same time, take full advantage of their states of disruption to gain meaningful insights into themselves and their lives.

Of course, psychobiological systems are never uniform. Everyone goes through episodes of disruption in his or her own way. The subjective perception of disruption can take forms other than depression—panic or bewilderment, for example. The most disadvantaged people are those who are so out of touch with themselves that they have no access to feelings that signal what is occurring.

An example is the alexithymic person. *Alexithymia* is a term coined by psychiatrists to describe lack of insight in its extreme form. The main features of alexithymia include great difficulty recognizing and expressing feelings in words and an utter lack of fantasies appropriate to, or expressive of, emotions and moods. Alexithymic individuals focus on the details of events that take place outside themselves, but betray little or no inner life. It is no coincidence that, since stress always takes it toll if not properly appraised and managed, alexithymic people have a very high incidence of stress-related physical illness, alcoholism, and drug dependency.

The so-called Type A personality who appears particularly vulnerable to heart disease is a first cousin of the alexithymic. Denial of feeling and lack of insight are the Type A personality's first lines of defense. Overactive, tense, pressured, impatient, struggling to get too much out of their lives in too little time, the Type A person is far more likely to drop dead of a heart attack on the tennis courts than to be caught, for one embarrassing instant, in something as unacceptable as an acknowledge state of acute depression.

Resilience Can be Learned

Can useful insight into oneself and into ways of effective coping be taught? Our own experience with teaching approaches to personal insight and stress management to medical students at Cornell University Medical College some years ago is one of many experiments that answer that question affirmatively. First-year students met in groups of eight under the supervision of psychiatrists participating in the program to discuss the stresses in going through medical school and in becoming physicians. The students not only had a chance to deal with the anxiety caused by both the nature and the amount of work demanded of them, but also had an opportunity to gain insights into emotional conflicts that might cause them difficulty in their later lives, personally and as physicians—handling anger and guilt, for example. Medical students, on the whole, have very high ideals that are difficult, if not impossible, to fulfill. They have a strong sense of responsibility that, in the practice of medicine, makes them especially vulnerable to unrecognized guilt and depression as they are relentlessly confronted year after year with patients who have chronic and fatal illnesses. The evidence of what unresolved conflicts can do to physicians can be seen by the time they are about to graduate from medical school. Freshmen enter as alert, energetic, humanistic young men or women; 4 years later, they already reveal a loss in their touch for human relationships, as well as in their flexibility and creativity. Educational efforts can clearly modify this risk.

Acute depression or some other signal of disruption often accompanies major changes in a people's lives. Not infrequently, their recovery and readjustment demand a reorientation and new way of living, such as: following divorce, the death of a husband or wife, having been fired from a job, or having one's business go bankrupt. Then they must face an unfamiliar, uncertain, as yet undefined future existence. At such times, people are especially at risk. At such times, defining the shape of the future and the steps required to move toward it demand the ability to think and act creatively.

Creativity is nothing more or less than the ability to come up with fresh solutions to problems for which there seem to be no answers. Psychiatrist Anthony Storr has pointed out that creativity is a vital part of personal coherence, "related to healing processes going on within the psyche." His observation has been experimentally confirmed; creative people score higher on items on the Minnesota Multiphasic Personality Inventory that predict the likelihood of recovery from states of anxiety and depression. Moreover, tests of ego strength—a key component of resilience—such as the use of the California Psychological Inventory to measure traits such as dominance, being in command, self-acceptance, responsibility, self-control, tolerance, and intellectual efficiency clearly indicate that creative people score significantly higher than those who are less creative.

For over 30 years, researchers at the Creative Education Foundation in Buffalo, New York, have been studying the nature of creative thinking and ways to enhance it. They have shown that creativity can be learned or sharpened by observing several basic rules, for example, the rule of *quantity* leading to *quality*.

Usually, the first ideas one comes up with in searching for solutions are the least original. Probably they have already been thought of, more than once, and found to be unworkable or inappropriate. As more ideas emerge—however silly, humorous, or remote from the problem at hand they may seem to be—a rich variety of options appears, so that farther down the road some genuinely unexpected answers become visible. These answers are not usually esoteric. In fact, they will often be rather obvious; they simply didn't come to mind before.

Deferring critical judgment until well into the process is another rule to follow. This prevents one from jamming the machinery of imagination by stopping to evaluate each idea as it occurs or by casting a negative pall on the whole operation so that the excitement and enthusiasm that stimulates creativity is too quickly dampened.

"Simmering" is another. Even after all the work has been done, no obvious solutions may be at hand. What then? Put the matter aside for awhile. Let the subconscious mind—the source of invention—work on it. In the subconscious, thinking is not limited by the pedestrian, literal restrictions of conscious language. At this level, one can rapidly mobilize large quantities of data more efficiently than any computer and superimpose dissimilar ingredients into new perceptual and conceptual patterns. At some point, solutions pop into the mind suddenly, as if from nowhere, and new directions can begin to take shape.

The time to cultivate creative problem-solving abilities is when we are not in the midst of a crisis, so that, when challenges do inevitably appear, we are better prepared to deal with them.

The Close Support of Others

What about the role of one's environment in surviving a period of clinical depression and staying well afterward? Careful studies have proven how important one's environment is to accomplish both these aims. The support of close family members is invaluable; friends, particularly empathetic confidants, are no less so. In spite of romantic notions to the contrary, no one person can ever fulfill all the needs of another. During any life crisis, a small group of people close to any person provide the maximum psychological support. After things have settled down, adding a broader, more diversified network of friends and acquaintances can offer new stimulation and the opportunity to gain fresh perspectives.

"During my divorce," one man said, "I became so depressed I had to go into a psychiatric hospital for a couple of months. There were times I wanted to kill myself. I was scared and lonely. The worst part of it was over in a few weeks, but the awful loneliness, the aching for someone to be close to, for a home, went on for months. I can remember lying in bed at night, sometimes fighting against the urge to rush to the window and jump out. I thought I had completely lost my mind.

"It was only months later, after I had begun to feel better, that I could see that one of the reasons things had gotten so out of hand was the fact that during my marriage I had allowed my wife to structure our whole social life. I'd lost contact with most of the old friends I'd had when I was single, and I hadn't made any new ones. My parents were dead. My only brother and I weren't close. So, when all hell broke loose, I literally had no one to turn to. My wife's friends—whom I had thought of as ours—vanished from my life. I'm convinced that if I had had someone then, I would never have ended up in such bad shape. Believe me, making a new set of friends and keeping them is number one on my list of priorities."

The willingness of key family members to cooperate with a patient's therapy has almost become a prognostic factor in evaluating the eventual outcome of the depression as well as of the family interactions. People who refuse to see their spouses' psychiatrists when requested to do so may be concealing something—an extramarital affair for example, or their fear of losing some measure of control over their spouses as a result of successful therapy. They may also feel embarrassed or guilty, with or without cause, about their complicity in provoking the depression, and at the same time they may lack the insight and flexibility required to change a longstanding habit of psychological sabotage. On the whole, the more cooperative and sincere family members are, the easier it is for depressed people to recover and remain free of undue depression, unless they choose to make serious, and sometimes very difficult, changes in their lifestyles.

Environments that Promote Resilience

The broader environment in which we all live is no less important in providing both the stability and flexibility to permit us to deal successfully with life crises. Restoring meaningful, constructive values to society is an important step toward reducing the depressogenic forces in our culture. In more specific ways, environmental modification can be applied to all kinds of organizations: private, governmental, educational. Many corporations, for example, have developmental programs designed to prepare employees to cope with stressful changes such as promotion, geographical relocation and retirement—changes that, if not adequately handled, can set the stage for chronic depression. However, in addition to paying attention to the needs of individuals, organizations should also consider ways to change environments that are depressogenic.

These changes should not be made in a haphazard way as many groups did some years ago when they used sensitivity training and awareness discussions and, having spent considerable money and exhausted a good deal of employee time, ended up disappointed by the lack of results. One must carefully define the nature, purpose, needs, and conflicts of the organization beforehand—making a diagnosis much as the physician makes a diagnosis—and then set priorities actively to apply methods that are designed to solve those issues that appear to be most relevant.

However, most people are not in a position to modify, by themselves, the overall quality of the organizations within which they work. For many whose depressions have been caused by a particular working environment, there may be no option but to leave. Many men and women who change jobs and create various reasons for doing so, are, in fact, attempting to escape depressogenic situations.

There is one place where everyone can do a great deal toward altering his or her environment: the home. Those who are depressed should consider what can be done to change the elements in family life that have been contributing to the depression. If someone else in the family is depressed, what might others be doing or not doing to add to the distress? Such questions should be asked not with the idea of placing blame and focusing guilt, but rather with the hope of turning an unrewarding situation into a rewarding one and of making an already satisfactory condition even more so.

An Opportunity for Change

If you are trying to change yourself or your life situation, you are bound to experience depression. If you are already depressed, you have an opportunity to make progress in three major areas: how you regard yourself, how you relate to other people, and how you may modify and cope with difficult environmental conditions.

How You Regard Yourself

A computer programmer commented: "Before my depression, I was always trying to win someone's approval. I worried about what my wife thought of me, what my employer thought of me, what impression I was making on other members of the department. I would go to almost any length to avoid being criticized. I needed constant feedback to reassure me that I was doing an adequate job.

"While I was depressed, none of this seemed to matter any more. For the first time, I saw my craving for approval as a recurrent pattern, one that dominated my life. It seemed irrational. Couldn't I define myself for myself? Couldn't I know and sense the person I am? As long as I relied on the definition of myself through others, it was as if I had no identity of my own.

"Now that I'm not depressed any more, I'm different. I know my abilities, and I know my limitations. I still want to please, but I'm more selective about it."

How You Relate to Other People

A woman described the following change in her marriage: "Before my depression, neither my husband nor I was aware of the way in which we were competing with each other all over the place—for the children's attention, careerwise. I used to resent his successes so much that I wouldn't let him talk about his work at all. And I felt that he had no appreciation for what I was doing at home. It was so bad that we would sometimes compete with each other for the affection of my parents and his.

"But we weren't aware of it until the marriage nearly fell apart. My becoming depressed forced us to take a new look at what was going on between us. It was a shock to realize that competitiveness had been wrecking the love and respect we had for each other. It had even messed up our sex life.

"Now the one-upmanship is gone. It didn't just disappear, of course. But we're aware of it when it creeps in and we can correct it. When I was depressed nothing mattered. Now that I'm not, I feel more able to share than I ever was."

Her husband commented, "We don't shove everything under the rug any more. I've learned to be more forthright, to say what I think and feel and try to say it so I can be understood. I wasn't as depressed as my wife, but I certainly was unhappy. I realized that things couldn't go on as they were. I would have to find new ways of dealing with issues, especially controversial ones, rather than passing them off time and time again."

How You Cope with Difficult Life Situations

Aging, the time in life over 60, can be a period of loneliness and unhappiness for many people. Retirement brings a halt to what is considered productive work. A sense of being useless moves in, and when idleness is compounded by health and financial problems, depression is common. "I used to lead a very active life," said one man. "Had my own consulting firm. I never was a roaring success, but we did well enough. Two years ago my partners insisted that I retire and gave me six months to do it in. At first I fought it. Then gave in.

"My wife and I moved to Phoenix. We didn't know anyone. Suddenly, after years of being up at six and working until seven and traveling everywhere, there was nothing for me to do. I dreaded the mornings. Going to buy *The New York Times* was the big event of the day. I lost interest in seeing anyone. Half the time I didn't want to eat. I was really morose and difficult to live with. I began to think there was something wrong with me physically.

"My family doctor assured me I was in good health. He made a few suggestions that proved invaluable—such as asking me what I had been interested in during my school years. I recalled that I would enter photography contests and that I had a rock collection. At one time I had even thought of being a geologist. Instead of sitting around thinking about doing things that didn't interest me, such as working for the local community chest, why didn't I pick up those old interests now that I had time to pursue them? I could feel myself coming alive again even as we talked about it."

How you regard depression depends on how you experience it. Because, by its very nature, it is associated with endings, and because each ending involves starting over, depression is itself a new beginning.

Selected Suggestions for Further Reading

Academy of Religion and Mental Health. *Moral values in psychoanalysis: Proceedings of the sixth academy symposium* (1963). New York: Author.

Affinson, T. J., & Robinson, R. G. (1992). Mood disorders following brain injury. *Directions in Psychiatry, 12*(3).

American Psychiatric Association (1994). *Diagnostic and statistical manual of mental disorders* (4th ed.). Washington DC: Author.

Andersen, A. E. (1989). Anorexia nervosa, bulimia, and depression: Multiple interactions. In F. F. Flach (Ed.), *Diagnostics and psychopathology* (pp. 131-139). New York: W. W. Norton & Company.

Bach, G. R., & Wyden, P. (1969). *The intimate enemy: How to fight fair in love and marriage.* New York: William Morrow.

Ban, T. A., & Ebert, M. H. (1988a). The diagnosis of depression in the elderly. In F. F. Flach (Ed.), *Affective disorders* (pp. 77-78). New York: W. W. Norton & Company.

Ban, T. A., & Ebert, M. H. (1988b). The treatment of depression in the elderly. In F. F. Flach (Ed.), *Affective disorders* (pp. 89-101). New York: W. W. Norton & Company.

Beck, A. T., Rush, A. J., Shaw B. F., & Emery, G. (1979). *Cognitive therapy of depression.* New York: Guilford.

Beitman, B. D. (1989). Combining pharmacotherapy and psychotherapy: process considerations. In F. F. Flach (Ed.), *Psychobiology and psychopharmacology* (pp. 75-89). New York: W. W. Norton & Company.

Binswanger, L. (1963). *Being-in-the-world.* New York: Basic Books, Inc.

Bradshaw, J. (1994). *Creating love.* New York: Bantam.

Braiker, H. B. (1988). *Getting up when you're feeling down.* New York: Pocket Books.

Branden, N. (1992). Working with self-esteem in psychotherapy. *Directions in Clinical Psychology, 4*(8).

Branden, N. (1993). The six pillars of self-esteem. New York: Bantam.

Bridge JA, S. Iyengar, C.B. Salary, R.P. Barbe, B. Birmaher, H.A. Pincus, L. Ren , D.A. Brent, MD. Clinical Response and Risk for Reported Suicidal Ideation and Suicide Attempts in Pediatric Antidepressant Treatment: A Meta-analysis of Randomized Controlled Trials. *Journal of the American Medical Association.* 2007; 297:1683-1696.

Brown, J. C. (1994). Adolescent suicide. *Directions in Child and Adolescent Therapy, 5*(1).

Browne, I. W., & Kenny, V. (1989). How does psychotherapy work? Part I: The new science paradigm for psychotherapy theory. In F. F. Flach (Ed.), *Psychotherapy* (pp. 1-15). New York: W. W. Norton & Company.

Burns, D. D. (1992). *Feeling good: The new mood therapy.* New York: Avon.

Burton, R. (1977). *The Anatomy of melancholia.* New York: Vintage (Original work published 1621).

Carr, J. E., & Vitaliano, P. P. (1985). The theoretical implications of converging research on depression and the culture-bound symptoms. In A. Klienman & B. Good (Eds.), *Culture and depression: studies in anthropology and cross-cultural psychiatry of affect and disorder.* Berkeley, CA: University of California Press.

Chopra, D. (1993). *Ageless body, timeless mind.* New York: Harmony Books/Random House.

Ciborowski, P. J. (1993). Counseling children of divorce. *Directions in Marriage and Family Therapy, 1*(1).

Cohn, H. W. (1989). Man as process: Existential aspects of psychotherapy. In F. F. Flach (Ed.), *Psychotherapy* (170-182). New York: W. W. Norton & Company.

Cole, T. R., & Winkler, M. G. (Eds.) (1994). *The Oxford book of aging.* New York: Oxford University Press.

Colgrove, M., Bloomfield, H., & McWilliams, P. (1991). *How to survive the loss of a love.* Los Angeles: Prelude Press.

Copeland, M. E., & McKay, M. (1992). *The depression workbook.* Oakland, CA: New Harbinger.

Cotton, N. S. (1989). A developmental model of self-esteem regulation. In F. F. Flach (Ed.), *Stress and its management* (pp. 37-57). New York: W. W. Norton & Company.

Deakin, J. F. W. (Ed). (1986). *Biology of depression.* Washington DC: American Psychiatric Press.

Delgado, P. L., & Gelenberg, A. (1994). Decision making in the use of antidepressants. *Directions in Psychiatry, 14*(21).

Demitrack, M. A. (1992). Chronic fatigue syndrome. *Directions in Psychiatry, 12*(15).

DePaulo, J., Jr., Raymond, A., & Keither, R. (1989). *How to cope with depression.* New York: Ballantine.

Downs, H. (1994). *Fifty to forever.* Nashville: Thomas Nelson.

Dubovsky, S. I. (1993). Diagnosis and management of psychotic depression. *Directions in Psychiatry, 13*(18).

Duguay, R. & Flach, F. (1964). An experimental study of weight changes in depression. *Acta Psychiatrica Scandinavica,* 40, 1-9.

Dunner, D. L. (1995). Diagnosing and treating bipolar II disorder. *Directions in Psychiatric Nursing, 1*(10).

DuPont, R. L. (1994). Facing and preventing teenage use of alcohol and other drugs. *Directions in Substance Abuse Counseling, 2* (3).

Dupont, R. L., McGovern, J. P. (1991). Co-Dependence. *Directions in Clinical Psychology, 2*(7).

Eisenberg, L. (1989). The meaning of illness. In F. F. Flach (Ed.), *Diagnostics and psychopathology* (pp. 3-13). New York: W. W. Norton & Company.

Erikson, E. H. (1950). *Childhood and society.* New York: W. W. Norton & Company, Inc.

Faragella, F., & Flach, F. (1970). Studies of mineral metabolism in mental depression. *Journal of Nervous and Mental Disease, 151*(2), 120-29.

Fieve, R. R. (1989). *Mood swings.* New York: Bantam Books.

Flach, F. F. (1964). Calcium metabolism in states of depression. *British Journal of Psychiatry, 110*(467) 588-93.

Flach, F. F. (1971). Group approaches in medical education. In H. I. Kaplan and B. J. Sadock (Eds.), *Comprehensive group psychotherapy.* Baltimore: Williams & Wilkins.

Flach, F. F. and Draghi, Suzanne (Ed.) (1975.) *The nature and treatment of depression.* New York: John Wiley and Sons, Inc.

Flach, F. F. (1988): *Resilience.* New York Fawcett Columbine. Revised edition (1997),Hatherleigh Press

Flach, F. F. (1990): *Rickie.* New York: Fawcett Columbine. (1991) paperback edition: Ballantine Books.

Flach, F. F. (1998): *The Secret Strength of Angels.* New York: Hatherleigh Press.

Flach, F. F.: (2000) *Faith, Healing, and Miracles.* New York: Hatherleigh Press.

Flach, F. F. et al. (1992). Visual perceptual dysfunction in patients with schizophrenic and affective disorders versus control subjects. *Journal of Neuropsychiatry, 4*(4), 422-427.

Flacht, F. (1620). *De melancholia et idiopathica et sympathica.* Basel.

Freeman, H. L. (1989). Mental health and the environment. In F. F. Flach (Ed.), *Stress and its management* (pp. 127-142). New York: W. W. Norton & Company.

Garbutt, J. C. (1989). L-Triiodothyronine and lithium in the treatment of tricyclic antidepressant nonresponders. In F. F. Flach (Ed.), *Psychobiology and psychopharmacology* (pp. 109-120). New York: W. W. Norton & Company.

Gaylin, W. (Ed). (1994). *Psychodynamic understanding of depression.* New York: Jason Aronson.

Gold, J. H. (1989). Premenstrual syndrome. In F. F. Flach (Ed.), *Diagnostics and psychopathology* (pp. 110-120). New York: W. W. Norton & Company.

Gold, M. S., & Herridge, P. (1988). The risk of misdiagnosing physical illness as depression. In F. F. Flach (Ed.), *Affective Disorders* (pp. 64-76). New York: W. W. Norton & Company.

Gold, M. S., & Morris, L. B. (1988). *The good news about depression.* New York: Bantam Books.

Goodwin, F. K., & Jamison, K. R. (1990). *Manic depressive illness.* New York: Oxford University Press.

Greenblatt, M., Becerra, R. M., & Serafetinides, E. S. (1989). Social networks, adaptibility to stress, and recovery from psychiatric illness. In F. F. Flach (Ed.), *Stress and its management* (pp. 117-126). New York: W. W. Norton & Company.

Gruen, P. H. (1991). Clinical use of fluoxetine hydrochloride (Prozac). *Directions in Psychiatry, 11*(25).

Hales, D., & Hales, R. E. (1995). *Caring for the mind.* New York: Bantam Books.

Hall, M. H., Dahl, R. E., Dew, M. A., & Reynolds, C. F. III. (1995). Sleep patterns following major negative life events. *Directions in Psychiatry, 15*(9).

Halpern, J. K., & Roose, S. P. (1990). The cardiovascular effects of tricyclic antidepressants. *Directions in Psychiatry, 10*(14).

Hammen, C. L. (1995). Stress and depression. *Directions in Psychiatry, 15*(22).

Healthyplace.com. List of Antidepressants—SSRIs, MAOIs, Tricyclics, Others. http://www.healthyplace.com/communities/depression/treatment/antidepressants/antidepressant_list.asp.

Healthyplace.com. Wellbutrin, Effexor, Remeron, Desyrel. http://www.healthyplace.com/communities/depression/treatment/antidepressants/other_antidepressants.asp.

Hoge, D.R. (1972) A validated intrinsic motivation scale. Journal for the Scientific Study of Religion, 11:369-376.

Howland, R. H. (1993). Psychotherapy of dysthymia. *Directions in Psychiatry, 13(*19).

Jenike, M. A. (1990). Depression in the elderly. *Directions in Psychiatry, 10*(1).

Jacobsen, F. M., & Rosenthal, N. E. (1988). Seasonal affective disorder and the use of light as an antidepressant. In F. F. Flach (Ed.), *Affective disorders* (pp. 215-310). New York: W. W. Norton & Company.

Jarrett, R. B., & Rush, A. J. (1992). Cognitive therapy for depression. *Directions in Clinical Psychology, 2*(3).

Keutzer, C. S. (1989). Synchronicity awareness in psychotherapy. How does psychotherapy work? In F. F. Flach (Ed.), *Psychotherapy* (pp. 159-169). New York: W. W. Norton & Company.

Kipfer, B. A. (1990). *14,000 things to be happy about.* New York: Workman.

Kraepelin, E. (1921). *Manic-depressive insanity and paranoia.* Edinburgh: E. & S. Livingstone.

Koenig, HG, McCullough, ME., Larson, DB. (2001) *Handbook of Religion and Health.* New York, NY: Oxford University Press.

Kramer, P. D. (1995). *Listening to Prozac.* New York: Penguin Books.

Larson DB, Lu FG, Swyers JP, eds. (1997) Appendix A: Questions for assessing patients' religious beliefs and their influences on patients. Model Curriculum for Psychiatric Residency Training Programs: Religion and Spirituality in Clinical Practice. Rockville, MD: National Institute for Healthcare Research.

Levy, E. M., & Krueger, R. (1988). Depression and the immune system. In F. F. Flach (Ed.), *Affective disorders* (pp. 186-198). New York: W. W. Norton & Company.

Malmquist, C. P. (1995). Depression and violence. *Directions in Psychiatry, 15*(21).

Manning, M. (1994). *Undercurrents.* New York: Harper Collins.

Marsella, A. J., Sartorius, N., Jablensky, A., & Fenton, F. R. (1985). Cross-cultural studies of depressive disorders: an overview. In A. Klienman & B. Good (Eds.), *Culture and depression: Studies in anthropology and cross-cultural psychiatry of affect and disorder.* Berkeley, CA: University of California Press.

Mayo Clinic. Deep brain stimulation: an experimental depression treatment. http://www.mayoclinic.com/health/deep-brain-stimulation/MH00114. Published July 24, 2006.

Mental Help Net. Rashmi Nemade, Ph.D., Natalie Staats Reiss, Ph.D., and Mark Dombeck, Ph.D. Biology of Depression—Neurotransmitters. http://www.mentalhelp.net/poc/view_doc.php?type=doc&id=12999&cn=5 Published July 20, 2007.

Mental Help Net. Rashmi Nemade, Ph.D., Natalie Staats Reiss, Ph.D., and Mark Dombeck, Ph.D. Biology of Depression—

Genetics and Imaging. http://www.mentalhelp.net/poc/view_doc.php?type=doc&id=13001&cn=5 Published July 20, 2007.

McAllister, R. J. (1988). Forgiveness. *Directions in Mental Health Counseling, 1*(7).

McCully, R. S. (1989). The almost forgotten dimension: Religion and the psyche. In F. F. Flach (Ed.), *Stress and its management* (pp. 91-102). New York: W. W. Norton & Company.

McGrath, E. (1994). *When feeling bad is good.* New York: Bantam.

Meissner, W. W. (1989). The dynamics of hope. In F. F. Flach (Ed.), *Stress and its management.* New York: W. W. Norton & Company.

Meissner, W. W. (1993). The psychodynamics of guilt and its management. *Directions in Psychiatry, 13*(8).

Meissner, W. W. (1995). The nature of trust and its management in therapy. *Directions in Psychiatry, 15*(6).

Menninger, K. (1963). *The vital balance.* New York: The Viking Press.

Meyers, J. E. (1994). Employment, retirement, and life career counseling for older workers. *Directions in Rehabilitation Counseling, 1*(6).

Miller, N. S. (1993). Pharmacotherapy in alcoholics. *Directions in Psychiatry, 13*(20).

Mintz, J. et al. (1994). Treatment of depression and the restoration of work capacity. *Directions in Rehabilitation Counseling, 5*(6).

Monk, T. H. (1988). Circadian rhythms in human performance. In F. F. Flach (Ed.), *Affective disorders* (pp. 199-214). New York: W. W. Norton & Company.

Moore, T. (1992). *Care of the soul.* New York: Harper Collins.

Nathanson, D. I. (1989). Understanding shame. *Directions in Mental Health Counseling, 1*(9).

Nemiah, J. C. (1989). Alexithymia and psychosomatic illness. In F. F. Flach (Ed.), *Stress and its management* (pp. 154-169). New York: W. W. Norton & Company.

O'Connell, R. A. (1988). Depression: Bipolar or unipolar? In F. F. Flach (Ed.), *Affective disorders* (pp. 29-37). New York: W. W. Norton & Company.

Papolos, D. & Papolos, J. (1992). *Overcoming depression.* New York: Harper Collins.

Papolos, F. & Lachman, H. M. (Eds.) (1994). *Genetic studies in affective disorders.* New York: John Wiley & Sons.

Paykel, E. S., Myers, J. K., Dienelt, M. N., Klerman, G. L., Lindenthal, J. J., & Pepper, M. P. (1969). Life events and depression. *Archives of General Psychiatry, 21*(6), 753-60.

Peale, N. V. (1987). *The power of positive thinking.* New York: Fawcett.

Peck, M. S. (1978). *The road less travelled.* New York: Touchstone.

Potter W. Z., Rudorfer M. V., & Manji, H. (1991). The pharmacological treatment of depression. *New England Journal of Medicine, 325,* 633-642.

Rabkin, R., & Rabkin, J. G. (1995). Management of depression in patients with HIV infection. In W. Odets and M. Shernoff (Eds.), *The second decade of AIDS.* New York: Hatherleigh Press.

Rainer, J. D. (1991). Genetics and psychiatric illness. *Directions in Psychiatry, 11*(25).

Redlich, F. C., & Hollingshead, A. de B. (1969). *Social class and mental illness: A community study.* New York: Basic Books.

Salzman, L. (1989). Terminating psychotherapy. In F. F. Flach (Ed.), *Psychotherapy* (pp. 223-230). New York: W. W. Norton & Company.

Seligman, M. E. P. (1992). *Helplessness.* New York: W. H. Freeman.

Sheehy, G. (1995). *New passages.* New York: Random House.

Sherlock, R. K. (1989). Values in psychotherapy. In F. F. Flach (Ed.), *Psychotherapy* (pp. 43-56). New York: W. W. Norton & Company.

Siegal, B. S. (1986). *Love, medicine, and miracles.* New York: Harper Collins.

Siegal, B. S. (1989). *Peace, love, and healing.* New York: Harper Collins.

Smith, H. (1991). *Depressed? Here's a way out.* New York: Harper Collins.

Society for Neuroscience. Depression and Stress Hormones. http://www.sfn.org/index.cfm?pagename=brainbriefings_depressionandstresshormones.

Spitz, H. I. (1988). Family and marital therapy in the treatment of depression. In F. F. Flach (Ed.), *Affective disorders* (pp. 128-139). New York: W. W. Norton & Company.

Storr, A. (1972). *The dynamics of creation.* New York: Atheneum.

Storr, A. (1988). Principles of psychotherapy with depressed patients. In F. F. Flach (Ed.), *Affective disorders* (pp. 102-113). New York: W. W. Norton & Company.

Storr, A. (1990). *The art of psychotherapy.* New York: Routledge.

Styron, W. (1990). *Darkness visible: A memoir of madness.* New York: Random House.

U.S. Food and Drug Administration. Questions and Answers on Antidepressant Use in Children, Adolescents, and Adults. http://www.fda.gov/CDER/drug/antidepressants/QA20070502.htm. Published May 2, 2007.

U.S. Food and Drug Administration. Consumer Update: Drug Approved for Two Psychiatric Conditions in Children and

Adolescents. http://www.fda.gov/consumer/updates/risperdal082207.html. Published August 22, 2007.

Weinberg, W. A., Harper, C. R., & Emslie, G. J. (1992). The effect of depression and learning disabilities on school behavior problems. *Directions in Clinical Psychology, 4*(14).

West, L. J. (1994). Principles in the psychotherapy of depression. *Directions in Clinical Psychology, 4*(1).

Whybrow, P. C. (1988). Affective styles in the etiology of depression. In F. F. Flach (Ed.), *Affective disorders* (pp. 1-9). New York: W. W. Norton & Company.

Williams, M. E. (1995). *American geriatric society's guide to aging & health.* New York: Harmony Books/Random House.

Winokur, G. (1995). Distinctions between manic-depressive illness and primary unipolar depressive disorder. *Directions in Psychiatry, 15*(8).

Wurtzel, E. (1994). *Prozac nation.* New York: Houghton Mifflin.

Organizations and Support Groups

Depressed Anonymous
c/o Depression Self-Help Services, Inc.
P.O. Box 17471
Louisville, KY 40217
(502) 569-1989

Depression After Delivery
P.O. Box 1282
Morrisville, PA 19067
1-800-944-4773 (information line) or (215) 295-3994

Depressives Anonymous (for women only)
For written information, send an SASE to:
329 E. 62nd Street
New York, NY 10021
(212) 689-2600

NAMI: National Alliance for the Mentally Ill
200 North Glebe Road, Suite 1015
Arlington, VA 22203-3754
1-800-950-6264 or (703) 524-7600

National Depressive & Manic Depressive Association
730 N. Franklin #501
Chicago, IL 60610
1-800-826-3632 or (312) 642-0049

National Mental Health Association

1021 Prince Street
Alexandria, VA 22314-2971
(703) 684-7722 fax: (703) 684-5968

National Mental Health Consumers Self-Help Clearinghouse
1211 Chestnut Street, Suite 1000
Philadelphia, PA 19107
1-800-553-4539 or (215) 751-1810

Postpartum Support International
927 N. Kellogg Avenue
Santa Barbara, CA 93111
(805) 967-7636

Index

About the Author

Frederic Flach, M.D., K.C.H.S. was an internationally recognized psychiatrist and author whose highly acclaimed books include *Putting the Pieces Together Again*; *A New Marriage, A New Life*; *Resilience*; *Rickie*; *The Secret Strength of Angels*; and *Faith, Healing and Miracles*. In 1996 he was awarded the Maxine Mason award by the National Alliance for the Mentally Ill. He appeared on numerous radio and television programs across the country including Today, Good Morning America, CBS This Morning, Good Day New York, and Donahue. Dr. Flach died in 2006.